T0181443

A European Perspective on Crisis Informatics

Christian Reuter

A European Perspective on Crisis Informatics

Citizens' and Authorities' Attitudes Towards Social Media for Public Safety and Security

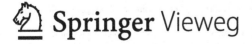 Springer Vieweg

Christian Reuter
Netphen/Siegen, Germany

Dissertation to obtain the degree of doctor from Radboud University Nijmegen on the authority of the Rector Magnificus prof. dr. J.H.J.M. van Krieken, according to the decision of the Doctorate Board to be defended in public on Tuesday, October 11, 2022 at 4:30 pm by Christian Reuter

ISBN 978-3-658-39719-7   ISBN 978-3-658-39720-3   (eBook)
https://doi.org/10.1007/978-3-658-39720-3

© The Editor(s) (if applicable) and The Author(s), under exclusive license to Springer Fachmedien Wiesbaden GmbH, part of Springer Nature 2022
This work is subject to copyright. All rights are solely and exclusively licensed by the Publisher, whether the whole or part of the material is concerned, specifically the rights of translation, reprinting, reuse of illustrations, recitation, broadcasting, reproduction on microfilms or in any other physical way, and transmission or information storage and retrieval, electronic adaptation, computer software, or by similar or dissimilar methodology now known or hereafter developed.
The use of general descriptive names, registered names, trademarks, service marks, etc. in this publication does not imply, even in the absence of a specific statement, that such names are exempt from the relevant protective laws and regulations and therefore free for general use.
The publisher, the authors, and the editors are safe to assume that the advice and information in this book are believed to be true and accurate at the date of publication. Neither the publisher nor the authors or the editors give a warranty, expressed or implied, with respect to the material contained herein or for any errors or omissions that may have been made. The publisher remains neutral with regard to jurisdictional claims in published maps and institutional affiliations.

Responsible Editor: Stefanie Probst
This Springer Vieweg imprint is published by the registered company Springer Fachmedien Wiesbaden GmbH, part of Springer Nature.
The registered company address is: Abraham-Lincoln-Str. 46, 65189 Wiesbaden, Germany

Acknowledgements

After finishing my first PhD (in information systems) at the University of Siegen (Germany) in 2014, with a thesis on software infrastructures for emergent collaboration, this work represents my second PhD thesis (in public administration and political science, especially the politics of safety and security) at Radboud Universiteit Nijmegen (The Netherlands) in 2022. It is based on parts of my research between 2014 and 2021 and addresses the use of social media for public safety and security. This thesis would not have been achieved without the help of others, and I would like to thank all the people and institutions that have made this possible.

My research activities were carried out in various settings: Firstly, this work was developed at University of Siegen in the research group "Computer Supported Collaborative Work and Social Media" of *Prof. dr. Volkmar Pipek* within the project *EmerGent* (2014–2017) on social media in emergency management funded by the European Union (No. 608352), as well as within my independent research group *KontiKat* (2017–2021) on civic societal and business continuity through socio-technological networking in disaster situations, which was gratefully funded by the German Federal Ministry for Education and Research (BMBF; No. 13N14351). Secondly, after becoming faculty member at Technical University of Darmstadt (Germany) in 2017, I conducted this work in my interdisciplinary research group "Science and Technology for Peace and Security" (PEASEC). This work was embedded in the *emergenCITY* centre (since 2020), focussing on emergency responsive digital cities, funded by the LOEWE initiative (Hesse, Germany) and was part of the National Research Center for Applied

Cybersecurity *ATHENE* (since 2019), also funded by the BMBF and the Hessian Ministry of Higher Education, Research, Science and the Arts.

This book has been prepared as a PhD thesis at Radboud Universiteit Nijmegen, and submitted in March 2022. First of all, I would like to thank my host and first supervisor *Prof. dr. Ira Helsloot* for his kindness to take over this position, his commitment and trust in my work. I appreciate that very much! I would also like to thank my second supervisor *Prof. dr. Kees Boersma* (Vrije Universiteit Amsterdam, The Netherlands) for his willingness to support this project and his valuable feedback. I would further like to thank the members of the manuscript committee for their efforts: *Prof. dr. Michiel de Vries* (Radboud Universiteit Nijmegen), *Prof. dr. Frédérick Benaben* (École Nationale Supérieure des Mines d'Albi-Carmaux, France), *Prof. dr. Tina Comes* (Technische Universiteit Delft, The Netherlands), *Prof. dr. Louise Comfort* (University of Pittsburgh, USA) and *Dr. Jelle Groenendaal* (3rdRisk, Amsterdam, The Netherlands). Furthermore, I would like to thank my former mentor *Prof. dr. Volkmar Pipek* (University of Siegen) for the freedom and environment he provided me with to do the things that I considered to be important and necessary.

With deep gratitude I thank my direct collaborators across different projects and institutions, who were involved in a large part of the research presented in this thesis. I would like to make special mention of *Dr. Marc-André Kaufhold* (Technical University of Darmstadt), whom I would like to thank for our 10 years of cooperation, first in Siegen and later, thankfully, also in Darmstadt. I am glad to have been able to work with him on various projects and to actively accompany him on his way from student assistant to post-doctoral researcher. Likewise, I would particularly like to thank all further co-authors of my journal articles, book chapters and conference papers, which form part of this thesis, for the valuable collaboration, and for their contribution to this work: *Stefka Schmid* (Technical University of Darmstadt), *Prof. dr. Volkmar Pipek*, *Prof. dr. Thomas Ludwig, Fabian Spahr* and *Michael Ritzkatis* (University of Siegen), *Dr. Thomas Spielhofer* and *Anna Sophie Hahne* (The Tavistock Institute of Human Relations, United Kingdom) as well as *Prof. dr. Amanda Lee Hughes* (Brigham Young University, USA). (Detailed descriptions of the contributions of the authors can be found in Section 1.4.)

Furthermore, I want to thank all the incredible members of my research group PEASEC, my colleagues in Siegen (until 2017) and Darmstadt (since 2017) and not to forget my (former) student assistants who have contributed in various ways, for example by practical work leading to the realisation of concepts, through joint research or proof-reading of publications. Moreover, I would like to thank the participants in my empirical studies and the reviewers of the underlying publications, who are both necessary and very valuable, but remain anonymous.

Last but not least, I would like to thank my family for their love and support— also during this second time. This thesis is dedicated to you.

Christian Reuter

Summary

Mobilising helpers in the event of a flood or letting friends know that you are okay in the event of a terrorist attack—more and more people are using social media in emergency, crisis or disaster situations. Storms, floods, attacks or pandemics (esp. COVID-19) show that citizens use social media to inform themselves or to coordinate. In addition, authorities use social media to warn the public, coordinate affected persons or helpers or enrich their situation assessment. In order to regulate and support this, knowledge about the actions of authorities and citizens as well as their perception on the role of social media for public safety and security is essential. However, there is a lack of comprehensive and representative empirical studies on this topic, especially those with a European focus.

This thesis contributes to this research gap by presenting empirical findings as well as strategies, concepts and technologies inspired by them. Based on the state of research in *crisis informatics* as a multidisciplinary field that combines computing and social science knowledge on disasters, and from the perspective of *public administration and political sciences*, this dissertation presents qualitative and quantitative studies on the attitudes of emergency services and citizens in Europe towards social media in emergencies. Across the individual sub-studies, almost 10,000 people are surveyed including representative studies in the Netherlands, Germany, the UK and Italy.

The work empirically shows that social media is increasingly important for emergency services, both for prevention and during crises; that private use of social media is a driving force in shaping opinions for organisational use; and that citizens have high expectations towards authorities, especially monitoring social media is expected, and sometimes responses within one hour. The work also shows that the spread of unreliable information is perceived as risk, most pronounced among respondents in Germany. Depending on the risk culture, the data show further differences, e.g. whether the state (Germany) or the individual (Netherlands) is seen as primarily responsible for coping with the situation. Furthermore, the thesis looks at novel concepts and technologies for citizens and authorities that have been developed and evaluated in the field. Although automation can help manage large amounts of data from social media, control and traceability are perceived as important, both in terms of tailorable quality assessment, aggregation and filtering for situational awareness and to support digital volunteers to coordinate across social media.

Samenvatting

Het mobiliseren van hulpverleners bij een overstroming of vrienden laten weten dat je in orde bent bij een terroristische aanslag – steeds meer mensen maken gebruik van sociale media in nood-, crisis- of rampsituaties. Stormen, overstromingen, aanslagen of pandemieën (zie COVID-19) laten zien dat burgers sociale media gebruiken om zichzelf te informeren of om te coördineren. Daarnaast gebruiken autoriteiten sociale media om het publiek te waarschuwen, getroffen personen of hulpverleners te coördineren of hun situatiebeoordeling te verrijken. Om dit te reguleren en te ondersteunen is kennis over de acties van autoriteiten en burgers, net zoals hun perceptie van de rol van sociale media voor de openbare veiligheid en bescherming van essentieel belang. Er is echter een gebrek aan uitgebreide en representatieve empirische studies over dit onderwerp, vooral deze met een Europese focus.

Deze dissertatie „*Een Europees Perspectief op Crisisinformatica: Houdingen van Burgers en Autoriteiten ten aanzien van Sociale Media voor Openbare Veiligheid en Beveiliging*" draagt bij aan deze onderzoekslacune door empirische bevindingen, alsook strategieën, concepten en technologieën die hierop geïnspireerd zijn voor te stellen. Gebaseerd op de stand van zaken in het onderzoek naar *crisisinformatica* als een multidisciplinair veld dat computer- en sociaalwetenschappelijke kennis over rampen combineert, en vanuit het perspectief van *bestuurskunde* en *politieke wetenschappen*, presenteert deze dissertatie kwalitatieve en kwantitatieve studies over de houding van hulpdiensten en burgers in Europa ten aanzien van sociale media in noodsituaties. In de afzonderlijke deelstudies worden bijna 10.000 mensen ondervraagd, waaronder representatieve studies in Nederland, Duitsland, het Verenigd Koninkrijk en Italië.

Het werk toont empirisch aan dat sociale media steeds belangrijker worden voor noodhulpdiensten, zowel voor preventie als tijdens crisissituaties; dat
privégebruik van sociale media een drijvende kracht is bij het vormen van meningen voor organisatorisch gebruik; en dat burgers hoge verwachtingen hebben
ten aanzien van autoriteiten, met name het monitoren van sociale media wordt
verwacht, en soms het reageren binnen het uur. Uit het werk blijkt ook dat de
verspreiding van onbetrouwbare informatie als risico wordt ervaren, het meest
uitgesproken bij respondenten in Duitsland. Afhankelijk van de risicocultuur
laten de gegevens verdere verschillen zien, bijvoorbeeld of de staat (Duitsland) of het individu (Nederland) wordt gezien als de hoofdverantwoordelijke
voor het beheersen van de situatie. Voorts worden in de dissertatie nieuwe concepten en technologieën voor burgers en autoriteiten bekeken die in het veld zijn
ontwikkeld en geëvalueerd. Hoewel automatisering kan helpen bij het beheren
van grote hoeveelheden gegevens uit sociale media, controle en traceerbaarheid
als belangrijk worden ervaren, zowel in termen van op maat gemaakte kwaliteitsbeoordeling, aggregatie en filtering voor situationeel bewustzijn als om digitale
vrijwilligers te ondersteunen bij de coördinatie via sociale media.

Contents

1 Introduction 1
   1.1 Motivation and Problem Statement 1
   1.2 Aim and Research Questions 6
   1.3 Content and Contributions 7
   1.4 Underlying Publications and Contributions of the Authors 13

2 The State of the Art in Crisis Informatics 19
   2.1 Case Studies of Social Media in Emergencies 20
   2.2 Types of Crisis Informatics Research 31
   2.3 Types of Interaction: Usage Patterns in Crisis Informatics 37
   2.4 Summary, Research Gaps and Next Steps 47

3 Attitudes by Emergency Services Staff in Europe 53
   3.1 Related Work 54
   3.2 European Emergency Services Perception in 2014 61
   3.3 Attitudes by Emergency Services Staff in Europe in 2014
        and 2017 86
   3.4 Summary and Next Steps 107

4 Citizens' Perception of Social Media in Emergencies in Europe 109
   4.1 Related Work 110
   4.2 Citizens' Perception of Social Media in Emergencies
        in Europe 112
   4.3 The Impact of Risk Cultures in Social Media Use
        in Emergencies 130
   4.4 Summary and Next Steps 157

5 Tailorable Situation Assessment with Social Media 159
   5.1 Related Work 160
   5.2 Social Media Assessment by Emergency Services 166
   5.3 EUD in Social Big Data Gathering and Assessment 170
   5.4 Evaluation: Tailorable Quality Assessment 182
   5.5 Design Requirements and Social Media Observatory 185
   5.6 Summary and Next Steps 188

6 Self-Organisation of Digital Volunteers across Social Media 191
   6.1 Related Work 192
   6.2 Empirical Study 197
   6.3 XHELP: Cross-Social-Media Application for Volunteers 223
   6.4 Design Requirements 233
   6.5 Summary 234

7 Discussion and Conclusion 237
   7.1 The State of the Art in Crisis Informatics 237
   7.2 Attitudes of Emergency Services' Staff 238
   7.3 Citizens' Perception towards Social Media in Emergencies 239
   7.4 Situational Assessment of Emergency Services 241
   7.5 Self-Organisation of Digital Volunteers with Social Media 242
   7.6 Policy Recommendations and Limitations 244

References 249

List of Figures

Figure 2.1   Crisis Communication Matrix (Reuter et al., 2012),
Adapted Concerning the Terminology 37

Figure 3.1   Country (Q8) 63

Figure 3.2   Age (Q6) 64

Figure 3.3   Organisations (Q1) 64

Figure 3.4   Years of Experience (Q5) 64

Figure 3.5   Role (Q2) 65

Figure 3.6   In my Private Life, I use Social Media Very Often
(Q7) 67

Figure 3.7   Attitudes of Emergency Service Staff (Q7) Depending
on their Age (Q4) 68

Figure 3.8   Attitudes towards Social Media (Q7) 68

Figure 3.9   Current Emergency Services' Social Media Use (Q9) 71

Figure 3.10 Usefulness of Different Types of Information Shared
on Social Media by the Public during Emergencies
(Q11) 75

Figure 3.11 Main Perceived Enabling Conditions for Social Media
Use (Q12) 76

Figure 3.12 Expected Increase of Future Social Media Use
in Own Organisation (Q14) 79

Figure 3.13 Emergency Management Cycle Enhanced with Social
Media (based on Q9 and Q14) 82

Figure 3.14 Internal and External Enablers and Barriers 83

Figure 3.15 Infographic of the Main Results 84

Figure 3.16 Attitudes towards Social Media for Private
and Organisational Purposes 94

Figure 3.17   Please Indicate how Strongly you Agree or Disagree
               with the following Statements (Q7—Cumulative
               Results 2014 and 2017)   95
Figure 3.18   Does your Organisation use Social Media?
               (Q9—Cumulative Results 2014 and 2017)   96
Figure 3.19   Which of the following Types of Information Shared
               on Social Media by the Public Would you find Useful
               to Receive during an Emergency? (Q11—Cumulative
               Results 2014 and 2017)   97
Figure 3.20   How Important do you Think are the following
               Factors to Ensure that Social Media is Widely Used
               by Emergency Services Like Yours? (Q12)   98
Figure 3.21   Please Indicate the Extent to which you Expect your
               Organisation to Increase its use of Social Media
               in Future (Q14)   99
Figure 3.22   Simple SEM on Private Experience
               towards the Attitudes (Description of the Fit
               Values in the Section 9.1.2.2)   103
Figure 3.23   SEM with the Moderator "Information expectations"
               (Description of the Fit Values in Section 9.1.2.2)   103
Figure 4.1   Countries   114
Figure 4.2   Age   114
Figure 4.3   Current use of Social Media (Q8)   116
Figure 4.4   Attitude towards Social Media (Q9)   117
Figure 4.5   Current Communication Channels in Use (Q10)   118
Figure 4.6   Current Use of Social Media for Information
               Gathering in Emergency situations (Q14)   118
Figure 4.7   Current use of Social Media for Information
               Gathering in Emergency Situations (Q15)   119
Figure 4.8   Future use of Social Media for Information Gathering
               in Emergency Situations (Q16)   119
Figure 4.9   Attitude towards Social Media as Information Source
               (Q21)   120
Figure 4.10   Current use of Social Media for Sharing Information
               Regarding Emergency Situations (Q17)   121
Figure 4.11   Current use of Social Media for Sharing Information
               regarding Emergency situations (Q18)   121
Figure 4.12   Future use of Social Media for Sharing Information
               Regarding Emergency Situations (Q19)   122

Figure 4.13   Perceived Social Media Integration of Emergency
              Services (Q22) 122
Figure 4.14   Knowledge about Social Media Services (Q23) 124
Figure 4.15   Future use of Apps for Information Exchange
              in Emergency Situations (Q13) 125
Figure 4.16   Infographic of Selected Survey Results 127
Figure 4.17   Infographic of Statistical Results of the European
              Survey 140
Figure 4.18   Use of Social Media during an Emergency (Q2) 141
Figure 4.19   Types of Information Shared (Q3) 143
Figure 4.20   Reasons for not Using Social Media
              during an Emergency (Q5; This would
              [definitely] put me off) 144
Figure 4.21   Expected Responsiveness of Emergency Services
              to Messages Posted via Social Media (Q4; Strongly
              agree, Agree) 146
Figure 4.22   Likelihood of Using an App in the Future
              for Different Purposes (Q8; Very likely, Quite likely) 147
Figure 5.1   Overall Architecture of Client Applications such
              as Social-QAS that use the Social Media API
              to Access Different Social Media over a Unified
              Interface 180
Figure 5.2   Quality Assessment Service Integrated
              into an Application 181
Figure 5.3   Search Results (left), Degree of Completion (Lower
              Left) and Map Presentation (Right) 182
Figure 5.4   Social Media Observatory (SMO) dashboard
              with interactive charts, feed and list view 188
Figure 6.1   Amount of Rainfall and Cases during the Floods 201
Figure 6.2   "Moms Help" Group Discussion 204
Figure 6.3   "Moms Help" List of Files 205
Figure 6.4   Photo with Emotional and Cohesive Appeal 207
Figure 6.5   Photo with Emotional and Cohesive Appeal 208
Figure 6.6   Google Maps in the City of Halle 211
Figure 6.7   MDR Live Blog and FluDDHilfe Website 212
Figure 6.8   Search Settings and Results 224
Figure 6.9   Geo-Localisation 225
Figure 6.10   Create new Posting 227
Figure 6.11   Dashboard with "My Postings" 228

List of Tables

Table 2.1   Overview of Some Case Studies in the Research
            Literature, Enhancement of Reuter & Kaufhold (2018a),
            updated for this thesis   21
Table 3.1   Structural Equation Model   102
Table 4.1   App-Categories and the Frequencies of Mentions (Q12)   125
Table 5.1   Excerpt of Source-Based Data Attributes   173
Table 5.2   Parameters for Social Media Search   175
Table 5.3   Implemented Quality Assessment Methods (Reuter
            et al., 2015c)   177
Table 6.1   Several Existing Approaches and Tools   195
Table 6.2   The Three Cases of Our Empirical Study   199
Table 6.3   Two Examples of Information Verification   207
Table 6.4   Positive Reception and Obstacles of Google Maps   210
Table 6.5   Identified Challenges and Actions   218

Introduction

1

1.1 Motivation and Problem Statement

Social media and collaborative technologies are nowadays part of everyday life and work. Out of 8 billion people on earth 5 billion use the internet, and 4,5 billion are active social media users, mostly mobile (Kemp, 2022). The predecessor concept *Web 2.0* was initially introduced as an architecture of participation with new possibilities for social interaction (O'Reilly, 2005). However, over the years, this interaction has increasingly been subsumed under the term *social media*, which is defined as a "group of internet-based applications that build on the ideological and technological foundations of Web 2.0, and that allow the creation and exchange of user-generated content" (Kaplan & Haenlein, 2010). Here, user-generated content refers to "the various forms of media content that are publicly available and created by end-users" (Kaplan & Haenlein, 2010). Allen (2004) noted that the "core ideas of social software itself enjoy a much longer history, running back to Vannevar Bush's ideas about the storage-device Memex in 1945 through terms such as augmentation, groupware, and *Computer Supported Cooperative Work* (CSCW) in the 1960 s, 70 s, 80 s, and 90 s". Similarly, Koch (2008) argued that "most of what […] is advertised as a revolution on the web has been there as CSCW applications years (or even decades) ago—however, not as nice and as usable as today".

According to recent statistics (Statista, 2022), the most frequently used providers of social media currently include *Facebook* with about 2.9 billion active

Supplementary Information The online version contains supplementary material available at https://doi.org/10.1007/978-3-658-39720-3_1.

© The Author(s), under exclusive license to Springer Fachmedien Wiesbaden GmbH, part of Springer Nature 2022
C. Reuter, *A European Perspective on Crisis Informatics*,
https://doi.org/10.1007/978-3-658-39720-3_1

users monthly, *YouTube* (2.6 billion), *WhatsApp* (2 billion), *Instagram* (1.5 billion), *WeChat* (1.3 billion), *TikTok* (1 billion) and *Twitter* (436 million). With such pervasiveness, social media is not only of relevance for ordinary routines; these media and technologies are also essential for public safety and security—such as during crises, emergencies, or disasters (Reuter & Kaufhold, 2018). This includes attempts to ensure, recover, and improve safety and security for humans, authorities, organisations, and companies. While dealing with such contexts and circumstances, applications should possess specific characteristics (Mendonça, 2007). They need to be able to deal with large volumes of data and traffic peaks, e.g., social big data; be reliable, e.g., prepared for unforeseen circumstances such as infrastructure disturbances or breakdowns; and attend to the fact that they may distribute information that can lead to panic or fear. Most importantly: The appropriate use of social media in such contexts is not just a technical question, but also an issue containing many social aspects. To sum it up: "big crisis data should not be considered as a magic bullet which can save lives just because they are available" (Boersma & Fonio, 2017).

One of the earliest examples of this kind of social media use occurred already more than 20 years ago, during the 9/11 attacks in 2001. During these attacks, the US Federal Emergency Management Agency (FEMA) and the Red Cross employed web-based technologies to disseminate information to the public and to report the status of the relief efforts externally and internally (Harrald et al., 2002). Additionally, citizens created wikis to gather information about missing persons (Palen & Liu, 2007). Since about 2006, the use of social media for managing crisis events has gained increasing interest among researchers, focussing on both human-induced disasters (e.g., shootings, terror attacks, political uprisings, conflicts, wars, such as the 2022 Russo-Ukrainian war) and natural hazards (e.g., tsunamis, hurricanes, earthquakes, floods), including long-term health crises like the COVID-19 pandemic (Haesler et al., 2021).

The area of study dealing with social media in emergencies is often called *crisis informatics*. The term established by Hagar (2007) and later expanded upon by Palen et al. (2009) "views emergency response as an expanded social system where information is disseminated within and between official and public channels and entities." Crisis informatics is a "multidisciplinary field combining computing and social science knowledge of disasters; its central tenet is that people use personal information and communication technology to respond to disaster in creative ways to cope with uncertainty" (Palen & Anderson, 2016).

It combines proceedings from many academic fields. From the *technical* perspective, *computer science* is the study of computation, automation and information. Advances in computer science are necessary in order to design and implement technical innovations. However, purely technical advances are not sufficient. In many cases, the design of concepts and technologies needs to be embedded in empirical work to ensure the applicability, wherefore interdisciplinary work, combining both sides, is necessary. The discipline of *information systems* focuses on the use of information technology in organisational settings; *human-computer interaction (HCI)* has a special emphasis on the various points of contact and interaction between human and computer; and *CSCW*, a sub-discipline of HCI, concentrates on computer-supported collaboration among different actors. From the *social science* perspective, focusing on the study of societies and the relationships among individuals, *psychology* studies the mind and behaviour of the individual, including individuals' attitudes towards an entity (such as social media), ranging from extremely negative to extremely positive. *Political science* addresses systems of governance and power. One important subdiscipline, public policy and administration or *public administration* (Rabin et al., 2007) deals with the actual implementation of government policy for public services, such as emergency services. Public administration is "what takes place after the election, in which the day-to-day business of governing actually occurs" (Reddick, 2012). Governments are increasingly able to use information and communication technologies (ICT) and therefore face a growing demand for open government (de Vries, 2016). This may include attempts to engage with the public, e.g., via social media.

When looking at social media in emergencies from a perspective of public policy and administration, theories on the relationship between technology and administration are of importance. According to Reddick (2012, p. 4) there are three common theories of public administration and IT, which all have in common that they examine the impact of technology on social and organisational change. *Technological determinism* (Marx & Smith, 1994) implies that the introduction of new technology creates change and will be adopted by public administration, its core argument being that technology itself causes social, political and cultural adjustments. *Reinforcement theory* (Sherrod, 1971) argues the opposite. It states that IT is implemented if it supports the perceived need for organisational change. Therefore, technology is not considered the driver, but organisational requirements. Based on perceived limitations of both theories, the *sociotechnical theory* (Pasmore, 1988) argues that "organisations are made up of people in the social system that use tools, techniques, and knowledge to shape the organisational change" and that "technical change is influenced by the demands of the external environment that impacts information systems change in an organisation" (Reddick, 2012, p. 5). According to Reddick (2012, p. 5) it is the most commonly used theory in public administration. It refers to the interrelation between social and technical aspects, in the sense that technological advancements, organisational requirements and peoples' attitudes influence the use of IT in an organisation and therefore social change. Accordingly, not just formal requirements, which may lead to decisions to implement a certain technology, are important. To implement public policy, legal authority is central. However, the *attitude*—referring to an individual's predisposed state of mind regarding a value of the stakeholders towards the problem or solution—in our case: social media in emergencies—has a great influence on the actual use.

Given the ubiquity of social media and considering all observed cases over the last 20 + years, it can certainly be stated without too much hesitation that social media indeed plays an important role for public safety and security (Reuter & Kaufhold, 2018). Considering a public administration and political science perspective as well as a sociotechnical perspective, the question remains how to implement social media for safety and security from both the technical side— the perspective of technological possibilities –, but also the social side, including organisational requirements and people's attitudes towards this technology. It's important to consider that these requirements and attitudes may differ among societies. The theoretical framework of *risk cultures* (Cornia et al., 2016; Dressel, 2015) concentrates on individuals' behaviour in and attitudes towards emergency situations. While *state-oriented risk cultures* point towards the state to solve the situation, they show high compliance with authorities' instructions. In *individualistic risk cultures* citizens still feel that they individually share responsibilities e.g. of being informed and prepared. Different risk cultures may lead to different requirements towards measures such as social media in emergencies.

It is also important, and comprehensive, to mention that the implementation of IT in organisations does not just lead to planned effects. Orlikowski and Hofman (1997) distinguish between three effects: *Foreseeable effects* are basically the reason why technology is implemented, such as the use of social media to be able to spread warnings very fast. *Opportunity-based effects* are not foreseeable, but are considered positive and then introduced purposefully and intentionally, such as the possibilities for two-way communication of social media during crises. *Emergent effects* are those, that arise spontaneously "out of local innovation and which are not originally anticipated or intended". They are sometimes based on local specifics, such as special skills or attitudes. Furthermore, besides the three described effects, there are challenging consequences that are neither foreseeable nor wanted, such as the excessive use of social media during crises, leading to information overload or misinformation. It is therefore interesting to research foreseeable, opportunity-based, emergent or challenging effects.

The challenges of effective use of social media in emergencies are not limited to emergency services. The Sendai Framework for Disaster Risk Reduction 2015–2030 (United Nations, 2015) emphasises that Disaster Risk Reduction (DRR) requires an intersectional approach which encompasses, e.g., establishing accessible and inclusive partnerships at all levels of society. In order to achieve the framework's goals, particular attention should be paid to ensuring and improving community resilience, e.g., by improving the organisation of citizens' voluntary work. Considering the emphasis placed on the role of social media as a means to promote awareness on DRR policies and strategies, on national and local, as well as global and regional levels, social media should thus also be considered essential for promoting citizens' resilience. The active role of ordinary citizens as volunteers "might be questioned if disaster response was a complex task", but this is not true for all tasks to be performed (Scanlon et al., 2014). In many cases citizens can be considered a valuable resource, as also emphasised by the Sendai Framework. Accordingly, a "paradigm shift in planning and implementing DRR is essential in international and national strategies. Knowledge in holistic disaster scenarios should be increased among actual citizens, which would ultimately motivate and enable them to reduce their own exposure and risk, instead of solely relying on law enforcement" (Parajuli, 2020).

Although a lot of research on social media in emergencies has already been published, from the perspective of public administration, the state of the art shows gaps (Reuter et al., 2018a; Reuter et al. 2018b; Reuter & Kaufhold, 2018) to be filled, as this thesis argues (Chapter 2):

1. Previous research often focuses on *either citizens or authorities*, with potentially diverging perspectives. The transfer of the functioning of social media in private contexts to the very different world of crisis situations and authorities with overstretched capacities harbours potential areas of tension. Nevertheless, speculating about these areas of tension is not helpful. Research integrating both perspectives is needed as a complement.
2. Previous research is often based on *smaller empirical samples*. Reliable or even representative empirical evidence on the attitudes of the authorities, e.g., emergency services on the one hand and the public, e.g., citizens on the other, possibly even based on data across different European countries, considering different *risk cultures*, is unfortunately still in short supply, and might be a complement.
3. Previous research also often focuses *on one particular crisis* event and researches the use of social media in this setting. Research independent of a single crisis is needed as a complement.

4. Research has *heavily emphasised Twitter*, mostly due to the ease of data collection and accessibility that the platform affords. Research not relying on Twitter, but on citizens self-disclosure might be a complement.
5. Previous research as well as datasets are often of *US origin* in the *English language*, which limits the diversity of research. Research of European origin and not just in the English language, but also e.g., Dutch, German, and Italian is needed as a complement.

1.2   Aim and Research Questions

This thesis contributes to the research on social media for safety and security with empirical findings regarding the use of social media and with concepts and technologies for support in such settings. This thesis aims to address authorities, such as emergency services, as well as the public, such as citizens, to deal with social media for safety and security, or: to implement the politics of safety and security. It aims to not focus just on Twitter, and to research more than one particular crisis, while including both perspectives of emergency services and citizens by utilising representative surveys across Europe. It has to be made clear that this work could not study the whole of Europe. Nevertheless, it aims to examine European disasters and European subjects, including a comparative study in selected European countries.

The main research question this thesis aims to answer from a European perspective is: **What are citizens' and authorities' attitudes towards social media for public safety and security?**

This leads us to the following sub-questions, which span the following two dimensions: stakeholders (authorities and citizens) and exploitation (passive usage and active benefits):

First, the thesis aims to research one of the central actors from a public administration perspective: authorities, especially emergency services and their actual use of social media in emergencies, as well as their attitude towards this technology. The thesis aims to consider a European perspective, as large differences between European countries are known. This leads to the first sub-question:

- **RQ1: What is the attitude of the staff of emergency services across Europe towards the organisational usage of social media?** How is social media used, what types of information are important, and what are important enabling conditions? Answers to these questions will be found in Chapter 3.

Second, citizens are also important stakeholders to consider, as long as the successful use of social media by emergency services depends on citizens' use, and also their expectations. This leads to the second sub-question:

- RQ2: **How do citizens across Europe**, especially in the Netherlands, Germany, Italy and the United Kingdom, **use social media during emergencies?** What are their expectations towards emergency services, what are perceived barriers, and what is their attitude towards mobile emergency apps? Answers to these questions will be given in Chapter 4.

Third, based on empirical evidence on both emergency services attitudes and citizens expectations, the thesis aims to analyse how situation assessment using social media might be implemented, which leads to the third sub-question:

- RQ3: **How can situational assessment of emergency services be supported by social media?** How can end-users articulate their personal quality criteria appropriately, and how can the selection of relevant data be supported by technology? Answers to these questions will be found in Chapter 5.

Fourth, the thesis also aims to find out how citizens might be supported by social media. Since this is a broad field, the thesis will focus on self-organising digital volunteers as an interesting use case, which leads to the fourth sub-question:

- RQ4: **How can self-organisation of digital volunteers be supported by social media?** How is social media used to organise volunteers, what are the challenges for collaboration support, and how might real and virtual relief activities be supported by specific tools? Answers to these questions can be seen in Chapter 6.

1.3   Content and Contributions

Following an introduction (Chapter 1) the thesis addresses current and potential practices and perceptions regarding the use of social media and interactive applications during crises and emergencies. Here, a European perspective is considered. In concrete terms, this means that central ideas were developed during a European project, and the empirical studies in particular were conducted not only in one nation state, but on a European level, including a large representative study in the Netherlands, Germany, the United Kingdom, and Italy.

Based on the state of the art in crisis informatics and the outline of future research potentials (Chapter 2), this thesis offers qualitative and quantitative studies on the attitudes of emergency services (Chapter 3) and citizens in Europe (Chapter 4) towards social media in emergencies. Furthermore, the thesis addresses empirical findings with novel concepts and technologies for citizens and authorities that have been designed and evaluated in this field. This includes applications to support tailorable quality assessment (Chapter 5) as well as to help digital volunteers to coordinate across social media (Chapter 6). Finally, a conclusion is drawn (Chapter 7). The methods used as well as the *research data management* will be described in detail in the methodology sections of the respective chapters, however also as a summary in Section 9.2. The main parts of Chapters 2 to 6 have already been published and resemble the accepted versions of reviewed journal articles or conference papers with minor to moderate changes and updates:

Chapter 2 (The State of the Art in Crisis Informatics) reviews the use of social media in emergencies since 2001 with view to case studies of social media use in emergencies, types of research in crisis informatics, as well as forms of interaction that have been researched. Particularly starting around 2006, many studies concentrated on the use of ICT and social media before, during, or after almost every emergency and crisis. These studies are sometimes summarised under the term crisis informatics. This chapter has been published to the *International Journal of Human-Computer Interaction* (Reuter et al., 2018b) (Paper A).

Contributions and highlights:

- Comprehensive overview of case studies of social media in emergencies.
- Detected biases of studies: Almost exclusive research focus on Twitter within the US, rather limited systematic European perspectives.
- Derived types of crisis informatics research and on usage patterns.
- Identification of areas for future research.

Chapter 3 (Attitudes by Emergency Services Staff in Europe) summarises the findings of a survey with 761 emergency service staff across 32 European countries. The main aims of the survey were to explore the attitudes expressed by emergency service staff towards social media for private and organisational use as well as the levels and main factors influencing the current and likely future use of social media in their organisations. Based on our results, we discuss possible enhancements of the emergency management cycle using social media. The first part of this chapter has been published in the *International Journal of Human-Computer Studies (IJHCS)* (Reuter et al., 2016b) (Paper B).

Contributions and highlights:

- A survey with 761 emergency service staff across 32 European countries (35% Germany, 18% Slovenia, 15% Poland, 16% Scandinavia, 5% Benelux, 11% others).
- The majority of emergency services have positive attitudes towards social media.
- Social media is used to share information (44%) than to receive messages (19%).
- A future increase is expected (74%), even more for organisations already using it.
- There is a huge gap between rhetoric (66%) and reality (23%) in social media use.

The chapter then presents a comparison with a second survey conducted across Europe with emergency services in 2014 and 2017 respectively, with additionally 473 answers. The analysis of both samples shows that personal experiences influence how organisational usage of social media is perceived and how emergency service staff view the future use of social media. Furthermore, an increase in use could be proven. This second part of this chapter has been published in the *International Journal of Disaster Risk Reduction (IJDRR)* (Reuter et al., 2020a) (Paper C).

Contributions and highlights:

- A survey with 473 emergency service staff in Europe.
- Interest of emergency staff in use of social media increased from 2014 to 2017.
- At the same time, more respondents pointed out to critical issues like reliability.

- Personal use does indirectly influence attitudes towards organisational use.
- The effect of personal on organisational use is moderated by "factors of meaning".
- Older participants are more interested in organisational social media usage.

Chapter 4 (Citizens' Perception of Social Media in Emergencies in Europe) first presents the findings of a survey of 1,034 citizens across 30 European countries to explore citizens' attitudes towards the use of social media for private purposes and in emergency situations. The aim of the overall study is to discuss citizens' attitudes towards social media in emergencies in order to derive challenges and opportunities for social resilience. This first part of this chapter has been published in the Journal *Technological Forecasting and Social Change (TFSC)* (Reuter & Spielhofer, 2017) (Paper D).

Contributions and highlights:

- Snowball survey with 1,034 citizens staff cross 30 European countries.
- Social media is rather used for searching (43%) than sharing information (27%).
- Emergency services are expected to monitor social media (69%).
- Mistrust turns out to be the main barrier to using social media in emergencies.
- Very little awareness exists regarding social media safety services and emergency apps.

Chapter 4 then researches the differences of social media usage during emergencies and respective perceptions across different countries. Our representative survey of 7,071 citizens in Europe (Germany, Italy, the Netherlands and the United Kingdom) shows differences of current use of social media in emergencies, expectations towards authorities monitoring social media, intensity of perceiving barriers regarding the use as well as variances concerning the (likelihood of future) use of mobile apps. Our comparison of the four countries allows for an interpretation of divergent behavioural patterns across countries with respect to risk cultures as well as expanding the respective model to social media contexts. At the same time, our findings stress that across the four European countries participants assessed similar advantages such as dissemination of information and barriers like false rumours with respect to the use of social media during emergencies. The second part of this chapter has also been published in the Journal *Technological Forecasting and Social Change (TFSC)* (Reuter et al., 2019b) (Paper E).

Contributions and highlights:

- Comparative representative evidence with 7,071 citizens in Europe (Germany, Italy, the Netherlands, and the United Kingdom).
- Almost half of respondents (45%) have already used social media during emergencies.
- Dutch and Italian respondents use social media comparatively frequently; German use is moderate; British participants have relatively low interest in future use.
- Risk cultures of social media use may account for the countries' diverging behaviour.
- Same barriers and advantages of social media were identified across risk cultures.

Chapter 5 (Tailorable Situation Assessment with Social Media) presents how a tailorable quality assessment service can support the use of citizen-generated content from social media. In particular, we studied how users can articulate their personal quality criteria appropriately. A presentation of related work is followed by an empirical study on the use of social media in the field of emergency management, focusing on situation assessment practices by the emergency services. Based on this, we present the tailorable *quality assessment service* (QAS) for social media content, which has been implemented and integrated into an existing application for both volunteers and emergency services. This chapter has been published in *New Perspectives in End-User Development* (Paper F) as well as the *Proceedings of the International Symposium on End-User Development (IS-EUD)* (Reuter et al., 2015c) (Paper G).

Contributions and highlights:

- The empirical study emphasises the range and quality assessment of citizen-generated content in emergencies.
- A technical concept for a tailorable social media gathering and quality assessment service for social media is presented.
- Formulation of a reference implementation of the gathering service as well as quality assessment service inside an existing web-based application for emergency services and an existing web-app for volunteers.
- A process from data selection presented to use from the perspective of end-user development.

Chapter 6 (Self-Organisation of Digital Volunteers across Social Media) first examines the actions of virtual communities in disasters using the case study of the 2013 European Floods. We conducted a qualitative analysis of selected emergent volunteer communities in Germany on Facebook and Twitter, among others, and subsequently conducted interviews with Facebook group founders and activists, focusing on the role of the moderator. Public coverage during the event indicated, and our analysis confirms, that Twitter, Facebook, Google Maps and other services were frequently used by affected citizens and volunteers to coordinate help activities among themselves. The first part of this chapter has been published in the *Journal of Homeland Security and Emergency Management (JHSEM)* (Kaufhold & Reuter, 2016) (Paper H).

Chapter 6 then introduces the novel cross-social media application "XHELP" for volunteers, which supports the process of both gathering and distributing cross-media and cross-channel information. The application is based on the results of a study on social media usage during the European Floods of 2013 which not only includes a comprehensive analysis of volunteer communities but also evaluates interviews with "digital volunteers" such as Facebook moderators of crisis-related groups. Furthermore, supporting designing implications for applications used by volunteer moderators during disasters are identified based on interviews with 20 users. The second part of this chapter has been published in the *Proceedings of the Conference on Human Factors in Computing Systems (CHI)* (Reuter et al., 2015b) (Paper I).

Contributions and highlights:

- The empirical study of the European floods 2013 emphasises the relevance of social media in Germany for the first time.
- "Moderators" mediate offers of and demands for help with the use of social media.
- Cross-platform search, especially with time and location filtering options, contributes to the channelling of the information flow.

Chapter 7 (Discussion and Conclusion) summarises the main findings of this thesis and discusses policy recommendations.

1.4 Underlying Publications and Contributions of the Authors

This thesis consists of the works that have been previously published as articles (journal articles, conference papers and book chapters), sometimes updated for this thesis. Main parts of this thesis are created by multiple authors. This section aims to state the independent academic contributions, which have been confirmed by all authors. For all papers, that are part of this thesis, I was the leading and corresponding author, however, the contributions of the co-authors, which have been gratefully provided, are very important as well, as I will describe in the following.

Paper A (in Chapter 2): **Reuter, C.,** Hughes, A. L. & Kaufhold, M.-A. (2018). Social Media in Crisis Management: An Evaluation and Analysis of Crisis Informatics Research. *International Journal on Human-Computer Interaction (IJHCI)*, vol. 34, no. 4, pp. 280–294. https://doi.org/10.1080/10447318.2018.1427832 [Impact Factor: 3.353]

This paper constitutes a joint work with Amanda Lee Hughes and Marc-André Kaufhold. As corresponding and leading author, I led the overall research design and was responsible for the management of the manuscript and the introduction (Chapter 1) of the paper. The analysis of published cases as well as the usage patterns of social media in emergencies were drafted by me and extended by Marc and Amanda. The types of crisis informatics research were mainly written by Amanda and extended by Marc and me. The discussion and conclusion were composed by contributions and reflections of all authors.

Paper B (in Chapter 3): **Reuter, C.,** Ludwig, T., Kaufhold, M.-A., & Spielhofer, T. (2016). Emergency Services Attitudes towards Social Media: A Quantitative and Qualitative Survey across Europe. *International Journal of Human-Computer Studies (IJHCS)*, 95, 96–111. https://doi.org/10.1016/j.ijhcs.2016.03.005 [Impact Factor: 3.632]

This paper constitutes a joint work with Thomas Ludwig, Marc-André Kaufhold and Thomas Spielhofer. As corresponding and leading author, I led the overall research design and was responsible for the management of the manuscript and the introduction of the paper. Thomas L. and I conducted the literature review. The representative survey was led by Thomas S. and me including methodology and questionnaire and was mutually designed by all authors. While I led the qualitative analysis with support of Marc, Thomas S. focused on the quantitative statistical analysis of collected data. Thomas L., Marc and I carried out the analysis and wrote the findings section. The discussion and conclusion were driven by Thomas L. and me.

Paper C (in Chapter 3): **Reuter, C.,** Kaufhold, M.-A., Spahr, F., Spielhofer, T. & Hahne, A. S. (2020). Emergency Service Staff and Social Media – A Comparative Empirical Study of the Attitude by Emergency Services Staff in Europe in 2014 and 2017. *International Journal of Disaster Risk Reduction (IJDRR)* vol. 46, no. 4. https://doi.org/10.1016/j.ijdrr.2020.101516 [Impact Factor: 4.32]

This paper constitutes a joint work with Marc-André Kaufhold, Fabian Spahr, Thomas Spielhofer and Anna Sophie Hahne. As corresponding and leading author, I led the overall research design and was responsible for the management of the manuscript and the introduction of the paper. I conducted the literature review, supported by Marc. The method and questionnaire was mutually designed by Thomas and me. While Thomas and Anna Sophie led the quantitative statistical analysis of collected data, Marc and I were responsible for the descriptive part. Fabian extended the analysis, focussed on the comparative analysis, and wrote the findings section in close collaboration with me. The discussion and conclusion were written by all authors.

Paper D (in Chapter 4): **Reuter, C.,** & Spielhofer, T. (2016). Towards Social Resilience: A Quantitative and Qualitative Survey on Citizens' Perception of Social Media in Emergencies in Europe. *Journal Technological Forecasting and Social*

Change (TFSC). https://doi.org/10.1016/j.techfore.2016.07.038 [Impact Factor: 8.593]

This paper constitutes a joint work with Thomas Spielhofer. As corresponding and leading author, I led the overall research design and was responsible for the management of the manuscript. The method and questionnaire were mutually designed by Thomas and me. While I focused on the qualitative analysis, Thomas led the quantitative statistical analysis of collected data. I wrote all sections of the paper, and Thomas contributed with continuous feedback.

Paper E (in Chapter 4): **Reuter, C.**, Kaufhold, M.-A., Schmid, S., Spielhofer, T. & Hahne, A. S. (2019). The Impact of Risk Cultures: Citizens' perception of social media use in emergencies across Europe. *Journal Technological Forecasting and Social Change (TFSC)*, vol. 148. https://doi.org/10.1016/j.techfore.2019.119724 [Impact Factor: 8.593]

This paper constitutes a joint work with Marc-André Kaufhold, Stefka Schmid, Thomas Spielhofer and Anna Sophie Hahne. As corresponding and leading author, I led the overall research design and was responsible for the management of the manuscript and the introduction. Marc and I conducted the literature review. The method and questionnaire of the representative survey was led by Thomas S. and me. While I focused on the qualitative analysis with support of Marc, Thomas and Anna Sophie conducted the quantitative statistical analysis of collected data. Stefka came in as an author at a later stage. While Marc introduced the risk culture perspective, Stefka reframed the paper to better address this theory. Hereby, Stefka re-interpreted the data with regard to risk cultures. The discussion and conclusion were driven by Stefka, Marc and me.

Paper F (in Chapter 5): **Reuter, C.**, Kaufhold, M.-A., & Ludwig, T. (2017). End-User Development and Social Big Data - Towards Tailorable Situation Assessment with Social Media. In F. Paternò & V. Wulf (Eds.), *New Perspectives in End-User Development* (pp. 307–332). Springer. https://doi.org/10.1007/978-3-319-60291-2_12

This paper constitutes a joint work with Marc-André Kaufhold and Thomas Ludwig. As corresponding and leading author, I led the overall research design and the conceptual idea and was responsible for the management of the manuscript. While I was responsible for the introduction, the literature section was drafted by me and extended by all authors. With regard to EUD in social big data gathering and assessment I was responsible for the pre-study, while Marc focused on big data gathering and I on big data assessment, based on a previous paper of mine.

Thomas provided supported in all chapters. Evaluation as well as discussion and conclusion were written by all authors.

Paper G (in Chapter 5): **Reuter, C.,** Ludwig, T., Ritzkatis, M., & Pipek, V. (2015). Social-QAS: Tailorable Quality Assessment Service for Social Media Content. In *Proceedings of the International Symposium on End-User Development (IS-EUD)*. Lecture Notes in Computer Science. https://doi.org/10.1007/978-3-319-18425-8_11 [Acc. 40%]

This paper constitutes a joint work with Thomas Ludwig, Michael Ritzkatis and Volkmar Pipek. As corresponding and leading author, I led the overall research design and concept development, and was responsible for the management of the manuscript. Michael created an earlier underlying draft of the manuscript and implemented the prototype. For the actual paper, I drafted the first half of the manuscript (introduction, related work, empirical study), and Thomas drafted the second half (concept, implementation, conclusion), however we mutually supported each other and worked together in all sections. Volkmar supported with helpful feedback.

Paper H (in Chapter 6): Kaufhold, M.-A., & **Reuter, C.** (2016). Digital Volunteers' Self-Organization across Social Media: The Case of the 2013 European Floods in Germany. *Journal of Homeland Security and Emergency Management (JHSEM)*, 13(1), 137–166. https://doi.org/10.1515/jhsem-2015-0063 [Impact Factor: 1.258]

This paper constitutes a joint work with Marc-André Kaufhold. As corresponding and leading author, I led the overall research design and was responsible for the management of the manuscript. While I had the initial idea to research self-organisation in this case, Marc conducted most of the practical work. Marc drafted an early version of the paper, on which I worked on extensively. I was responsible for the introduction, related work and method, and Marc was responsible for the results. Challenges and derived patterns were developed in close collaboration.

Paper I (in Chapter 6): **Reuter, C.,** Ludwig, T., Kaufhold, M.-A., & Pipek, V. (2015). XHELP: Design of a Cross-Platform Social-Media Application to Support Volunteer Moderators in Disasters. In *Proceedings of the Conference on Human Factors in Computing Systems (CHI)*. Seoul, Korea: ACM Press. https://doi.org/10.1145/2702123. 2702171 [CORE-A*]

This paper constitutes a joint work with Thomas Ludwig, Marc-André Kaufhold and Volkmar Pipek. As corresponding and leading author, I led the overall research design and concept development and was responsible for the management of the manuscript and the introduction (Chapter 1). I came up with the initial idea to research volunteering during the European floods, what kind of study we should do, as well as what kind of supportive prototype might be our design intervention (embedded in Facebook). I was responsible for related work, but existing approaches were analysed by Marc. The study case as well as the empirical study were drafted by Marc and improved by Thomas and me. The concept was also drafted by Marc and extended by Thomas and me. The evaluation was conducted by Marc and me. Discussion of design requirements was done by Thomas and Marc. The conclusion was written by mes. Volkmar contributed with helpful support.

The State of the Art in Crisis Informatics

2

Social media in crisis management has become an important research topic. Since the terrorist attacks of 9/11, the use of social media in emergency and crisis situations has greatly increased. Particularly in the period from 2007 until today, many studies have concentrated on the use of ICT and social media before, during, or after numerous emergencies and crises. These studies are sometimes summarised under the term crisis informatics. In conferences like the International Conference on Information Systems for Crisis Response and Management (ISCRAM), many papers deal with social media from various perspectives and major journals in HCI and other fields publish related special issues. This chapter reviews research focused on the use of social media in emergencies since 2001, trying to look at case studies of social media use in emergencies, on types of research in crisis informatics, as well as forms of interaction that have been researched. The purpose of this chapter is to review the crisis informatics research literature, report trends, summarise the achievements and offer a perspective on the future of this research.

We begin with an overview of the many case studies of social media use in emergencies (Section 2.1). Many crisis informatics studies focus on specific events, such as 2011 London riots, 2012 Hurricane Sandy, the 2013 European floods, 2017 Manchester bombing or the COVID-19 pandemic. We provide a sample of the many different kinds of events that have been studied and summarise trends across these events. Next, we examine the different types of research that can be found in the crisis informatics literature with the aim of helping the reader understand the most common approaches to research in this area (Section 2.2). We then break down the literature by the different types of interaction studied and derive use patterns (Section 2.3). Finally, we discuss research gaps (Section 2.4).

© The Author(s), under exclusive license to Springer Fachmedien Wiesbaden GmbH, part of Springer Nature 2022
C. Reuter, *A European Perspective on Crisis Informatics*, https://doi.org/10.1007/978-3-658-39720-3_2

This whole chapter has been published as an article: "Social Media in Crisis Man-
agement: An Evaluation and Analysis of Crisis Informatics Research" by Christian
Reuter, Amanda Lee Hughes and Marc-André Kaufhold in the International Journal on
Human-Computer Interaction (IJHCI) (Reuter et al., 2018b) *[Paper A]. This chapter*
has been updated with regard to new findings after publication of the article.

2.1   Case Studies of Social Media in Emergencies

The World Disaster Report (IFRC, 2015) states that between 2005 and 2015 there
have been an average of about 631 disasters per year, including 83,934 deaths,
193,558 persons affected and estimated damage of 162,203 million US dollars
per year. The World Disaster Reports (International Federation of Red Cross
and Red Crescent Societies, 2020) focuses on climate-related events and states:
"In the past ten years, 83% of all disasters triggered by natural hazards were
caused by extreme weather- and climate-related events, such as floods, storms
and heat-waves." (p. 4).

Since 2001, social media has played an increasingly important role in how
people respond to and communicate around these worldwide disasters. For example, after the 9/11 attacks, people used photo repository sites for information
exchange after the 2004 Indian Ocean tsunami (Liu et al., 2008) and the 2007
Southern California wildfires (Shklovski et al., 2008). A prior study on Hurricane Katrina in 2005 looked at the use of PeopleFinder and ShelterFinder
(Murphy & Jennex, 2006). What all of these studies have in common is that
they have all found that social media has become an evolving and meaningful
form of backchannel communication and public participation for disaster events
(Palen, 2008). Here, we take a closer look at the many different disaster events
that have been the subject of crisis informatics research over the years.

In recent years, also various studies have emerged that deal with the use of
social media in emergencies. Journals worldwide have taken up the topic in special issues (Hiltz et al., 2011; Imran et al., 2020; Pipek et al., 2014; Reuter et al.,
2015d; Reuter et al., 2020b) as well as tracks at various conferences, such as
CSCW and *ISCRAM* (Reuter et al., 2018a). Recently, corresponding researchers
developed and published a literature resource on crisis informatics research to
support research on the COVID-19 pandemic (Palen et al., 2020).

2.1.1 Chronological Overview of Case Studies

Table 2.1 provides a chronological overview of studies regarding social media use across a wide variety of emergency and disaster events0F[1]. When compiling this list, the emphasis was to provide a representative sample of the types of events that have been studied since 2001. It was not our aim to provide a comprehensive list of all the research on this topic. Following the methodology of vom Brocke et al. (2015), we used Google Scholar to identify research studies by searching for the keywords "social media", "Web 2.0", "Twitter", "Facebook", "emergency", "disaster", and "crisis" in singular and plural forms without temporal limitations. Additionally, we used backward and forward searches. For larger, more well-known crises, we concentrated on studies about the use of social media while using a search term for that event (e.g., "Paris shootings 2015").

While we oriented our literature review on methodological guidelines, our aim was not to conduct a systematic literature review as such (e.g., with a selection of journals and conferences and the pure consideration of defined keywords). Our aim was more to comprehend the development of an emerging field (crisis informatics) among different terms, journals and disciplines. For each study, Table 2.1 lists a reference, the event that was examined and the contribution of the study. The table gives an overview of the detected cases during our literature study and serves as a summary, giving some structural aspects for each case. Several studies are analysed more precisely in the following sections. The studies are sorted by the year of occurrence.

Table 2.1 Overview of Some Case Studies in the Research Literature, Enhancement of Reuter & Kaufhold (2018a), updated for this thesis

Event of Study	Contribution	Reference
2001 9/11	Describes the use of wikis to collect information about missing people.	(Palen & Liu, 2007)
2001 9/11	Explains how FEMA and the Red Cross used web-technologies to inform the public and to provide status reports.	(Harrald et al., 2002)

(continued)

---

[1] This table extends an earlier version (Reuter & Kaufhold, 2018).

Table 2.1 (continued)

Event of Study	Contribution	Reference
2004 Indian Ocean tsunami	Describes citizens' use of photo repository sites to exchange information.	(Liu et al., 2008)
2005 Hurricane Katrina, 2010 volcano Eyjafjallajökull in Iceland	Shows that the credibility of social media information is less than that of printed, official online or televised news and information from family, relatives or friends.	(Endsley et al., 2014)
2007 Southern California wildfires	Describes how citizens use social media to seek and share information that builds community during a disaster event.	(Shklovski et al., 2008)
2007 Southern California wildfires	Suggests that community information resources and other backchannel communications activity enabled by social media are gaining prominence in the disaster arena.	(Sutton et al., 2008)
2008 Hurricanes Gustav and Ike	Highlights differences between the use of Twitter in crises and general use.	(Hughes & Palen, 2009)
2008 Sichuan earthquake	Outlines how people gather and synthesise information through social media.	(Qu et al., 2009)
2008 Tennessee River technological failure	Describes how official responders broadcast emergency-relevant information via Twitter.	(Sutton, 2010)
2009 Lakewood attack on police officers	Shows the ability of Twitter to organise and disseminate crisis-related information.	(Heverin & Zach, 2010)
2009 Oklahoma fires	Discusses the role of retweeting for information processing, especially filtering and recommendation.	(Starbird & Palen, 2010)

(continued)

Table 2.1 (continued)

Event of Study	Contribution	Reference
2009 Red River floods	Delineates the different ways people use social media during an event, including information broadcasting, directing, relaying, synthesising and redistributing.	(Vieweg et al., 2010)
2010 earthquake in Chile	Shows that the propagation of tweets that correspond to rumours differs from tweets that spread news because rumours tend to be questioned more than news by the Twitter community.	(Mendoza et al., 2010)
2010 Bornholm blizzard	Examines two Facebook groups and finds that geographical location and self-selection into groups creates different views of a crisis.	(Birkbak, 2012)
2010 Deepwater Horizon oil spill disaster	Demonstrates that BP's corrective action as the dominant image restoration strategy caused high presence of negative emotion.	(Muralidharan et al., 2011)
2010 Haiti earthquake	Analyses how people helped translate information during the earthquake and reveals the phenomenon of "digital volunteers".	(Starbird & Palen, 2011)
2010 Love Parade mass panic in Germany, volcano Eyjafjallajökull in Iceland	Systematises the communication between authorities and citizens during emergencies, outlining the need for duplex communication.	(Reuter et al., 2012)
2010 Haitian earthquake	Presents a case study of how social media technologies were used and how they influenced knowledge sharing, reuse, and decision-making.	(Yates & Paquette, 2011)

(continued)

Table 2.1 (continued)

Event of Study	Contribution	Reference
2010 San Bruno Californian gas explosion and fire disaster	Illustrates that sentiment analysis (analysis for identifying and extracting subjective information) with emotions performed 27% better than Bayesian Networks alone.	(Nagy & Stamberger, 2012)
2011 large-scale fire in Moerdijk, the Netherlands	Explains that most tweets do not contain new relevant information for governments; tweets posted by governments were buried in an avalanche of citizen tweets.	(Helsloot & Groenendaal, 2013)
2011 Egyptian uprising	Shows how the crowd expresses solidarity and does the work of information processing through recommendation and filtering.	(Starbird & Palen, 2012)
2011 Great East Japan earthquake	Emphasises the use of Twitter to provide emotional support and mentions the problem of widely publishing obsolete or inaccurate information and the unequal distribution of useful information.	(Wilensky, 2014)
2011 Norway attacks	Finds that the notion of peripheral response has evolved in relation to emergent forms of agile and dialogic emergency response.	(Perng et al., 2012)
2011 San Diego / Southwest blackout	Discusses the limitations of using social media to contact friends and family when the cell phone network did not function as expected.	(Jennex, 2012)
2011 Shadow Lake fire	Analyses the deployment of trusted digital volunteers as a virtual team to support an incident management team.	(St. Denis et al., 2012)

(continued)

Table 2.1 (continued)

Event of Study	Contribution	Reference
2011 Super Outbreak	Distinguishes groups of twitterers, such as helpers, reporters, retweeters and repeaters.	(Reuter et al., 2013)
2011 Tunisian revolution	Describes how social media linked young activists with actors in other cities and stimulated participation in weekly demonstrations.	(Wulf et al., 2013)
2011 Escherichia coli contamination crisis	Illustrates how social media can act as a complementary information channel, but that it is not a substitute for traditional or online media.	(Kuttschreuter et al., 2014)
2011 Fukushima Daiichi nuclear disaster	Contrasts effects of medium and crisis type in an online experiment.	(Utz et al., 2013)
2011 Tohoku earthquake and tsunami Japan	Sent open-ended questionnaires to a randomly selected sample of Twitter users and analysed the tweets sent from the disaster-hit areas.	(Acar & Muraki, 2011)
2012 hurricane Isaac	Demonstrates which classification algorithms work best in each phase of emergency.	(Yang et al., 2013)
2012 hurricane Sandy	Shows that few departments used online channels in their response efforts and that communication differed between fire and police departments and across media types.	(Hughes et al., 2014)
2012 Madrid Arena tragedy	Discusses opportunities for social media to support local communities using the Crisis Communication Management theory.	(Medina & Diaz, 2016)

(continued)

Table 2.1 (continued)

Event of Study	Contribution	Reference
2013 Colorado flood	Highlights the blending of online and offline expertise to evacuate horses from an isolated ranch.	(White & Palen, 2015)
2013 European flood in Germany	Identifies challenges of public response among emergent groups and digital volunteers, highlighting the role of moderators.	(Kaufhold & Reuter, 2014)
2013 European flood in Germany	Analyses one of the Facebook groups used during the flood in Dresden, by categorizing different posts according to their function to examine how the so-called "switchboard mechanism", whereby citizens in need of help could be connected to those offering it, is works.	(Albris, 2017)
2013 European flood in Germany	Finds that messages from users located near severely flooded areas have a much higher probability of being relevant.	(de Albuquerque et al., 2015)
2013 Woolwich (London) terrorist attack	Shows that the sentiment expressed in tweets is significantly predictive of both size and survival of information flows.	(Burnap et al., 2014)
2014 Carlton Complex Wildfire	Examines who contributes official information online during a crisis event and the timelines and relevance of the information provided.	(Chauhan & Hughes, 2017)
2014 Sydney siege	Provides a system to analyse posts about a special topic and visualise the emotional pulse of a geographical region.	(Wan & Paris, 2015)

(continued)

Table 2.1   (continued)

Event of Study	Contribution	Reference
2015 Cyclone Pam 2014 Kashmir floods, Indonesia landslide	Collects data via Twitter for exploration of the ICT infrastructure for disaster management.	(Chaturvedi et al., 2015)
2014 Ebola fear in the USA	Examines the amplified fear of the imported Ebola virus through social media.	(Fung et al., 2014)
2015 Amtrak derailment, Baltimore protests, hurricane Joaquin floods	Examines the use of the live-streaming application Periscope by both citizens and journalists for information sharing, crisis coverage and commentary.	(Fichet et al., 2015)
2015 Nepal earthquake	Investigates the work of mapmakers and outlines factors contributing to the emergence of infrastructure around their work practice.	(Soden & Palen, 2016)
2015 Nepal earthquake, 2013 Philippines typhoon, 2011 Japan tsunami	Investigates how "Ambient Geographic Information" via social media (Twitter and Flickr) can be used in crisis management.	(Zipf, 2016)
2015 Charlie Hebdo shooting	Examines sociological theories in terms of the social factors that contribute to online individual behaviour.	(An et al., 2016)
2015 Tianjin blasts	Provides a clustering analysis and time series analysis of social network Weibo's rumour management strategies.	(Zeng et al., 2017)
2015 Paris shootings	Examines the velocity of newsworthy content and its veracity with regard to trusted source attribution.	(Wiegand & Middleton, 2016)

(continued)

Table 2.1 (continued)

Event of Study	Contribution	Reference
2015/2016 Syrian refugee Crisis	Explores sentiments towards Syrian refugee crisis in a comparative way.	(Öztürk & Ayvaz, 2018)
2016 Roanu cyclone in Sri Lanka	Explains how Twitter and Facebook were used to help flood-affected victims with disaster warnings, relief information and weather alerts.	(Sagar, 2016)
2016 Jammu and Kashmir conflict	People use Twitter to make their own point of view clear to others and discredit the opposing party; at the same time, tweets reflect the antagonism between the two parties to the conflict, India and Pakistan.	(Gabel et al., 2019)
2017 Manchester bombing	Individual role types are initiators of sense-breaking in early crisis stages when uncertainty is at its height.	(Mirbabaie & Marx, 2020)
2017 Hurricanes Harvey, Irma, and Maria	Different crisis response strategies are prioritized differently over multiple crisis stages.	(Alam et al., 2020)
2017 Storm Cindy	Explores connections and patterns of the social network created by the aggregated interactions in Twitter during disaster responses.	(Kim et al., 2018)
2018 Gulf of Alaska earthquake	Investigates a Facebook discussion group for disaster risk communication in Alaska, comparing patterns of use during periods of low magnitude activity.	(Lambert, 2020)
2020 COVID-19	Investigates communication and sense-giving through social media in times of crisis.	(Mirbabaie et al., 2020)

(continued)

Table 2.1 (continued)

Event of Study	Contribution	Reference
2020 COVID-19	Show that the organizational aim of coordinating help was successfully achieved by connecting heterogeneous actors through digitization and institutionalization.	(Haesler et al., 2021)
2021 COVID-19	Offer a critical sociotechnical perspective on tracing apps to understand how social, technical, and institutional dimensions form the ingredients for increasing surveillance.	(van Brakel et al., 2022)
2022 Russo-Ukrainian War	Examine how Nigerian refugees use social media storytelling for seeking and receiving help and found a significant positive correlation as well as that communication systems determined the promptness in receiving help	(Talabi et al., 2022)
2022 Russo-Ukrainian War	Conduct a case study on the dynamics of the public opinion fighting regarding the Russo-Ukrainian war in Chinese Weibo texts	(Chen et al., 2022)

2.1.2 Observation of Trends in Social Media Case Studies

When looking at these case studies, we observe several trends.

- First, there is *wide diversity in the different types of events that have been studied*, with the representation of both human-induced disasters (e.g., shootings, terror attacks, political uprisings, conflicts, wars) and natural hazards (e.g., tsunamis, hurricanes, earthquakes, floods, pandemics). As more events are studied, we can better understand how social media is used in different types of disaster events. This diversity also allows researchers to look for patterns or trends in the research by comparing how social behavioural patterns might differ from each other or resemble one another across events.

- Second, most studies listed here (and in the crisis informatics literature more generally) *almost exclusively concentrate on Twitter as a medium of study* (Hughes et al., 2016), only sporadically studies focus on other platforms (e.g., Reddit (Leavitt & Robinson, 2017) and newer studies, mainly studying COVID-19, on TikTok (Bukar et al., 2022; Kuhn, 2022) or Telegram (Bukar et al., 2022; Khan et al., 2022). While Twitter is a popular social media site, other social media sites, such as Facebook attract more users. But why is Twitter still the focus of so many crisis informatics studies? There are several reasons for this inconsistency. First, it is easier for researchers to obtain public data from Twitter than from other sources. Twitter has a public API and more open terms-of-use agreements for how its public data can be used. Obtaining a statistically sound data sample is also easier to achieve with Twitter (Reuter & Scholl, 2014). Moreover, limitations on the amount of content that can be contained in each message (280 characters, 140 characters until 2017) make Twitter messages easier to store, process and analyse. While a growing number of studies looks at social media data beyond Twitter, most of the research only focuses on Twitter, which is a limitation of the crisis informatics literature.

- Finally, these case studies reflect a *bias towards the study of US-based events as well as the examination of social media data in the English language.* The focus on US-based events has largely been a result of who has conducted the research; researchers tend to study events they have ready access to, and in the early years most of the crisis informatics research was carried out by US researchers. Over time, the research field has attracted researchers from around the globe, and thus a wider variety of international disaster events has been studied (see Table 2.1). The abundance of research on English-language social media data is a more pronounced trend that continues to persist. Again, this trend is mostly a result of who is performing the research (i.e., English-speaking researchers), but also a reflection of the techniques and tools that researchers use to make sense of this data. For example, Natural Language Processing (NLP) techniques are far more developed and sophisticated for the English language. That is an important gap to fill but requires ongoing efforts from those who either know other languages or have access to translation services which can make the research cost prohibitive.

2.2 Types of Crisis Informatics Research

In this section, we describe four broad types of research commonly found in the crisis informatics literature. Based on the analysis of Section 2.1 *"Case Studies of Social Media in Emergencies"*, we intended to cluster the results and identified approximate research types. These types are not meant to be inclusive of all possible research in the field, but rather to serve as a guide for understanding the typical scope and variety of research that has appeared in relevant conferences, such as ISCRAM conference, and research publications, including diverse special issues on the topic in international journals (Hiltz et al., 2011; Pipek et al., 2014; Reuter et al., 2015d; Reuter, 2018). These types of research employ different methods and approaches and reflect the multidisciplinary nature of crisis informatics research.

2.2.1 Empirical Investigation of Social Media Use

The focus of empirical work in crisis informatics has been to observe and enumerate how social media is used and the many different types of behaviours that social media can support. Most studies of this type collect social media datasets concerning a particular disaster event or user group and then analyse these datasets looking for patterns or interesting phenomena.

Empirical investigation in crisis informatics was particularly common when social media was new, and researchers were still trying to figure out how they could be used during a crisis event (Palen & Liu, 2007). Through these early empirical investigations, most of which are descriptive in nature, researchers learned much about how social media is used during emergencies. For instance, researchers discovered that social media has increased the rate and scale at which information seeking and production can take place (Hughes et al., 2008; Palen & Liu, 2007). Emergency responders use social media as a means to communicate with the public by distributing important information and making themselves available for questions and feedback (Chauhan & Hughes, 2016; Hughes et al., 2014). Responders also increasingly use social media as a way to understand the public information space around a crisis—looking for information that could help in response efforts as well as false rumours and misinformation that need correction (Andrews et al., 2016; Denef et al., 2013; Hiltz et al., 2014; Hughes & Palen, 2012; Latonero & Shklovski, 2011; Sutton et al., 2012). Those directly affected by a crisis event seek, provide, and exchange information through social media as they attempt to rapidly assess the impact of the event on themselves and their social network, determine what to do, and meet the needs of others affected with information and other types of assistance (Bruns & Burgess, 2012; Hughes et al., 2008; Liu et al., 2008; Palen et al., 2009; Perng et al., 2012; Qu et al., 2009; Semaan & Mark, 2012; Starbird et al., 2010). Interested members of the public outside the impacted area can monitor the event from around the world using social media (Bruns & Burgess, 2012), which has enabled groups of interested bystanders to help in the response, relief and recovery efforts through acts of digital volunteerism (Starbird & Palen, 2011).

As empirical work in crisis informatics matured beyond the initial focus of what social media could do, researchers began to look more deeply at the socio-technical phenomenon and challenges that were introduced by social media. For example, a number of research studies employed interviews and surveys with emergency responders to better understand the challenges responders face when using social media (Hughes & Palen, 2012; Latonero & Shklovski, 2011; Plotnick et al., 2015). Such challenges include the lack of organisational support, poor training, and insufficient time and resources. Several studies tried to understand how citizens perceive social media communications in emergencies (American Red Cross, 2012a; Canadian Red Cross, 2012; Flizikowski et al., 2014; Reuter & Spielhofer, 2017). Other research explored what kinds of citizen-generated social media information could contribute to situational awareness around a crisis event and how that information could be extracted and used (Cameron et al., 2012; Saroj & Pal, 2020; Vieweg et al., 2010). Another rich area of research centred on understanding the credibility of social media sources and the information they provide (Arif et al., 2016; Castillo et al., 2011; Starbird et al., 2014; Tapia et al., 2013). Such research seeks to detect and prevent or correct false rumour and misinformation that could be damaging to crisis response and relief efforts. Also, the perception towards fake news (Reuter et al., 2019a) was researched. As a last example, many empirical studies assess and analyse the uses and effectiveness of different social media platforms, such as Flickr, Twitter, Facebook and Periscope (Fichet et al., 2015; Hughes et al., 2014; Liu et al., 2008).

The empirical investigations discussed in this section often tie to HCI traditions of understanding users and user behaviour—giving us insight into how we might build and shape future technologies, as well as how human processes and practices might be better adapted to work with social media technologies.

2.2.2 Collection and Processing of Social Media Data

The crisis informatics research in this category focuses on collecting, sorting and making sense of the large amounts of social media data that people generate regarding a crisis event (Castillo, 2016). Making appropriate choices about how to collect relevant social media data can be challenging, and study of large-scale data sets requires increasingly sophisticated software infrastructure to collect and store the data (Anderson & Schram, 2011). Keywords and hashtags are often used to find relevant messages to study, but there are limitations to this approach because the queried keywords and hashtags may not be explicitly included in messages about an event and they tend to evolve over time (Reuter et al., 2016c). One approach for finding relevant social media data is to search for messages that originate from the location of study. However, only a small subset of social media data contains geo-location information, so samples collected in this manner are necessarily limited. Temporal problems with data collection can also arise, because social media data is often ephemeral and access to the data can quickly disappear if it is not collected right away—furthermore less and less data is provided by some services (Reuter & Scholl, 2014). Some meta-data (EXIF data with pictures) are no longer provided, or services ask for payment to provide them. When collecting social media data to study, researchers must carefully consider these challenges and choose research questions that can be answered given the limitations of the collected data.

Researchers employ a variety of methods for processing social media data, including NLP techniques and machine learning classification (Imran et al., 2015). The goal of this type of research is to make data more accessible and to provide solutions that can help people make sense of data in real-time. By examining data from Twitter and a crowdsourcing app, Wang et al. (2018) highlight that big data, for example, can complement existing means of flood data collection. Despite growing usefulness and accuracy of these approaches, there are still many challenges for this kind of research. For example, computational processing and analysis have been difficult to do in real-time. Most research is done post hoc, months, or even years after the occurrence of the event, which limits the usefulness of the research findings for more current events. Thus, moving towards real-time analysis is an important goal for this type of research. Researchers are also seeking ways to improve the classifying process and better sort and filter relevant information. Accuracy varies widely, and it is unlikely that a single approach will work for all types of events; it likely needs to be adapted to fit the context of the crisis event being monitored. Another big challenge is to detect malicious behaviour, identifying false rumour and misinformation (Starbird, 2017; Starbird et al., 2014; Starbird 2019) including the aim to find efficient and accepted measures to counter fake news (Kirchner & Reuter, 2020)

Researchers have developed several systems that employ these data processing techniques to make useful information more readily available to emergency responders and members of the public (Caragea et al., 2011; Imran et al., 2014; Yin et al., 2012). For example, Alam et al. (2018a) propose a model for performing adaptation based on adversarial learning. Kaufhold et al. (2020c) suggest the semi-automatic creation of alerts in order to address information overload of crisis data on social media. Another approach applies an algorithm for relevance classification of social media posts (Kaufhold et al., 2020a). We discuss development of such systems in more detail in the next section.

2.2.3   System Design, Building and Evaluation

Another common type of crisis informatics research is one where researchers design, build and/or evaluate technical solutions that address the problems that users encounter with social media during a crisis event. These solutions encompass a growing number of systems that originate from researchers in fields such as computer science and HCI.

When designing systems, researchers have taken different approaches. Some researchers take a participatory approach, where the potential users of the system are directly involved in the design process as co-participants (Hughes, 2014; Hughes & Shah, 2016; Kristensen et al., 2006). Other researchers engage in more theoretical design work. In this kind of work, researchers propose a model or framework for understanding social media communications in crises (Liu, 2014; White & Plotnick, 2010). These models or frameworks typically lead to design implications and recommendations for systems that support social media use in a disaster.

Examples of systems that have been built include a growing number of public, scientific and commercial applications for managing social media in crisis. Pohl (2013) compares and classifies these applications by whether they (a) consider one or several social media platforms for monitoring, (b) were directly or indirectly developed for crisis management and (c) perform different kinds of analysis, such as monitoring or sentiment analysis. Many systems support some of these requirements (e.g. Ushahidi (Okolloh, 2009), TweetDeck (Twitter, 2014), Twitcident (Terpstra et al., 2012), Tweak the Tweet (Starbird & Stamberger, 2010), TwitInfo (Marcus et al., 2011), SensePlace2 (Robinson et al.,

2013), XHELP (Reuter et al., 2015b), CrowdMonitor (Ludwig et al., 2015c), Image4Act (Alam et al., 2017), and PIO Monitoring Application (Hughes & Shah, 2016)). However, these systems are limited as many of them have syntactical requirements for the user, do not provide cross-platform structures, just focus on Twitter (Marcus et al., 2011; Terpstra et al., 2012), or require the use of a new platform and therefore fail to integrate ICT for volunteers into existing networks (Marcus et al., 2011; McClendon & Robinson, 2012; Robinson et al., 2013; Terpstra et al., 2012; Twitter, 2014). Thus, there continues to be a need for new and improved systems that support social media use in times of crisis and for better communication between emergency responders and experts for specialized emergency management software (Hiltz et al., 2020).

After these systems are built, they are usually tested with their target audience. Evaluation procedures vary widely. Often, evaluation is limited, done in a tightly controlled environment or a less than realistic situation (e.g., a simulation). Other times, evaluation takes place during an actual event. Unfortunately, testing during an actual emergency event can be challenging since emergency responders typically do not want to rely on an untested system. Therefore, researchers must focus on establishing relationships with emergency responders before an event begins so that the responders will trust them enough to use a new, untested system (Hughes & Shah, 2016).

2.2.4 Cumulative and Longitudinal Research

Now that the field of crisis informatics has begun to mature, works that summarise or synthesise existing research into new theoretical or practical perspectives have appeared. These works include research survey articles like this one and others (Hughes et al., 2014; Veil et al., 2011) that orient practitioners and researchers to the field of crisis informatics and the developments found there. Synthesising research also includes papers that focus on summarising research around a particular problem, such as the issue of including the work of digital volunteers into formal response work (Hughes & Tapia, 2015) or the challenges of processing and making sense of large amounts of social media data in crisis (Imran et al., 2015). These are usually problems that cannot be solved with one study and so, it is important to draw conclusions across a wide body of research.

The field of crisis informatics has begun to accumulate a large enough body of research that longitudinal research is starting to become possible. Such research promises to answer questions such as the following: How do people use or not use social media during different types of crisis events (e.g., terrorist attacks, hurricanes, wildfires, etc.)? What type of social media is more or less effective for emergency management? Longitudinal research can still be challenging to conduct because social media platforms continue to rapidly evolve and the context in which the platforms are used also changes quickly. For instance, different platforms grow and ebb in popularity based on location, time or other social factors. Thus, it is important that crisis informatics researchers distinguish between findings that are generalisable versus those findings that are tied to a specific social media platform or crisis context.

2.2.5   Summary of Research Types

The research covered in this section of the chapter is meant to give the reader perspective on the different kinds of research typically found in the field of crisis informatics. The research employs a wide array of methods and techniques that fall across a variety of academic disciplines.

- For instance, much of the empirical work (e.g., social media content analysis, interviews with social media users, etc.) is conducted by *social science* researchers or those who use social science methods (e.g., human-computer interaction or information science researchers).
- The application of big data methods to issues of social media use in crisis tends to come from computational scientists in fields like *computer science* and *data science*.
- Researchers in fields like *computer science* and *HCI* are typically the ones that build and evaluate systems that support social media use during crisis events.

Because the field of crisis informatics is multi-disciplinary, relevant research can be diffuse and difficult to find, appearing in the journals, conferences, and other publication venues of the many disciplines that engage in this research. The diversity of crisis informatics research highlights the importance of interdisciplinary publication venues, such as the ISCRAM conference, that bring together researchers from different disciplines to discuss common concerns and research interests. Here, we have discussed which academic disciplines engage in crisis informatics research and provided examples so that the reader can better understand the scope of research done in the area and where to find it.

2.3 Types of Interaction: Usage Patterns in Crisis Informatics

Another way to understand the crisis informatics literature is to distinguish between different types of use, aka use patterns (Reuter & Kaufhold, 2018). The use of social media requires classification due to the range of diverse emergencies and their responses. Classification can ease the utilisation and development of qualified technology and promote interaction and systematic analysis of behaviours. Reuter et al. (2012) created a classification matrix for cooperation in crises, which depends on the sender (X-axis) and the recipient (Y-axis) of digital content. Considering citizens (C) and authorities (A), such as emergency services, the crisis communication matrix differentiates between four observed information flows or patterns of social media use in emergencies (see Figure 2.1).

At the inter-organisational level, crisis response organisations communicate with each other (A2A). Citizens and volunteers communicate with each other face-to-face or virtually via social media such as Facebook or Twitter on the public level (C2C). Crisis response organisations investigate this citizen-generated

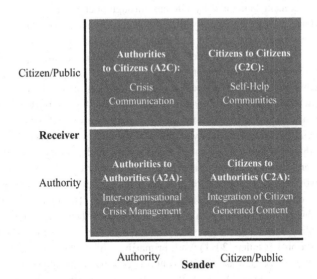

Figure 2.1 Crisis Communication Matrix (Reuter et al., 2012), Adapted Concerning the Terminology

content (C2A). Not only citizens talk to each other, but also organisations responsible for recovery work keep the public up-to-date (A2C). The categories are inspired by the "categories of organisational behaviour" of Quarantelli (1988). The 2×2 matrix has to be understood as a simplification of reality and it is clear that the dimensions can be divided arbitrarily. Categories like volunteers, organisations, or media might be worth considering. In this matrix, depending on the respective context, voluntary helpers and other organisations might be classified into either the public or the authority level. It is important to notice that in any case, the analysis has to remain manageable. Therefore, we decided to work with this 2×2 matrix.

In the following sections, we discuss each of the four classifications in the crisis communication matrix (see Figure 2.1) in more detail and offer examples of crisis informatics literature that fall into each of these classifications.

2.3.1   From Citizens to Citizens (C2C)—Self-Help Communities

Most of the content generated by citizens through social media is intended for other residents and not necessarily for emergency services. Social media enable people to help each other and to coordinate among themselves, but these types of activities are not new. Quarantelli and Dynes (1977) and Stallings and Quarantelli (1985) describe "emergent groups" like these as "private citizens who work together in pursuit of collective goals relevant to actual or potential disasters but whose organisation has not yet become institutionalized." Quarantelli (1984) defines important conditions for the emergence of such groups: a legitimising social environment, the availability of specific non-material resources, a perceived threat, a network of social relationships and a supporting social climate. Research has found that citizens can significantly contribute to rescue and response work because, contrary to popular opinion, they tend to react rationally to a crisis, rarely panic or loot, and are not helpless (Helsloot & Ruitenberg, 2004). In this context, Reuter et al. (2013) differentiate between activities in the 'virtual' online world and the physical location of a disaster. Virtual "digital volunteers" (Starbird & Palen, 2011) work primarily online, while on-site "emergent groups" (Stallings & Quarantelli, 1985) normally work at the physical site of the crisis event. Recent research shows that response organizations may be "able to transcend the boundaries between different types of organized behaviour during disaster" (Schmidt et al., 2018).

Several studies have examined citizens' and communities' activities in social media during emergencies. One study that concentrates on hurricanes Ike and Gustav from 2008 distinguishes between the use of Twitter in crisis and non-crisis times and reports that information brokerage and broadcasting can be found more often in Twitter use during crises (Hughes & Palen, 2009). Against the backdrop of the earthquakes in Nepal in 2015, one study investigates how these disasters are represented visually through Twitter-shares images, hereby, differences in the communication of images shared within global versus local populations are examined (Bica et al., 2017). Further, social media provides ordinary people with the capacity to share news globally and to keep not only a local community but potentially the world informed about current events, acting as local journalists from afar, as citizen journalism being enabled akin to data-driven investigative news (Norris, 2017). During the 2008 Sichuan earthquake, people collected and synthesised information (Qu et al., 2009). Another study about the Tennessee River technological failure in 2008 discovers that social media could be used to raise emergency awareness among citizens and exceed the boundaries of locally limited networks (Sutton, 2010).

During the Yushu earthquake in 2010, people used microblogging to obtain information about people or the status of the emergency (Qu et al., 2011). Another study shows that after the 2011 Tohoku earthquake and tsunami, citizens of the affected areas used Twitter to communicate their uncertain situation, while users in other areas informed their followers via Twitter that they were safe (Acar & Muraki, 2011). By analysing Twitter usage with "Tweak the Tweet" translators, the concept of "digital volunteers" converging to strongly intertwined networks was discovered during the Haiti earthquake in 2010 (Starbird & Palen, 2011). Digital volunteers relay, amplify, synthesise and structure information in emergency situations (Starbird, 2013). Additionally, they perform tasks which are usually not executed by official emergency services, for instance, the recovery of lost animals during hurricane Sandy in 2012 (White et al., 2014). The convergence of geomobile technologies and crowdsourcing methods has opened up multiple forms to participate in disaster management tasks, relevant variables in this context are the type of data to be processed, as well as the participation of the crowd (Poblet et al., 2018). Moreover, often citizen-led groups emerge to assist with disaster response, if official agencies cannot provide enough assistance during widespread disasters. With citizens using diverse apps and social media-related platforms, different challenges, like incomplete feedback loops, unclear prioritization, and communication overload, can be identified (Smith et al., 2018).

Another function of social media allows users to serve as supporters in crisis situations by expressing solidarity as in the 2011 Egyptian uprising (Starbird &

Palen, 2012) and giving emotional encouragement as in the 2010 Great East Japan Earthquake (Wilensky, 2014). Analysing the timeline of the 2011 Super Tornado Outbreak (Reuter et al., 2013), those affected by the tornados retweeted warnings and crisis tracking activities during the preparedness and response phases of the event. Also, virtual self-help communities started their relief operations in the recovery phase along with a relatively growing number of external source links. But not only Twitter is used in emergencies: In the 2010 Bornholm blizzard, the use of two Facebook groups indicates that self-selection into groups generates various opinions (Birkbak, 2012). Goolsby (2010) concentrates on ad-hoc crisis communities using social media to create community crisis maps. Until now, seven different crisis-mapping practices in OpenStreetMap are known (Kogan et al., 2016). Furthermore, technology can also help with coping with disrupting and debilitating events that happen as part of everyday life. Here, Semaan (2019) investigates so-called *routine infrastructuring* in order to build a kind of everyday resilience through technology use.

If there is uncertainty caused by extra information and misinformation because of chaotic "unorganised" online behaviour of the volunteers, "there will be a larger amount of collaboration on the platform" (Valecha et al., 2013). Research on the COVID-19 pandemic found "mutual aid organizing in relation to disaster is growing practice but remains evolving" (Soden & Owen, 2021) and how neighbourhood groups build up a virtual network (Haesler et al., 2021). Possible ways to improve the organisation of online volunteers include cross-platform moderators (Reuter et al., 2015b) or the installation of public displays for volunteer coordination (Ludwig et al., 2017). Even though Purohit et al. (2014) propose a system designed to identify seekers and suppliers of information and resources in social media communities to encourage crisis coordination, many challenges remain. Cobb et al. (2014) suggest connecting different tools and tasks, coordinating and integrating voluntary activities, and the opportunity to share one's own activities so that spontaneous and less experienced volunteers may learn something new. Nespeca et al. (2020) present a "framework for disaster management information systems that embraces an actor-centred perspective to explicitly support coordination and self-organization". Furthermore, Kaufhold and Reuter (2014) determine ways to ease procedures of moderation and independent work, to encourage digital and on-site volunteers in providing clarification and representation of important content, to support feedback as well as updates in interaction relationships and to include technologies and interaction types.

Another trend is the use of rather closed platforms, such as Telegram (Bukar et al., 2022; Khan et al., 2022). Furthermore newer social media are studied:

A recent study examines the factors and influencing mechanisms related to citizen engagement with the TikTok account of the National Health Commission of China during the COVID-19 pandemic by analysing 355 short videos (including number of likes, shares and comments) from the Healthy China account on TikTok, showing that the content significantly influenced the level of citizen engagement (Chen et al., 2021).

2.3.2 From Authorities to Citizens (A2C)—Crisis Communication

Today and increasingly in the future, authorities include social media into their crisis communication efforts to disseminate information to the public on how to behave during emergencies and how to prevent accidents or emergencies (Reuter et al., 2016b).

Already the 2009 case study of Public Information Officers (PIO) of the Los Angeles Fire Department emphasises the significance of the information evangelist, who supports the use of new forms of media and technology within authorities to attain an efficient organisational application of social media (Latonero & Shklovski, 2011). According to Hughes and Palen (2012), members of the public "have a changed relationship to the institution of emergency response" through the authorities' use of social media. In this context, increasingly data-driven instruments are used, e.g. for early warning systems, whose effectiveness are influenced by various actors (van Esch et al., 2021). Authorities also correct misinformation caused by the "emerging risks of the chaotic use of social media" (Kaewkitipong et al., 2012), as shown in a study about the Thailand flooding disaster in 2011 or the 2011 Norway attacks (Perng et al., 2012), and the purposeful dissemination of misinformation, which was also termed *infodemic* during the COVID-19 pandemic (Cinelli et al., 2020), emergency services require suitable crisis communication strategies to serve their primary purpose of saving lives. Jiang and Tang (2022) studied 189 cities in China during COVID-19 and found positive effects that crisis-related social media posts published by local government agencies has on citizen compliance. They conclude that social media are a "efficient and low-cost tool to assist local government agencies to achieve public administration objectives during crises, and its efficacy is largely dependent on regional socioeconomic status" (Jiang & Tang, 2022). A recent study identified a number of vulnerable groups of citizens, e.g. elderly people with low incomes or people of foreign origin with limited language skills (Rudolph-Cleff et al., 2022).

Against this backdrop, Mirbabaie et al. (2020) investigate how to reduce social media distrust and facilitate sense-making. They analysed the potential impact of sense-giving from Twitter crisis communication generated during Hurricane Harvey. They emphasise the importance of information-rich actors in communication networks and the leverage of their influence in crises such as the COVID-2019 pandemic. Similarly, Gui et al. (2017) investigate how people cope with uncertainty during public health crises by using social media. Additionally, a study investigating crisis communication in the context of the Fukushima Daiichi nuclear disaster demonstrates that crisis communication through social media can be more effective than via traditional media (Utz et al., 2013). In crisis communication, instrumental and public-including expressive communication approaches through Twitter have been implemented by police units in the 2011 London riots (Denef et al., 2013). Nonetheless, another study on 2012 hurricane Sandy demonstrates that communication in fire and police departments and across media types differs (Hughes et al., 2014) and therefore, they recommend new features and tools "to better track, respond to, and document public information." Moreover, there is an overview by Veil et al. (2011), which shows recommendations for practitioners, best practices and examples of social media tools.

Regarding different relevant actors, Chauhan and Hughes (2017) identify four different types of official information sources, i.e., event-based resources, local responders, local news media, and cooperating agencies. At the same time, Bukar et al. (2020) find that stakeholder interaction during crises is an under-researched area. Morss et al. (2017) highlight that the distribution of crisis information is never a linear process but rather an interconnected dynamic system in which information can evolve along with people's risk perceptions. This becomes particularly evident in a case study of a refugee shelter in the Netherlands, which was initially managed with a firm top-down approach, but eventually the residents of the shelter connected themselves with the local community via social media (Smets et al., 2021). Accordingly, Zhang et al. (2019) emphasise the various functions of information distribution on social media, including the acquisition of situational awareness, the support of help activities, and the enabling of communication between agencies and the public. This variety of approaches is also evident regarding theoretical models in the area of social media crisis communication and management. Here, Bukar et al. (2020) conducted a systematic literature review and identify situational crisis communication theory, social-mediated crisis communication, and integrated crisis mapping models as the most frequently applied models. Time-series analyses expose that relevant information becomes less dominant as the crisis moves from the prodromal to acute phase and that information regarding individual remedial behaviours decreases analogously (Spence et al., 2015).

Authorities must deal with many hurdles concerning the use of social media. An exploratory study investigates the collaboration among humanitarian aid organisations and Volunteer and Technical Communities (V&TCs) classifying the latter into software platform development communities, mapping collaborations, expert networks, and data aggregators (Gorp, 2014). In this study, six barriers of collaboration with aid organisations are identified: the management of volunteers, different levels of engagement, the level of commitment by V&TCs, diverse ways of working, limited resources, and the aid for organisations' limited knowledge about the V&TCs' expertise.

Plotnick and Hiltz (2016) demonstrate how county-level US emergency managers use social media, review barriers to efficient social media use and offer suggestions to improve use: For both disseminating information (A2C) and collecting information (C2A) lack of sufficient staff is the most important barrier. However, lack of guidance/policy documents is the second highest rated barrier to dissemination via SM. Lack of skills and of the training that could improve these skills is also important. Grace (2021) further investigated these barriers, suggesting that overcoming barriers to social media use resulting from a lack of tools, staff, and trust requires new and existing sociotechnical infrastructures that facilitate intra- and inter-organizational processes of multisensory integration across periods of stability and crisis. Here, Eriksson (2018) conducts a systematic content analysis of pieces of advice for effective social media crisis communication and identifies five central aspects: "(1) exploiting social media's potential to create dialogue and to choose the right message, source and timing; (2) performing pre-crisis work and developing an understanding of the social media logic; (3) using social media monitoring; (4) continuing to prioritize traditional media in crisis situations; and finally, (5) just using social media in strategic crisis communication".

Kaufhold et al. (2020b) examined the attitudes, expectations, and use of mobile crisis apps in Germany and conclude, that people want to have one central app to get information on crisis but in addition to emergency and weather warnings, crime- and health-related warnings are also desired by many, as is the possibility for bidirectional communication. While introducing apps to help during crisis brings a lot of advantages, there are also critical aspects: In the course of the COVID-19 pandemic contact tracing apps were widely used. Brakel et al. (2022) offer a critical, sociotechnical perspective by looking closer at two of those tracing apps introduced in the Netherlands and Belgium to understand how social, technical, and institutional dimensions pose a risk of increasing surveillance.

2.3.3 From Citizens to Authorities (C2A)—Use of Citizen-Generated Content

The use of citizen-generated content is also essential besides the communication from authorities to citizens. Emergency services can use data from social media to calculate statistical measures, e.g., estimate citizen alertness, by using data mining (Johansson et al., 2012). The high number of social media posts might improve the accuracy of the statistical measures in this case. Potentials are to analyse problematic situations based on diverse content, including text, pictures and videos taken with mobile phones. Such information is often unreliable and a significant obstacle in investigating such possibilities (Mendoza et al., 2010). Crowdsourcing strategies may relieve this to improve the reliability of visible information in a picture (Reuter et al., 2012). For instance, based on prior research of the crowds' self-correcting capabilities, Arif et al. (2017) propose a model for twitter rumour correction and emphasise the locus of responsibility, corrective objective and perceptions of the audience to choose the correcting action. However, the perceived unreliability and sheer volume of such information during large-scale emergencies is a major obstacle to exploring such opportunities (Kaufhold et al., 2020a; Mendoza et al., 2010). Hughes and Palen (2014) identify the challenges of verification, liability, credibility, information overload and allocation of resources in a broad literature review about the integration of social media content. Moreover, a study on the 2010 Haiti earthquake demonstrates possible ways in which social media can be used for disaster relief with respect to donations towards the Red Cross (Gao et al., 2011). Akhgar et al. (2013) explain how security organisations and public safety are increasingly aware of social media's added value proposition in times of crisis. Meanwhile, another study recommends that volunteer groups in emergencies in the future must mature and improve according to these enhanced opportunities, so that "professional responders will begin to rely on data and products produced by digital volunteers" (Hughes & Tapia, 2015).

Emergency responders "critically depend upon the situation awareness the team members have acquired" (van de Walle et al., 2016). Many methods and applications have been investigated in social media research to include citizen-generated content and encourage authorities in processing social media content. An entire special issue on citizens in crisis and disaster management aims to understand barriers and opportunities for citizen inclusion (Ferguson et al., 2018). To evaluate situated crowdsourcing mechanisms, Ludwig et al. (2016) execute a public display application with a reliable communication infrastructure. Furthermore, Castillo (2016) collects methods (e.g., NLP, semantic technologies, data mining) to process social media messages under time-critical limitations. Various research studies seek to extract situational awareness from social media. For example, Vieweg et al. (2010) identify categories of information found on Twitter that could improve situational awareness. Pohl et al. (2015) show clustering approaches for sub-event detection on Flickr and YouTube to automate the processing of data in social media. Meanwhile, Sakkaki et al. (2010) offer an algorithm that integrates Twitter users as social sensors for real-time event detection concerning the Japanese earthquakes in 2009. Additionally, de Albuquerque et al. (2015) prove that geographical approaches for quantitatively assessing social media messages might be helpful to enhance important content. Moi et al. (2015) suggest a system to process and investigate social media data, transforming the high volume of noisy data into a low volume of rich content that emergency personnel can use. To succeed, they categorise the steps of information gathering and data preparation, information mining, data enrichment, alert detection, information visualisation, semantic data modelling with ontologies and information quality assessment. Coche et al. (2021) presents an "attempt to shift from data to information exploitation" and proposes a way to automatically organize information from social media data up to decision-makers. Therefore, the approach uses the coding scheme of the 6 W (where, what, weapons, when, who, why) applied to social media (Kropczynski et al., 2018).

To examine challenges and future research directions involving techniques for data characterisation, clustering, acquisition, classification, preparation, event detection and tracking, extraction, summarisation as well as semantic technologies, Imran et al. (2015) provide a comprehensive overview of managing social media messages. Humanitarian organizations are also confronted with the challenges of "near-real-time information processing, information overload, information extraction, summarization, and verification of both textual and visual content" (Imran et al., 2020). Another study by Pohl (2013) concentrates on tools and existing frameworks developed in the context of non-crisis related (e.g., Twitinfo) and crisis related (e.g., Twitcident or "Tweak the Tweet") research work to investigate social media or to integrate new features into the social media usage for crisis management. Starbird and Stamberger (2010) suggest using structured crisis-specific Twitter hashtags to ease machine parsing, processing and re-distribution for the proposed micro syntax "Tweak the Tweet" and to make information, which was generated during emergencies, more useful. In this comparison, they detect that there are systems for diverse applications, reflecting one or various social media platforms for monitoring, especially developed for crisis management, and executing different kinds of analysis: event-detection, sentiment analysis and monitoring. A study on the perceptions of police technology use found that perceptions differ according to experience of unfair treatment by the police (Haunschild & Reuter, 2021).

In the course of the COVID-19 pandemic, Criado et al. (2020) have investigated how digital platforms have been used to offer an agile response to COVID-19 by analysing how the Spanish authorities have encouraged citizen-networked co-production for communication and crisis coordination. Nevertheless, other studies have demonstrated simultaneously that not all responders use such data during disasters, as there are complications with the obtaining and filtering of large amounts of data in emergencies (Hughes & Palen, 2012; Reuter et al., 2016a). The Plotnick and Hiltz (2016) study of county-level U.S. emergency managers states that after lack of staff, the most important barriers to collecting information (C2A) are trustworthiness of the data and information overload issues, which points to the need for appropriate software support to deal with these system-related issues. Fathi et al. (2020) investigate so-called Virtual Operations Support Teams (VOSTs). These teams are set up in the effort to be able to deal with massive data overload during crises and to increase situational awareness.

2.3.4   From Authorities to Authorities (A2A)—Organisational Crisis Management

Social media platforms, such as Twitter or Facebook often do not encourage the inter- and intra-organisational cooperation (A2A) of authorities. Nonetheless, social media may help to enhance informal processes and inter-organisational awareness. White et al. (2009) investigate the capabilities of online social networks with emergency management students: The most popular functions were the distribution of information, communication and networking. Additionally, it is demonstrated that, for instance, information integrity, user identification, privacy and technology reliability are potential issues with those systems. Experiences show that inter-organisational social networks for authorities could create potential value (Pipek et al., 2013; Reuter, 2014b; Schmidt et al., 2018). Authorities can also use social media for internal communication. A study on 2010 Haiti Earthquake shows how social media technologies such as wikis and collaborative workspaces can be employed as knowledge sharing systems (Yates & Paquette, 2011).

2.3.5 Summary of Usage Patterns

Looking at the different types of interaction, as defined by Reuter et al. (2012), we summarise what can be learned about the four usage patterns from the crisis informatics literature:

- *Citizens to Citizens (C2C):* Most people use social media during crises to communicate with other citizens. In this context, social media serves for self-coordination purposes. Additionally, they are mainly used among citizens for information sharing and obtaining, especially information about people's well-being and the status of uncertain situations, and for providing or receiving emotional support. However, there are still some challenges to be met to simplify social media use during crises and increase their reliability.
- *Authorities to Citizens (A2C):* Social media is increasingly used by authorities for their crisis communication with the public. In this context, a variety of studies investigates how social media is actually used and how they should be used and demonstrate the importance of social media for disseminating information to the public. Nevertheless, barriers, such as a lack of staff and reliability are still challenging for efficient social media use by authorities.
- *Citizens to Authorities (C2A):* The integration of citizen-generated content is important for authorities. Through data mining, important information can be gathered from the mass number of posts on the Internet and strategies such as crowdsourcing can counteract the unreliability of such information. Research in this area concentrates on methods and applications that promote both an efficient collection and use of social media data.
- *Authorities to Authorities (A2A):* Social media can be used in inter- and intra-organisational cooperation for distributing information, communicating, networking and knowledge sharing.

2.4 Summary, Research Gaps and Next Steps

Over the last 20 years, social media has had an increasing impact on crisis management. In particular, major events such as Hurricane Sandy in 2012, the 2013 European floods or the ongoing COVID-19 pandemic, have shown that citizens are not passive victims but active participants who use social media for crisis response. Accordingly, the interdisciplinary research field of crisis informatics emerged, combining both computer science and social science knowledge of disasters (Palen & Anderson, 2016). This chapter contributes to this by analysing the use of social media during different crises and emergencies (Section 2.1), discussing different types of crisis informatics research (Section 2.2) and discussing usage patterns of authorities and citizens in social media in emergencies (Section 2.3). In this final section, we summarise the findings of our overview of crisis informatics literature and explore the future of this research.

Social media continues to evolve, and so does their use in emergency and crisis events. Since the first recorded case of disaster relief with social media in 2001, the use of social media before, during, and after crisis events has become more and more pervasive. Emergency and disaster management as well as defence and security management are more and more converging. In the field of crisis informatics, studies have investigated various cases, methods, practices, tools and users in different crises, disasters and emergencies of all types and scales.

Other review studies systematically analysed social media use across multiple emergencies or technologies. Olteanu et al. (2015) report on the average prevalence of various information types, sources and their temporal distribution across a variety of crisis situations. Moreover, Eismann et al. (2016) executed a systematic literature study on collective behaviour identifying seven key findings concerning the event, impact, social units and response. From a technological perspective, Imran et al. (2015) surveyed "the state of the art regarding computational methods to process social media messages and highlight both their contributions and shortcomings". Likewise, Castillo (2016) highlights computational methods "focusing on methods that are commonly used for processing social media messages under time-critical constraints". This chapter aims to contribute by examining case studies and identifying use patterns that describe the interactions among authorities and citizens.

The first section *"Case Studies of Social Media in Emergencies"* (Section 2.1) surveys studies focusing on the use of social media during many of the most significant emergency events to happen worldwide since 2001. Initial research focused on events that took place in the USA, but more recently there have been a growing number of studies based on crisis events in other countries. This increasing diversity has enabled more comparative and systematic analysis across diverse types of emergency contexts. The crisis informatics literature continues to heavily emphasise Twitter (possibly overestimating its importance in crisis management), mostly due to the ease of data collection and accessibility that the platform affords as well as datasets in the English language, which limit the diversity of research. Future research should look more broadly at all the variations of social media as well as different languages to represent a more complete picture of how social media is used in crises around the world. This is why we will focus on studying the situation from a European perspective, including quantitative empirical studies with authorities (Chapter 3) and citizens (Chapter 4).

The second section *"Types of Crisis Informatics Research"* (Section 2.2) provides an overview of the different types of research that can be found in the crisis informatics literature. Much of this research is empirical, where researchers collect social media data or conduct interviews with social media users to better understand the behaviours that social media support in crisis management. Other research seeks to address the task of collecting, processing and making sense of large amounts of social media data. Still, other research involves designing, building and testing systems that help users use social media more effectively in times of crisis. The final type of research discussed in this section takes a broader view of the crisis informatics field by summarising and pulling together research across the field to address larger problems and research questions.

In the third section *"Types of Interaction: Usage Patterns in Crisis Informatics"* (Section 2.3), the analysis attaches importance to various *use patterns*, involving the communication among citizens (C2C), with concepts of self-coordination and help, emergent groups, and (digital) volunteers; the communication from authorities to citizens (A2C), involving concepts of crisis communication; from citizens to authorities (C2A), involving concepts like big data or social media analysis, crowdsourcing and crowd tasking; and among authorities (A2A), involving inter-organisational social networks. Despite an increasingly broad scope of crisis informatics literature, there are still many areas open for future practice and research:

- *Crisis communication* (A2C) is still a challenge. Pursuant to particular studies, many citizens anticipate that authorities will respond to their messages within one hour (Reuter & Spielhofer, 2017). Spokespeople must conform to a new role, which contains more dynamics in comparison to pre-social media times. To meet these expectations, spokespeople must take the time to carefully word their posts. Taking this time will not be conducive to responding, as expected by the public, immediately. Thus, types of communication, such as instrumental or public-including expressive communication approaches (Denef et al., 2013), must be further investigated to recommend smaller authorities additional ways of crisis communication. Furthermore authorities' (Chapter 3) and citizens' (Chapter 4) needs and their compatibility must be explored.
- Different algorithmic approaches have been applied to study and *include citizen-generated content* (C2A) from social media (Imran et al., 2015). On

the one hand, they are supposed to identify or predict critical events and to convert the high volume of big and noisy data that cannot be managed by emergency managers in a short time before or during large-scale emergencies, to a low volume of rich and thick content (Moi et al., 2015). On the contrary, algorithms are supposed to identify underlying patterns (e.g., mood or geospatial correlations) applying statistical approaches or visual analytics (Brynielsson et al., 2014; Fuchs et al., 2013). Fake news and social bots complicate these efforts, but one should take bigger incidents as well as smaller emergencies with suitable algorithms and various granularities and thresholds into account. Emergency managers are sometimes not convinced of the quality of citizen-generated content and social media (Hughes & Tapia, 2015; Reuter et al., 2016b) and see major risks in the inappropriate use of social media (e.g. accident gaffers). Still, they might trust in the quality of algorithms as an additional filtering layer, e.g., by offering a particular degree of customizability and transparency (white-box approach). In addition to that, research investigated crowd-sensing approaches to attaching the authorities' importance to citizens' activities (Ludwig et al., 2015b; Sakaki et al., 2010). Possibilities to support enhanced situation assessment need to be researched (Chapter 5).

- *Self-coordination and help* (C2C) have been assumed to be very important, but it has been identified in some studies that chaos is a consequence of this interaction. In this context, the question arises, how this can be addressed. While flexibility is also necessary, the automatic cross-media recommending of relevant posts pursuant to crises dynamics (Kaufhold & Reuter, 2016) of interest or the adjusting of needs and offers (Purohit et al., 2014) could help to structure communication. The granularity of citizen activities is also essential to define appropriate work practices and organisation: The question is whether groups of citizens, such as soccer clubs or single citizens, should be included in crisis management. To ease appropriation of existing tools amongst citizens and, long-term, to enhance disaster preparedness, the visibility of various practices that proved their functionality appears essential. One example includes the automatic matching of offers and demands in social media (Purohit et al., 2014; Reuter et al., 2015b) and their communication with the help of bots that provide automatic posts to highlight possible matches (Chapter 6).

In summary, *crisis informatics* has established itself as an important research area in the ever-increasing complexity of the cyber world, which is amplified by the time-critical constraints of emergencies and disasters. However, crisis informatics will be challenged to evolve quickly to tackle global-scale emergencies, such as the ongoing COVID-19 pandemic and the increasing risks of natural hazards due to the climate crisis.

After having presented the state of the art, the following chapter will focus on the attitudes of emergency services staff (Chapter 3) and citizens' perception (Chapter 4), before concepts for tailorable situation assessment (Chapter 5) and the self-organisation of digital volunteers (Chapter 6) are presented.

Attitudes by Emergency Services Staff in Europe

3

Finding a way to ensure an effective use of social media has become increasingly important to emergency services over the past decade. Various studies show that social media is used in emergencies—and that in spite of possible challenges for emergency services, beneficial use cases can be identified. However, relatively little empirical data is available regarding the attitudes of emergency services towards social media, and almost none of a comparative nature. Across various studies of emergencies numerous positive and negative aspects of social media have been identified. Existing studies either focus only on citizens, only on the emergency services in the US, or only on one particular emergency service. Therefore, an open question remains concerning the perception of different emergency services in Europe towards the use of social media. We assume that different cultural—even within Europe—as well as legal backgrounds have a significant influence on the emergency services' opinions and attitudes. The survey we describe below tests that hypothesis. Additionally, different countries in Europe have been affected by different types of crises ranging from natural disasters to terrorist attacks, which may have led to different types of experiences, responses, and attitudes.

Within this chapter, we seek to explore the attitudes of European emergency service staff towards social media for private and organisational use as well as the levels and main factors influencing their current and likely future use in their organisations. To provide empirical evidence, we present a comparison of two surveys, conducted across Europe with emergency services in 2014 and 2017

Supplementary Information The online version contains supplementary material available at https://doi.org/10.1007/978-3-658-39720-3_3.

© The Author(s), under exclusive license to Springer Fachmedien Wiesbaden Gmbh, part of Springer Nature 2022
C. Reuter, *A European Perspective on Crisis Informatics*, https://doi.org/10.1007/978-3-658-39720-3_3

respectively, with a total of 1,169 answers. The analysis shows that personal experience has an effect on how organisational usage of social media is perceived and how emergency service staff view the future use of social media. Furthermore, the use has increased. This study not only shows emergency services what their staff think about their social media usage but also discusses challenges and directions for the design of systems that can be useful for further development of optimised organisational social media usage.

This chapter has been published as two articles: "Emergency Services Attitudes towards Social Media: A Quantitative and Qualitative Survey across Europe" by Christian Reuter, Thomas Ludwig, Marc-André Kaufhold and Thomas Spielhofer in the International Journal on Human-Computer Studies (IJHCS) (Reuter et al., 2016b) [Paper B] as well as "Emergency Service Staff and Social Media—A Comparative Empirical Study of the Perception by Emergency Services Members in Europe in 2014 and 2017" by Christian Reuter, Marc-André Kaufhold, Fabian Spahr, Thomas Spielhofer and Anna Sophie Hahne in the International Journal of Disaster Risk Reduction (IJDRR) (Reuter et al., 2020a) [Paper C]. The introduction contains content from both papers, related work mainly from Paper B, however Section 3.1.2 is published as part of Paper C and 3.1.3 contains content from both papers. Section 3.2 has been published as Paper B, and Section 3.3 as Paper C.

3.1   Related Work

Today, we find a broad strand of literature on the use of social media in emergencies, including potentials and barriers of social media use in emergencies (Section 3.1.2). In giving an overview of the vast body of literature we also present results of surveys which have already been conducted, focusing specifically on social media use and related attitudes of emergency services (Section 3.1.2) to clarify the research gap this study aims to fill (Section 3.1.3).

3.1.1   Emergency Services' Potentials and Challenges of using Social Media

Based on qualitative data on emergency services' attitudes towards volunteer activities, studies by Reuter et al. (2013) claim that "additional information provided by volunteers can improve the work of emergency services". A contribution on the 2013 German centennial flood further confirms the potential of Twitter as a distributed 'social sensor' by analysing spatio-temporal clusters of tweets. Yet it also highlights some caveats in interpreting immediate results: As not every disaster is represented by a cluster, some clusters occur in places and times where no disaster happens and some clusters may not refer to disaster events but are consequences of these (Fuchs et al., 2013). However, volunteer activism—also in social media—may have a negative impact. For instance, a case study on microblogging during the 2011 Norway attacks found that public rescue efforts and public opinion—both possibly influenced by microblogging activities—made disaster response more complex for professionals and increased the pressure on emergency services to act according to public discourse dynamics rather than outcome-oriented (Perng et al., 2012). Therefore, in several past cases such as the 2011 Shadow Lake Fire, volunteers are actively deployed as "trusted volunteers"—a virtual team designed to manage and monitor social media communications in support of emergency incident response (St. Denis et al., 2012, p. 1). A study of the 2011 Thailand flooding disaster highlights that authorities could have taken actions to correct mistakes caused by the "emerging risks of the chaotic use of social media" (Kaewkitipong et al., 2012). Regarding the advantages of social media, Rexiline Ragini et al. (2018) emphasise that such platforms can be used for data mining to locate people who might be in danger.

Group interviews in Virginia with 25 county officials about their social media use and community involvement led to the identification of challenges, such as the overwhelming amount of data as well as recognising relevant information accurately and in a timely manner (Kavanaugh et al., 2011a). Hughes and Palen (2012) underlined that the speed and reach of social communication results in new demands and expectations by the public, putting pressure on emergency responders to find ways to receive and filter a substantial amount of incoming information. Limited resources that hamper the collaboration of humanitarian aid organisations and Volunteer and Technical Communities (V&TCs), i.e. technically trained volunteers, via social media (Gorp, 2014) have also been under examination. According to a study comprising eleven semi-structured interviews with US public sector emergency managers, the barriers to use social media are mainly organisational rather than technical (Hiltz et al., 2014). The two most reported statements concern a lack of personnel or time to work with social media, as well as a lack of policies, and guidelines for its use. Further responses identify a lack of appropriate technology and training as well as issues of trustworthiness. Therefore, they stress that the information system designers need to provide structures and features for collecting, validating and transmitting citizen-generated information, in order to improve usability. Nonetheless, Hiltz et al. (2014) report that interviewees were 'enthusiastic' about the potential usefulness of prototypes.

Social media offers potential across the entire emergency management cycle (EMC), which comprises the phases of mitigation, preparedness, response and recovery (Baird, 2010). In an interview study with emergency service staff, Reuter et al. (Reuter et al., 2015a) outline potentials for bidirectional communication between authorities and citizens, including the identification of potential hot spots and informing the public about emergencies (prevention or mitigation), certain warnings or directions (preparedness), forthcoming evacuations (response) as well as medical aid and further behaviour (recovery). Furthermore, citizens' information needs differ in the EMC's phases (Fischer et al., 2016), i.e. they require instructional information during the preparation phase as well as orientational information in the response phase (Coombs, 2009; Kaufhold et al., 2018b; Nilges et al., 2009). Correspondingly, a survey with 761 emergency service staff found that emergency services disseminate preventive information on how to avoid incidents (44%) (preparedness), share information on how to behave during an incident (31%), monitor social media activities (23%), receive messages (19%) (response), write reports enriched with media or coordinate clean-up activities (recovery) (Reuter et al., 2016b). However, the type of disaster has implications for the potentials of social media use: In contrast to less predictable disasters such as wildfires, predictable disasters such as floods allow the timely distribution of preparatory information via social media (Vieweg et al., 2010). Despite different information needs across the EMC, a comparison of fifteen social media guidelines for emergencies showed that only six guidelines differentiated their recommendations with regard to the EMC (Kaufhold et al., 2018a).

3.1.2   Related Survey Studies on Social Media Use and Attitudes of Emergency Services

As outlined above, qualitative studies on social media in emergencies provide an in-depth approach to the practices of various parties in relation to specific events. However, due to the eclectic nature of these events, generalising about overall attitudes towards social media use is difficult. Thus, quantitative studies complement the important qualitative work that has already been done so as to provide a more general understanding of attitudinal tendencies with respect to how often social media is used and for what purposes (Reuter et al., 2017b).

For instance, in 2013 the American National Emergency Management Association (NEMA) published a comparative study on the current degree of social media usage in crisis situations by emergency services and the organisations' perspectives on its future use. The web-based survey was sent to all 50 state emergency agencies and resulted in responses from 41 (San et al., 2013). Considering the trustworthiness of citizen-generated information, 75% of the respondents mentioned that their agency would not take action on social media information unless it was verified by a trusted source. The main barriers to the agencies' use of social media were identified as a lack of personnel, experience and knowledge to take on additional responsibilities, although the "largely untapped resource" of digital volunteers could "help to alleviate some personnel issues" (San et al., 2013). Moreover, the study revealed that all state emergency management agencies use social media in some capacity, as do 68% of county emergency management agencies and 85% of local response agencies.

A 2014 survey investigated the current status of 241 US county-level emergency managers' social media usage. About half (52%) of the respondents reported that staff of their agency use social media (SM) for job-related activities (Plotnick et al., 2015). Only a few have formal policies and procedures guiding the use. Of those that do have formal policies, about one quarter implemented policies preventing social media use. A lack of staff, guidance and skills have been identified as the main barriers for A2C. The main barriers for C2A constitute a lack of staff, the trustworthiness of public generated content and information overload (Kaufhold et al., 2020c). The authors conclude that "the agencies and their representatives are not yet ready to embrace social media and use it to its fullest potential. For the most part, current social media use is for dissemination of information, not the collection of it" (Plotnick et al., 2015). Furthermore, "in addition to technological advances, policy and management changes are needed as well, to remove the 'red tape' (lack of guidelines or even prohibitions against use) that impedes the effective use" of social media (Plotnick et al., 2015).

Since 2010, the International Association of Chiefs of Police (IACP) has conducted an annual quantitative survey about law enforcement agencies' use of social media, addressing "the current state of practice and the issues agencies are facing in regard to social media" (International Association of Chiefs of Police, 2015). With more than 500 participating law enforcement agencies across the United States each year, the survey provides comparable results on how attitudes and adoption rates shifted in the last six years. Comparing the first (International Association of Chiefs of Police, 2010) and last surveys, the agencies' use of social media increased from 81% (77% Facebook, 37% Twitter and 16% YouTube) to 96% (94% Facebook, 71% Twitter and 40% YouTube) and the share of agencies implementing social media policies has increased from 35 to 78%. The 2015 survey also highlights that 74% of responding agencies not using social media were considering its adoption; 86% reported that social media helped solving crimes and 84% stated that social media improved police-community relations in their jurisdiction. However, agencies were "very concerned" about online radicalisation and violent extremism (26%), criminal use of social media (25%), fake accounts (25%), privacy (22%), employee safety (21%) and staying informed about technological changes (21%).

Flizikowski et al. (2014) conducted the only recent survey among European citizens (317 respondents) and emergency services (130 respondents plus 33 interviews from Finland, France, Portugal, Norway, Ireland, Great Britain and Poland). The study identifies preliminary end-user requirements concerning crisis management in online and mobile communication. Generally, a high share of respondents claimed that they use social media, expressing a positive attitude towards its use for crisis management purposes and considering it a good way for distributing and receiving information. Accordingly, emergency services acknowledge the potential of citizens contributing to disaster response by providing "photos of the situation, video and audio messages, and information about location of events" (Flizikowski et al., 2014). Both citizens and emergency services identified similar challenges. These include a lack of knowledge, guidelines on how to use social media and trained personnel, the reliability of citizen-generated content, concerns about security and personal data protection as well as accessibility for older generations. Finally, the authors highlight that the type of emergency service had no significant influence on the respondents' opinions.

Summarising the current studies on citizens' attitudes, it has been shown that there is a positive attitude towards the use of social media in general (San et al., 2013) with regard to both personal and organisational use (Reuter et al., 2016b). Most US authorities already use social media, valuing its usefulness for information dissemination (San et al., 2013). This includes warnings and advice as well as guidance on how to cope with and prevent emergencies. For example, emergency services can offer advice on how to behave during an emergency, coordinate the help of volunteers, summarise information or coordinate the clean-up activities (Reuter et al., 2016b). Therefore, a further increase of social media usage can be expected, as 74% of agencies currently not using social media are considering its adoption (Reuter et al., 2016b).

On the other hand, there are some restrictions regarding the use of social media: First, despite the overall positive attitude towards social media for obtaining an overview of the situation in emergencies, only a few agencies have in fact often or sometimes used social media sites for this purpose. Thus, there is a huge gap between rhetoric and reality (Reuter et al., 2016b). This can be attributed to social media being predominantly used to share (Reuter et al., 2016b; San et al., 2013) rather than receive information (Reuter et al., 2016b). Furthermore, only a modest use of social media was observed; ground-breaking, crowdsourcing and crisis-mapping activities are neglected (San et al., 2013). In addition, about 20% of the local and about 30% of the county agencies surveyed by NEMA "had not identified a goal for social media operations" at all (San et al., 2013). Also, the study of Plotnick et al. (2015) found that about half of the county-level emergency agencies observed had not used social media at all. Identified barriers to usage included a lack of dedicated personnel (San et al., 2013), doubts about credibility and reliability (Reuter et al., 2016b; San et al., 2013), concerns about privacy issues (Reuter et al., 2016b) and a lack of formal policies to guide it (Plotnick et al., 2015). As the NEMA survey indicates, the constrained usage of social media in the field of emergency management could be based on limited reach and insufficient resources for the collection and analysis of data (San et al., 2013). However, organisational culture and skills, which can also be the key to the verification of citizen-generated content (San et al., 2013), were identified as enabling conditions for the organisational use of social media (Reuter et al., 2016b).

3.1.3 Research Gap

It has been shown that social media is used "with pockets of use and acceptance among organisations" (Tapia & Moore, 2014). Benefits, such as additional information, or pictures that are of particular value; and challenges, such as the pressure to act, chaotic use, overwhelming amount, limited resources, appropriate technology and trustworthiness, have been summarised. Findings regarding the perception of emergency services are often based on small numbers of qualitative interviews (Hiltz et al., 2014; Kavanaugh et al., 2011; Tapia & Moore, 2014).

A few quantitative studies concerning social media and emergency services already exist. Surveys with several hundred responses often focus on citizens' perception (American Red Cross, 2012b; Canadian Red Cross, 2012). Just four of the studies focus on the attitudes of the emergency services: The first one is an annual survey conducted in the US since 2010 (International Association of Chiefs of Police, 2015); the second one builds on a survey conducted in the US in 2012 (San et al., 2013); the third was conducted in the US as well in 2014 (Plotnick et al., 2015), and only the fourth was conducted in Europe (Flizikowski et al., 2014). All studies attest a positive attitude towards social media and all identify challenges in terms of credibility, knowledge and personnel. San et al. (2013) reference the knowledge required to take on additional responsibilities, and

Flizikowski et al. (2014) acknowledge a lack of uniform terms of use. However, there is clearly a lack of recent strong evidence of attitudes towards social media usage in Europe, with most of the evidence coming from the US.

While the study by Flizikowski et al. (2014) imparts insights about social media use and challenges across multiple European countries utilising mainly qualitative survey questions (open questions, the main intention of which is to identify respondents' ideas and opinions on how social media can be used in crisis response efforts), our study seeks additionally to build on this by providing a combined analysis of qualitative and quantitative survey questions as well as shifting the focus to private and organisational attitudes because we assume that differences exist between acting as a private person and acting as an emergency service unit. We also use methods of utilisation with regard to both private and organisational social media usage in the present and in the future. With this study, we therefore provide a recent insight into the attitudes towards the current and future social media usage during emergencies from the perspective of European emergency services.

Research suggests that citizens share information across multiple platforms during crises (Hughes et al., 2016), indicating that both crisis communication and monitoring are required to encompass cross-platform interactions despite the observed lack of skills and staff by emergency services (Plotnick & Hiltz, 2016). Therefore, it is important to not only analyse attitudes of organisations in Europe but to focus especially on staff attitudes regarding organisational social media usage. This is necessary because they will implement, evolve and work with instruments concerning the usage of social media in emergency service organisations. Hence, is it our goal—and the research gap we aspire to fill—to provide a better understanding of the emergency services' staff attitudes concerning the organisational use of social media platforms.

We acknowledge that, as mentioned above, studies on this issue have already been conducted. Yet we offer novel insights into European developments with regards to personal and organisational social media use, key factors of effective utilisation as well as opinions on future use before, during and after emergencies. Comparing the surveys' results and observing trends is important to align organisational and technological developments with staff needs, perceptions and their practice (Rohde et al., 2009). At the same time, we suggest building our analysis on plausible assumptions regarding individual processes of knowledge and reality formation. Particularly due to experiences in the staff's personal lives and their increasing use of social media platforms, they are more willing to use social media in organisational contexts. Thus, our perspective offers a first examination of the hypothesised causal relationship between private and organisational social media usage.

3.2 European Emergency Services Perception in 2014

The research question reads as follows: *What is the attitude of the staff of emergency services across Europe towards the organisational usage of social media platforms?* This question aims for the very organisations and individuals which would work with the various social media platforms in the event of an emergency to inform the public or facilitate help among civilians. In order to gain a more detailed insight into their attitudes regarding organisational social media usage, we asked why and how they (would) interact with the public in a case of emergency, what types of information are important and what they would require from their organisation to ensure an effective use of social media. Assuming a correlation between private and organisational use, in our questionnaire we included questions regarding, e.g., own experiences with social media or the amount of time spent on social media platforms, as these potentially influence the attitudes of both current private and organisational use as well as views on future developments of organisational social media usage.

3.2.1 Methodology

Based on our goal to produce a comparative analysis of emergency services' attitudes towards social media across several European countries, we decided to conduct an online survey with closed (quantitative) as well as open-ended (qualitative) questions. The survey was conducted as part of the EU funded project "EmerGent". This section presents the methodology of our study, whereby we will first present the survey design (Section 3.2.1.1), including questions, technical realisation and channels of distribution. Then we will present a characterisation of our participants (Section 3.2.1.2) followed by a description of our quantitative (Section 3.2.1.3) and qualitative (Section 3.2.1.4) analysis design.

3.2.1.1 Survey Design
Our survey aimed to identify the attitudes of emergency services, both as a whole as well as individual staff, towards their own and their organisation's current and future use of social media. The survey was designed with the aim of collecting

a mixture of quantitative and qualitative evidence. It consisted of four parts (see Appendix for details), as follows:

- Part I: Demographic details of survey participants (age, gender, country of origin, role, type of organisation) to explore any differences in responses depending on the characteristics of participants.
- Part II: Attitudes towards social media—a combination of closed questions (eight-point Likert scale (Likert, 1932) asking participants to rate on a scale of 1 to 5 how much they agree with a series of statements) and open-ended questions.
- Part III: Use of social media by one's own organisation—three sets of closed questions to gauge current usage, what information is seen as useful and the main factors to ensure the use of social media by the organisation. This was supplemented by two open-ended questions to provide further details.
- Part IV: A series of closed questions and one open-ended question to explore expected changes in the future use of social media.

We designed the survey based on a strategy aimed at triangulation of micro- (referring to individual perceptions) and macro-level (referring to organisational responses) attitudes. This methodological triangulation involved a combination of questions that focus on more qualitative aspects of the emergency services' intentions towards social media and their usage before, during and after an emergency at a micro-level as well as more quantitative aspects to obtain a comprehensive picture of emergency services' attitudes towards social media within emergencies at a macro-level.

The survey was created using the open-source survey application LimeSurvey (http://www.limesurvey.org). In early September 2014, we sent out the link to the online survey to different networks of emergency services as well as to different national / international mailing lists, like the Federation of the European Union Fire Officer Associations, various Fire and Rescue Units (e.g. Fire Brigade Ljubljana and also Dortmund), Firefighters 112 Social Network, EENA Emergency Services Staff Network (ESSN) and Norwegian regional authorities, the civil defence department at the County Government and others.[1]

---

[1] We would like to thank all members of our project for their remarks and for distributing our survey within the following networks: Federation of the European Union Fire Officer Associations (FEU), EENA Emergency Services Staff Network (ESSN), German Federal Agency of Technical Relief (THW), Fire Brigade Ljubljana, Slovenia Firefighters 112 Social Network, District Headquarters of the SFS (Poland), Fire Department Dortmund (FDDO), German Fire Service Association (DFV), German Fire Protection Association (vfdb), Association of Fire

3.2.1.2 Characteristics of Survey Participants

We received 761 survey responses from emergency service staff across 32 countries. It is important to emphasise that the sample of emergency service staff responding to this survey represents an opportunity sample and, as such, provides a heuristic device for exploring some questions which are relevant to this study. The largest number of respondents came from Germany (269) followed by Slovenia (134), Poland (117), Denmark (65), Finland (28), Norway (28), Belgium (23), Italy (17), the Netherlands (11) and other countries (70) (Figure 3.1). 310 participants (40%) also answered at least one of the qualitative free-text fields. The large majority of respondents (92%) were male, although the survey did include 54 female emergency service staff (8%). The largest proportion of respondents was aged 30–39 years old (29%) and the smallest aged less than 20 years old (6%), although, overall responses were fairly well distributed across age groups, with similar proportions of responses (around 20%) received from those aged 20–29, 40–49 and 50 years or older (Figure 3.2).

Figure 3.1 Country (Q8)

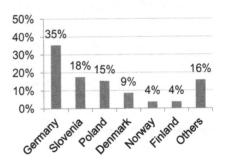

The majority of survey participants were full-time employees in Fire Departments (39%), Volunteer Fire Brigades (23%) or the German Federal Agency for Technical Relief ('Technisches Hilfswerk') (23%). The remaining 16% of participants included a relatively small number of staff working at Public Service Answering Points (PSAPs), for Emergency Medical Services, the police and other relevant organisations (Figure 3.3). The largest proportion of respondents described themselves as 'members of the crew' (31%), while 23% were Heads/Supervisors of their particular emergency service. This, as well as the average experience (Figure 3.4), suggests that the survey achieved a

---

Departments in North-Rhine Westphalia (VdF), Association of heads of German fire services (AGBF), Norwegian regional authority, and the Global Fire Service Leadership Alliance.

Figure 3.2 Age (Q6)

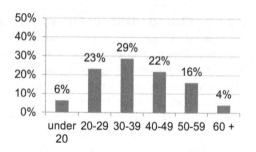

good cross-section of senior as well as more junior and supervisory-level staff (Figure 3.5).

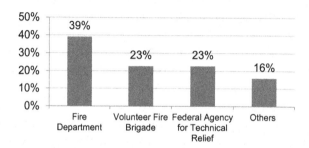

Figure 3.3 Organisations (Q1)

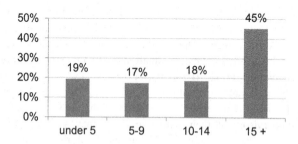

Figure 3.4 Years of Experience (Q5)

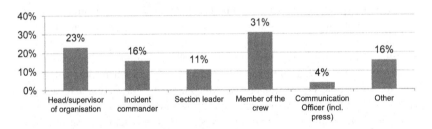

Figure 3.5 Role (Q2)

3.2.1.3 Quantitative Analysis

For the quantitative analysis, the survey data was extracted and analysed using Excel, a free software environment for statistical computing and graphics called "R" (http://www.r-project.org) as well as Statistical Package for the Social Sciences (SPSS, a software package for analysing quantitative data (IBM, 2014)). The analysis consisted of three key steps:

1. *Exploring basic frequencies* for each question and *using cross-tabulations* to explore any significant differences across different types of respondents.
2. *Factor-analysis of the eight Likert scale questions* (see above) on participants' attitudes towards social media. To measure respondents' attitudes towards the use of social media for both private and organisational purposes, we used the statistical technique of factor analysis. Factor analysis is a technique used in research to identify groups or clusters of variables, which, taken together, represent an underlying construct or variable of interest in the study (Field, 2009). The analysis showed that the factor, consisting of the eight questionnaire items, had high reliability with a Cronbach alpha score $\alpha = 0.774$ (Cronbach, 1951), which is used to indicate reliability of the scale used.
3. One-way Analysis of Variance—ANOVA (Field, 2009) was then used to measure any significant differences between the types of respondents in relation to this factor.

3.2.1.4 Qualitative Analysis

The analysis of our free-text survey questions was based on the inductive approach of *grounded theory* (Strauss, 1987). We used *open coding* associated with grounded theory to derive categories from the more qualitative free-text answers by careful reading and the aggregation of categories.

The first step was to extract the entire dataset from the survey platform into an Excel (*.xls) output file. Accordingly, a second sheet was added which contained only the qualitative results including the response identifier and original language identifier. As the survey had been distributed all across Europe, responses made by the emergency service staff were in different languages wherefore there was a need for translation. For each question, two columns for translation and categorisation were added. Thereafter each response was read manually and translated into English, if required. The translation was performed by native speakers of the respective languages. Easy translations were performed by translation services, such as Google Translate and supplemented with dictionaries, if single words could not be translated automatically or the translations needed manual adjustment for better intelligibility. These translations have later on been checked by a native speaker.

To use the grounded theory-oriented method, the open-ended questions were coded openly, and participants' statements were divided into categories. Each response was then assigned to one or multiple categories to achieve a quick overview of the interesting and relevant topics. The previously acquired knowledge from the literature review and quantitative analysis was used to increase theoretical sensitivity. Within the next section, we only present those responses that show both positive and negative perceptions of social media and its use by emergency services from an organisational as well as individual perspective. Each quotation is referenced with the participants' response identifier (e.g., R391). Several similar answers are indicated with a number (e.g., 12).

3.2.2 Empirical Results

In the following sections, we present the results of our survey. First, we present results regarding personal attitudes towards the use of social media (Section 3.3.2.1), then on the current organisational use (Section 3.2.2.3), types of information (Section 3.2.2.5), important factors (Section 3.2.2.7), and insights about the future use of social media (Section 3.2.2.8).

3.2.2.1 Attitudes Towards Social Media Use (Q7)

Following our questions focusing on the characteristics of the participants themselves (Section 3.3.2), the second step was to obtain insights into their attitudes towards the use of social media for private purposes. We asked them to rate their agreement or disagreement on a scale from 1 to 5 to a series of statements. Figure 3.6 shows, for example, that almost two thirds (66%; 27% strongly agreed and 39% agreed) of respondents stated that they used social media very often in their private life. As described in Section 3.2.1.3 above, eight of these statements were combined using factor analysis to provide an overall factor score for each respondent on their attitudes towards the use of social media for both private and organisational purposes.

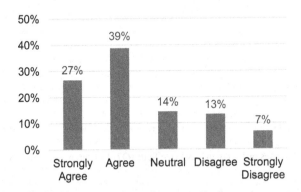

Figure 3.6   In my Private Life, I use Social Media Very Often (Q7)

We identified significant differences between different types of emergency service staff in their attitudes towards the use of social media for private purposes (as measured by this 'factor'). We found out that female emergency service staff are much more open-minded and have a more positive attitude towards social media than their male counterparts ($p < 0.05$). The significance of the statement, however, is mitigated by the low number of female participants (8%). In addition to gender, it is unsurprising that the age of the participants has an impact on the attitudes concerning social media usage. As Figure 3.7 shows younger emergency service staff are more positive towards using social media than older staff members ($p < 0.01$)—this difference was particularly significant when comparing those aged less than 20 years with those aged 50 or over. Emergency service staff in countries with high levels of social media use(We Are Social, 2014) were, on average, more positive than those living in countries with lower levels of use ($p < 0.001$, Kruskal–Wallis test; see Field (2009) as well as Kruskal and Wallis (1952)).

Almost 60% of all emergency service staff think that social media is important for their organisation (Figure 3.8). They thought that potential use cases could be sharing information with citizens (83%), keeping in touch with citizens (67%) and

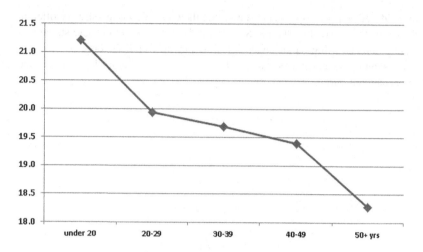

Figure 3.7 Attitudes of Emergency Service Staff (Q7) Depending on their Age (Q4)

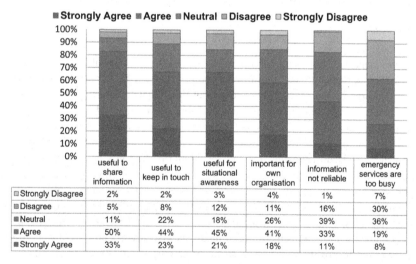

	useful to share information	useful to keep in touch	useful for situational awareness	important for own organisation	information not reliable	emergency services are too busy
Strongly Disagree	2%	2%	3%	4%	1%	7%
Disagree	5%	8%	12%	11%	16%	30%
Neutral	11%	22%	18%	26%	39%	36%
Agree	50%	44%	45%	41%	33%	19%
Strongly Agree	33%	23%	21%	18%	11%	8%

Figure 3.8 Attitudes towards Social Media (Q7)

improving the overview of a situation and therefore raising situational awareness (66%). However, 44% state information is not reliable and 27% thought that emergency services are in general too busy to use social media data (Figure 3.8).

When we asked for further comments to explain the participants' attitude (either positive or negative) towards the use of social media for private purposes, most of them answered this question from the point of view of their professional role of their particular emergency service unit. There were no significant differences in attitude depending on the staff role of the respondents, although, unsurprisingly, communications officers appeared to have a more positive attitude than other staff members—although the sample only included 28 staff working as press or communication officers.

3.2.2.2 Additional Comments on the Participants' Attitude towards Social Media (Q8)

The open-ended responses asking participants to provide additional comments about their attitude showed that, for some emergency service staff, social media provides the opportunity for organisational self-presentation (n = 10), such that citizens can better appreciate the work of the emergency services (R130), have a closer relationship with emergency services (R127), and potentially develop a more positive attitude towards institutional emergency service activities:

> *"A safe community must communicate! It's our job to stay in touch with those we serve each and every day, proving ourselves to be a reliable service for prevention and also to overcome challenges and crises. We have the knowhow, it's worth sharing. Save lives and spare suffering, at almost no cost. To make sure the public trusts us and to maintain their confidence we have to communicate with them wherever they are 24/7!" (R1901).*

While one participant pointed out that "these days, radio and television are no longer sufficient" as "more and more people use social media" (R391), another argued that social media needs to be used to deliver information and save lives:

> *"Social media is a valuable part of an emergency organisation [...] because it is quite useful to deliver information to the population as well as providing them with a wider view of the situation. We need to integrate this channel because it helps to save lives and it is a very valuable tool for civil protection, given the citizens' tools to protect themselves before, after, during and in the aftermath of a disaster" (R632).*

In Germany in particular, the fire brigade mainly relies on volunteers. On the one hand, it is usually difficult for them to assign additional personnel to handle social

media (R2101). Often, this is the result of a lack of time and required expertise among staff (R3164). On the other hand, social media offers an "important
medium to recruit voluntary helpers" (R2708). However, the survey participants
mentioned some caveats regarding data quality as well as privacy and issues of
social media adoption. In some instances, it cannot be guaranteed that the data is
correct as the individuals' perception may complicate the situation:

> "How useful data in social networks is depends on who gives this information to the
> public. It also depends on the very technical possibilities of information transfer and
> public access to this data on social networks. So, information [...] is always provided
> by very different people [...]. It can happen that the information is inaccurate, accidents
> exaggerated or data is incorrect [...]" (R327).

The information provided by unauthorised people or unofficial sources might be
unreliable (R848, R1733) and could mislead organisations (n = 33). Therefore,
"emergency services must be very careful about using information received on
social media during emergencies" and "information may be inaccurate and may
not provide a sufficient overview of what is actually happening" (R562). Another
challenge is the issue of privacy (n = 6), "because information is disseminated
within seconds and also victims have a right to privacy" (R1028) and organisations possibly "have no experience in media ethics" (R1246). For instance,
"the right of control over a picture of your own body could be compromised"
(R1041). To overcome some issues, participants argued for the standardisation of
information processing (n = 6):

> "There is a need for standards. The use could be very reliable and important but it
> must be very well organised" (R635).

Moreover, other participants argued that the wider adoption of social media by
emergency services is likely to take time (R861) and secondly that "communication concerning major events is reserved for state authorities" and "it is unlikely
they will give it up and we are not certain of being competent" (R654). Further
participants appraise social media as a useful technology that they "inevitably
[...] have to deal with" (R885), without mentioning a precise idea of its use
(n = 18):

> "It is really hard to ignore the impact social media has on the way we communicate
> today; it can be a powerful tool in shaping the way we want to be perceived and the
> relationships we have with others" (R884).

3.2.2.3 Current Organisational Use (Q9)

In contrast to the general positive attitudes towards social media, the actual organisational use paints a different picture, and it has been shown that only a relatively small proportion of respondents utilised such data frequently, particularly during an emergency. As Figure 3.9 shows, almost half share (A2C) information with the public 'sometimes' or 'often' before an emergency occurs (44%); most organisations have never actually shared any information with the public during emergencies (34%) and 83% (Q7) of emergency services staff nevertheless think sharing information with citizens is an important use case.

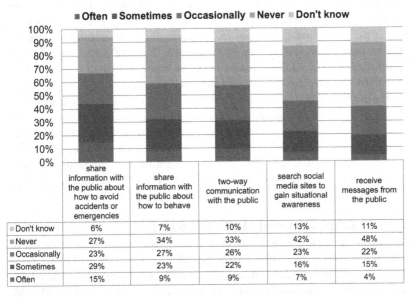

	share information with the public about how to avoid accidents or emergencies	share information with the public about how to behave	two-way communication with the public	search social media sites to gain situational awareness	receive messages from the public
Don't know	6%	7%	10%	13%	11%
Never	27%	34%	33%	42%	48%
Occasionally	23%	27%	26%	23%	22%
Sometimes	29%	23%	22%	16%	15%
Often	15%	9%	9%	7%	4%

Figure 3.9 Current Emergency Services' Social Media Use (Q9)

The survey also showed that 19% of the respondents said that social media was used 'sometimes' or 'often' for receiving messages from the public during emergencies (C2A) and only 4% said this happened often in their organisations. This is also the case for situational awareness. Although 66% (Q7) of emergency services think social media can be used to obtain an overview of the situation and to raise situational awareness, actually only 23% have often or sometimes used social media sites for this purpose. Such results clearly show that there is a huge gap between rhetoric and reality in the use of social media by emergency services within emergency management.

However, at the same time, analysis of the data suggested that overall, those emergency service staff already using social media frequently in their organisations were significantly more likely to indicate that they expected their organisations to increase their use of social media than other respondents. For example, of 112 emergency service staff who said they were already using social media to share information with the public about how to avoid accidents or emergencies, 109 (97%) said they thought that their organisations were likely to increase their use of social media for this purpose in the future. In contrast, among the 206 who said their organisation currently never did this, only 95 (46%) thought their organisation would do so in future. This contrast was even more striking concerning messages received from the public during emergencies: 94% of the 34 who said they received messages from the public often thought their organisation would increasingly do so in future, compared with only 37% of the 364 who said this was not currently their practice.

The qualitative analysis revealed that 18% (26 of 138) of those who answered the question about personal attitudes towards the use of social media in emergencies have concrete concerns regarding the credibility of citizen-generated content. Simultaneously, 21% (29 of 138) argued in favour of one-way communication towards citizens. There was little overlap between the two groups (only 5 individuals belonged to both groups), implying that overall levels of concern were appreciably higher than might be apparent at first glance.

3.2.2.4 Examples Social Media Use (Q10)

As part of the survey, participants were asked to provide concrete examples of some of the ways in which their own organisations had recently used social media during the emergency management cycle. Overall, their comments suggested that such use most commonly included: (a) providing warnings, advice and guidance to citizens on how to cope with or prevent emergencies or disasters; (b) disseminating hints and advice on how to behave during an emergency as well as coordinating the help of volunteers; and (c) sharing summary information or reports with citizens after the emergency and coordinating clean-up activities.

While most participants named several activities, their organisation had undertaken generally or explicitly before (n = 37), during (n = 64) or after (n = 62) an emergency, others either reported that their organisation did not use social media (n = 25), did not specify the use (n = 11) or answered with "do not know" (n = 5). Although partially covered by the quantitative questions, many participants mentioned the dissemination of preventive measures (R560) and, respectively, general behavioural advice (n = 12), information (R688) or warnings (n = 13), and media, like videos (R146) before an emergency. One participant said that their organisation used Virtual Operations Support Teams (VOST) which "provide recommendations about how to act before a disaster strikes (for instance, what to do in case of floods or heavy rain)" (R632).

During an emergency, information about the forwarding of units (R280), status updates on the current state of emergency (R2647) on the one hand (n = 16), or general tips (R560) relating to different kinds of safety advice (R2102) and recommendations regarding citizens' behaviour on the other hand (n = 10) were disseminated. One participant also mentioned "early warning of upcoming hazards" and using social media to refer "spontaneous volunteers to existing coordination initiatives" (R688), thereby providing an example of how volunteers could be integrated into relief efforts. Further important tasks were seen to be countering criticism and providing trusted information to citizens: *The most important task is countering criticism during a disaster* [for instance during a forest fire], *so as to provide trusted information and avoid the collapse of motorways or hospitals, which should be available for the emergency services" (R632).*

For the purpose of information, documentation or posting of equipment, participants' organisations shared photos (n = 12): "Updated information on the transportability of the main roads during the flood (approx. 15-min interval). Documented with photographs. The response was excellent" (R1522).

A widespread use of social media was the publication of a report (n = 45)—sometimes supplemented with pictures (n = 11)—after the emergency; for example, press releases that recap the emergency to "avoid countless questions about what happened" (R146). Moreover, clean-up activities were part of the effort, for instance "after storms when power lines are down and roads are closed" to locate "fallen trees in a large area" (R1072) or to provide guidance in terms of reconstruction:

"After an emergency, we share information. If recovery and rebuilding is necessary, we provide information on damage assessment, how citizens can indicate their losses to the authorities, what the official procedures are, where and how donations can be made and what kind of help is needed, and so on" (R1733).

Furthermore, from a more general perspective, some participants reported to represent the organisations' work practices (R173) or to get information by reading feeds from other authorities (R912). Also, the use of social media was said to serve as an additional channel supporting internal organisational communication

(R2911); for instance, to exchange experiences of former similar cases prior to an emergency (R2573).

To prepare for a possible electricity shortage in Belgium, an organisation processed social media data: *"Extracted the useful data gained from monitoring social media, and converted it into information to communicate advice at the federal crisis centre" (R547).*

Although not specified in detail, one participant mentioned the way social media could be used to control the spread of rumours (R891) to diminish the dissemination of misinformation. Other participants simply gave examples of recent incidents in which they had used social media, including wildfires, floods, pier or city fires, freezing rain, traffic management during incidents and rescue efforts. However, some participants reported the use of specific social media platforms (Facebook (n = 23), Twitter (n = 11), YouTube (n = 2), and WhatsApp (n = 2)). Although the sets are rather small, Facebook was used to provide information and updates (n = 5), disseminate articles or reports (n = 3), and to seek or monitor information (n = 4): *"When it rains heavily, it is soon reported on Facebook which city has been worst affected and you can see the first images of the actual situation of the people affected"* (R3176). In one case the police asked for information about a car accident via Facebook (R3435). Twitter was mostly used to provide information and updates (n = 6) and to disseminate alerts (n = 2).

From a more critical point of view, a participant identified issues concerning the reachability, information reaction and overload: *The problem I see with my experience working with poor or lower social classes is that many times they do not have the chance to access any type of information or technology. At other times, they can ignore or over-react to information. I would say that the emergency organisations are overcrowded with useless information and are too close to the sources of information. So, we cannot build a system that includes a useful social media tool"* (R720).

Among those answering that their organisation did not use social media, few mentioned a concrete reason. Either (political) authorities prevent or prohibit the use (R1417) or the perceived unreliability influences them: "Social media is too unreliable as a source of information on the latest threats. In addition, you cannot reach everyone this way" (R3142). 20% of those answering (26 from 130) mentioned barriers in terms of trust in citizen-generated content.

These key issues or attitudes mentioned above might hamper the successful integration of social media into the relief efforts of emergency services; a point to be discussed within the following survey question.

3.2.2.5 Types of Information (Q11)

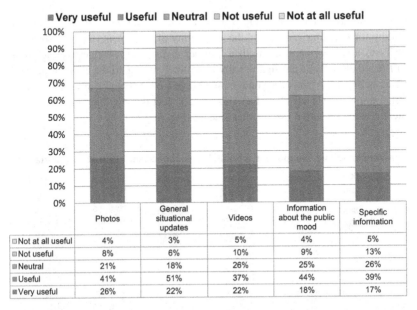

	Photos	General situational updates	Videos	Information about the public mood	Specific information
☐ Not at all useful	4%	3%	5%	4%	5%
☐ Not useful	8%	6%	10%	9%	13%
▣ Neutral	21%	18%	26%	25%	26%
▣ Useful	41%	51%	37%	44%	39%
▣ Very useful	26%	22%	22%	18%	17%

Figure 3.10 Usefulness of Different Types of Information Shared on Social Media by the Public during Emergencies (Q11)

Our survey researched what types of information shared on social media by the public would be useful during emergencies (Figure 3.10). It reveals, unsurprisingly, that general situational updates on a current emergency are considered to be more useful or very useful (73%) than specific information such as details about injuries or damage to property. Almost two thirds of the respondents consider both photos (67%) and videos (59%) important information to be shared on social media during an emergency. However, once again further analysis suggested that all types of information were most likely to be seen as useful by those already using social media to receive or share information with the public often (or at least sometimes).

3.2.2.6 Important Enabling Conditions (Q12)

Since we assumed a gap between the potential use and the actual current use of social media, we asked which conditions could ensure that social media is widely

used by the emergency services within one's own organisation (Figure 3.12). The
analysis suggested that the most important enabling conditions were organisational culture (78%) as well as the skills of staff in using social media (77%).
The conditions which were deemed to be less important were the provisions of
funding for staff time (56%), and the availability of equipment (68%) or software
(68%) to access or analyse the data. Further analysis also suggested that older
staff (aged 30 to 49) were significantly more likely to regard the skills of personnel as being important than younger staff (aged 29 or below) in enabling their
organisations to use social media—this could reflect the fact that older staff have
lower confidence in the use of social media (Figure 3.11).

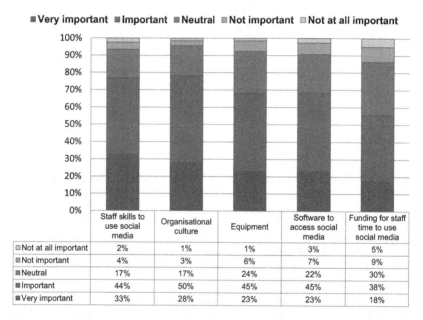

Figure 3.11 Main Perceived Enabling Conditions for Social Media Use (Q12)

3.2.2.7 Other Important Conditions enabling Social Media use (Q13)

In summary, the open-ended responses largely reflected those of the quantitative
survey in that participants emphasised the importance of staff skills and knowledge to ensure that information from social media is accessed and used in their

organisations. In addition, qualitative responses highlighted the need for good practice examples and awareness of recent trends and legal frameworks to ensure social media is used effectively by emergency services.

To ensure the wider use of information from social media, participants pointed out the importance of experience, which requires training (n = 9). They designated personnel (n = 8) to be responsible for the access of such information. For example, as one participant observed, this could include "a person with knowledge in this field or a responsible member of society (a volunteer in our case) who has the appropriate knowledge and equipment to communicate with the public" (R391), or staff "training and guidance for simple use" (R877) and "online identity, credibility and excellent communication skills" (R635). Concerning technical requirements (10), a reliable Internet infrastructure (R2708) and accessibility to the scene of the incident must be ensured (R2573). In addition, there is the need for software to enable the easy dissemination of messages into multiple social media networks:

> "Software should be designed to access all selected social media directly whenever it is used, and to enable the one-click dissemination of text into all (selected) networks" (R1414).

Besides those action- and technology-oriented factors, several participants emphasised the importance of the organisational culture (n = 13); for instance, personnel having a positive attitude (R861) or even enthusiasm (R2102) towards using social media, supplemented by knowledge of "examples of good practice, to encourage the development of using such social networks" (R487). Moreover, a participant quoted the requirement of rethinking emergency management scenarios:

> "Understanding that the rules have changed and we live in a completely new scenario, where citizens expect to receive advice and help through social media and where first responders and authorities listen to what the citizens' share [...], because those affected by a disaster are an important source of information. This is a two-way channel and it should not be used only to extract information as it has been traditionally done with press, radio and other communications technologies" (R632).

On the other hand, survey participants identified factors that could limit organisational use, including the possibility that interacting with the public through social media might be restricted for legal reasons:

"A clear allocation and restriction of access to the accounts of the emergency services (is required). It must be clearly defined which employees can and may perform the information disclosure and publication. Free communication between all employees on behalf of the ES is not allowed! Specific information is sometimes very important and sometimes also punishable by law!" (R1034).

In our context, participants also name issues regarding data credibility and protection (n = 5). Requiring that "the privacy and data protection must be ensured", especially "photos of the danger area (no matter from which side) may constitute a problem" (R2973). Additionally, there are risks that "information is manipulated in social media, or a one-sided depiction takes place" (R2865) and that "few posts in social media are objective and effective" (R3562), which is why "you cannot rely unrestrictedly on them" and "you must also provide your own impression" (R2865). Also, the compliance with the command structure is important; for instance, there must be clear rules regarding whether a WhatsApp message constitutes an official order or not (R2215). A participant furthermore emphasised the complexity of the information space with its dimensions and possible risks, whose questions must be answered with maximum importance (R1075):

"When we talk about social media and players, we're not talking about people, information, explanation, mediation, reality. The timing of the information may not match reality [...]. Also, we may believe that we are delivering great information and often we forget the other side (recipient) of the information [...]." (R1075).

In any case, a "backup plan" was always said to be required in case the internet infrastructure or social media communication failed (R2215).

3.2.2.8 Future Social Media Use (Q14)

The majority of emergency service staff said they expected their organisations to increase their use of social media in future, particularly in relation to sharing information with the public before and during emergencies (Figure 3.12). Thus, around three quarters of respondents thought that their organisation would increase their use of social media to share information with the public about how to avoid accidents (74%) and how to behave during an emergency (73%). A lower proportion, but still more than half (54%), also thought that their organisation would be more likely to utilise social media to receive messages from the public during emergencies.

However, at the same time, analysis of the data suggested that overall, it was the emergency service staff already using social media often in their organisations

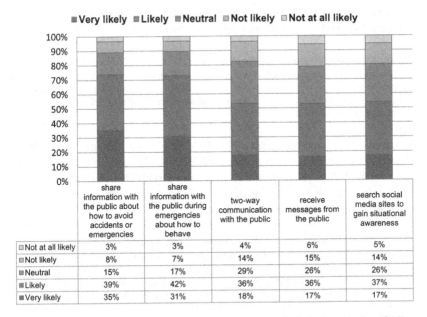

Figure 3.12 Expected Increase of Future Social Media Use in Own Organisation (Q14)

who were significantly more likely to indicate that they expected their organisations to increase their use of social media than other respondents. This suggests that although there is a willingness even among those who currently only seldom use social media in the emergency services to expand their use of social media, the growth of this practice and the uptake of more sophisticated systems is likely to be greatest among so-called 'early adopters' or 'converts' (Rogers, 2003)—who already use such technology and have the most positive attitudes towards social media.

3.2.2.9 Comments on the Role of Social Media for Organisations in 5–10 Years' Time (Q15)

Reflecting the findings of the quantitative survey, most responses to a qualitative open-ended question asking participants to explore the role social media might play for their organisations in a horizon of 5–10 years' time, highlighted the way social media was likely to play an increasingly important role. Concrete scenarios of the expanded use of social media in future included using it to recruit employees (R2880) and as the "main communication channel to promote volunteers" (R3021) or to coordinate their involvement during emergencies:

> *"The floods in 2013 showed that Facebook and others can reach broad bands of the population, who, however, tried to help spontaneously in quite an uncoordinated way. At this point, control centres and headquarters could intervene to lead such volunteers to some extent or to keep them away from incident scenes in especially dangerous situations [...]" (R1414).*

Participants also anticipated that "the advent of younger generations" (R280) working for emergency services would inevitably lead to an increasing role for social media. Others emphasised that emergency service staff of all ages needed to keep up with the latest social trends, including the use of social media, to ensure effective emergency management:

> *"The public are increasingly using social media and therefore emergency services have to work with this- In the UK, younger people use mobile phones less often to make a person-to-person telephone call, but they make use of a wider number of apps to connect with a large audience. Emergency services need to keep up with developing social trends, to find out how our communities communicate with each other" (R562).*

In contrast, the participant also commented on the fact that access to technology is limited in some areas and that social media is not used throughout society, which means that emergency services should not rely solely on information derived from social media when making decisions:

> *"However, we must remember that not everyone uses social media in the same way and some of the older generation use social media less frequently, if at all. Emergency services need to recognise the diverse communities they serve as well as the technological difficulties in some areas, where mobile phone signals and 3G or 4G is poor" (R562).*

Other survey participants indicated that the adoption of social media depends on "...the future decision-makers. Today's generation is denied the current possibilities of active communication with citizens; a short introduction to these information and communication channels is unlikely" (R1034). According to one participant, the process of adoption itself and responsible subsequent use must be planned precisely to ensure social media complements existing practices effectively:

"Firstly, we must create a map of risks on social media. Then we have to draw up a strategy for 15–20 years. We also need to create tactics that correspond to each one of the dangerous situations, disasters or incidents which can arise. Create all the mechanisms for integration into contingency plans, etc." (R1075).

3.2.3 Discussion and Conclusion

Recently, by using social media, citizens have acquired new means of communication both within their daily lives and as a means of mobilisation during emergencies. Emergency services are confronted with the problem of how to integrate such new methods of communication into their work practices. As other studies have already revealed, it is quite obvious from the citizens' point of view that the professional emergency services are expected to recognise citizen-generated content within social media (American Red Cross, 2012b; Canadian Red Cross, 2012). As San et al. (2013) have shown, most emergency services within the US (85%) already use social media, compared to approximately 19–44% of emergency service staff (Q9) found in this survey focusing on Europe: 19% often or sometimes receive messages (C2A); 31% do two-way communication and 32% share information with the public about how to behave or 44% how to avoid accidents or emergencies.

Thus, with regard to attitudes towards social media, the emergency services in the US cannot necessarily be compared to those of Europe. How European emergency services are disposed towards the use of social media for private and organisational use as well as the levels and main factors influencing their current and likely future use of social media in their organisations is therefore still an open question, which we tried to address within this chapter.

3.2.3.1 Main Results

Emergency service staff reported that their organisations were currently most likely to use social media to share information with the public (A2C) about how to avoid accidents or emergencies (Q7). However, only 15% (Q9) of respondents said they did this often. Less than half the respondents said social media was used to receive messages from the public (C2A) at least occasionally and only 5% said this happened often in their organisations (Q9). Nevertheless, the survey—and especially the qualitative answers (Q10)—revealed several organisations already use social media in several phases of the emergency management cycle (Figure 3.13).

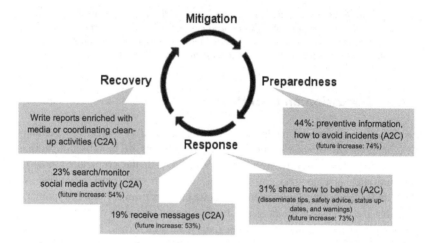

Figure 3.13 Emergency Management Cycle Enhanced with Social Media (based on Q9 and Q14). (Own Illustration)

European emergency service staff uses social media for different purposes within different phases of an emergency: (a) Before an emergency, they tend to use it to release preventive information and recommendations; (b) During an emergency, organisations disseminate tips, safety advice, status updates and warnings, or they monitor social media activity. Moreover, social media is sometimes used for internal communication and sharing experiences; (c) After emergencies, it is used to share reports enriched with multimedia content or to coordinate clean-up activities through social media. Problems discussed here are the unequal reachability of citizens, as lower social classes or older generations potentially have no or only limited access to social media.

The majority of emergency service staff expected their organisations to increase their use of social media in future (Q14), particularly to share information with the public about how to avoid accidents and how to behave during emergencies. However, the emergency service staff already using social media 'often' in their organisations were significantly more likely to indicate that they expected their organisations to increase their use of social media than other respondents. This means that while some emergency services are likely to increase their usage over the coming years, others may not do so at all or only in small incremental ways.

The main factors seen as enabling the use (Q12) of social media by emergency services were seen to be staff skills and an organisational culture open to the use of such information (Figure 3.14). The open-ended question (Q13) exposed additional enabling conditions: To ensure wide use, trained personnel, appropriate knowledge and excellent communication skills are required. On the technical side, it demands an available and reliable Internet infrastructure, including software artefacts that support a user in dealing with multiple social networks. A positive attitude and examples of good practice could influence the use of social media positively. Moreover, emergency services must keep up with changing scenarios, trends and habits of communication in social media. Barriers of usage may result from legal concerns such as data protection, internal organisational compliance issues or mistrust, as well as from the perceived complexity of social media information spaces.

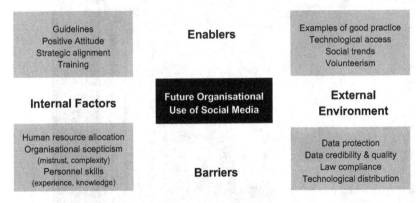

Figure 3.14 Internal and External Enablers and Barriers. (Own Illustration)

The study's key findings are summarised in Figure 3.15.

This study also has limitations: We do not differentiate between different social media services. Furthermore, we do not analyse differences between answers from the 32 countries, since the number of participants of each country was not high enough to draw clear conclusions from it. Because participants from certain countries and emergency service roles as well as females were rather underrepresented in this sample, and since we do not distinguish between different social media services, upcoming studies should take these issues into account to be able

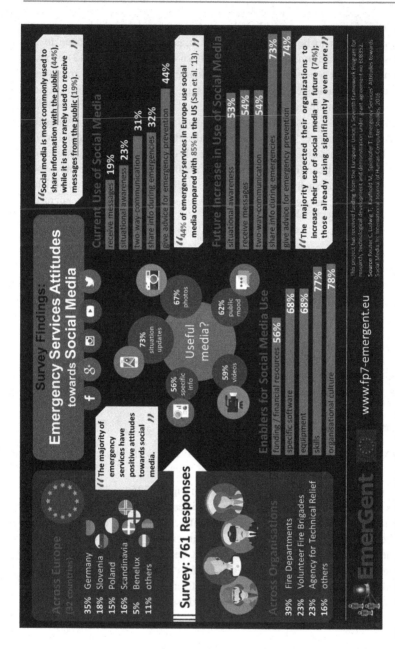

Figure 3.15 Infographic of the Main Results. (Own Illustration)

to compare e.g., culture-, role- and social media-specific differences. Also, further in-depth research is required to analyse how to overcome negative attitudes towards social media use.

3.2.3.2 Relationship with Related Work

We partly confirmed the results previously obtained by Flizikowski et al. (2014) and extended them in relation to the way in which current usage tended towards one-way communication, i.e., the provision of information (A2C) and the collection of information as part of the monitoring process (C2A). Also, both studies conclude that the use of social media is generally regarded positively. We also obtained results with regard to the concerns and challenges regarding future use. Challenges for the future use became apparent from the statements expressed by the respondents: In both cases, lack of expertise and human resources as well as uniform usage conditions were expressed. Similarly, a lack of trust in relation to citizen-generated information was mentioned.

A comparison with the study of the Canadian Red Cross (2012) is more difficult, as the geographical and cultural conditions differ from those in Europe. This can lead to different results when evaluating the surveys, particularly as not only natural disasters but also cultural and political events such as riots or attacks are very different from those in Europe. Consequently, the local emergency services and citizens experience such exceptional situations in a very different manner too (Flizikowski et al., 2014). Furthermore, both studies differ in that in Canada only citizens were interviewed about their expectations regarding the use of social media in relation to the emergency services. However, the case studies contained in the paper are particularly interesting: They show not only an example of how social media is already being used in Canada, but they draw parallels between the Canadian and European authorities. The police in Toronto trained 300 employees to deal with social media to improve the response to disaster situations in terms of providing situational information (A2C) as well as for monitoring social media (C2A) to respond to emergency calls if necessary or to correct misinformation (two-way-communication). This shows that at least in some Canadian emergency services there is a demand for skills in dealing with social media. Meeting these needs is, according to our study, one of the main prerequisites to enable its future use.

The study published by the American National Emergency Management Association (San et al., 2013) as well as the study on US emergency managers (Plotnick et al., 2015) are geographically and thus also culturally and politically based in the US. However, they are similar in so far as both surveys are addressed towards emergency services and include both quantitative and qualitative questions which have many substantive parallels. When comparing the results of these studies, it becomes apparent that there are many similarities in the use of social media by the emergency services in America and in Europe, despite the varying environmental conditions. Most obvious is the pace—but not the direction—of change and that it varies a great deal as a result of cultural and organisational factors.

Thus, all studies conclude that the setting for the use of social media is generally positive, even if the widespread implementation of their use is often hampered by a lack of resources, experience or lack of knowledge, or is at least limited by these shortcomings. The most important factor is staff time as the monitoring and the active use of social media is time consuming. Organisations, especially in larger or more protracted civil cases, cannot use social media without additional, competent, staff. Similarities can also be found regarding concerns about trust: 75% of respondents wanted to check the messages first before responding (San et al., 2013, p. 50). In our survey, one of the most frequently mentioned concerns was the trustworthiness of social media data.

One major difference was found: While the details of the attitudes of European and US authorities towards social media in disaster situations are mostly similar, the main difference is the extent of their practical implementation: As already stated, within the American study all national and 85% of local authorities reported already using social media (San et al., 2013). The regular use rate detected in our study however lies between just 19% – 44% of emergency service staff, depending on the application. The type of use, the authorities are agreed, still resides mainly in the dissemination of information to the population (A2C).

3.3 Attitudes by Emergency Services Staff in Europe in 2014 and 2017

Our first survey from 2014 shows that at that point in time only 44% of the organisations' staff were saying that their organisation is giving advice for emergency prevention (Reuter et al., 2016b). The staff also stated that skills and the organisational culture are in need of improvement in order to increase the effectiveness of social media usage. However, most of the participants only thought of sharing information rather than extracting it. But since 2014 the virtual landscape of social media has changed, as has the view of emergency organisations regarding their social media presence and interaction. In our second round of surveying in 2017 this questionnaire was used again, thus building a survey with two waves although it did not cover the same set of respondents. Nonetheless, the comparison of the respective results allows for a presentation of developments from 2014 to 2017. As a first step, the comparison's presentation will be operationalised with a basic descriptive comparison of the two datasets. Shifting the perspective towards a more causal analysis, this will be followed by combining the two sets to one big dataset with an ANOVA and a Mann–Whitney test for parametric and non-parametric correlations. The analysis concludes with a structural equation model to get a brief idea of how the given answers are dependent on a knowledge-based structure.

By analysing the survey results, we want to generate a baseline of European emergency service staff usage of social media. Our survey results may prove valuable in terms of social media usage across various disaster or emergency scenarios and phases, focusing on emergency services' staff's general views on organisational use. This in turn will help us to develop ideas of how to increase the effectiveness of social media usage of emergency services in Europe during extreme events. The chapter is structured as follows: In the following we describe the method of our survey including a dataset comparison, subgroup analysis and structural equation model (Section 3.3.1) and present our results thereafter (Section 3.3.2). As a last step, the findings are discussed within the scope of the emergency management cycle before concluding (Section 3.3.4).

3.3.1 Methodology

Based on our goal to produce a comparative analysis of emergency services' staff attitudes towards social media across several European countries in the years 2014 and 2017, this section presents the method of our study. First, we will present the survey design (Section 3.2.1.1). This is followed by a characterisation of our participants (Section 3.3.1.2) and a description of the design of our quantitative analysis (Section 3.2.1.3).

3.3.1.1 Survey Design

Our survey aimed to identify the attitudes of emergency service staff towards their own and their organisation's current and future use of social media. The survey was designed with the aim to collect a mixture of quantitative and qualitative evidence. It consisted of four parts, as described below (also see Section 9.1):

- Part I: Demographic details of survey participants (age, gender, country of origin, role and type of organisation) to explore any differences in responses depending on the characteristics of participants.
- Part II: Attitudes towards social media—a combination of closed questions (five-point Likert scale (Likert, 1932) asking participants to rate on a scale of 1 to 5 how much they agree with a series of statements) and open-ended questions.
- Part III: Use of social media by one's own organisation—three sets of closed questions to gauge current usage, what information is considered useful and the main factors to ensure the use of social media by the organisation. This was supplemented by two open-ended questions to provide further details.
- Part IV: A series of closed questions and one open-ended question to explore expected changes in the future use of social media.

We designed the survey based on a strategy aimed at triangulation of micro- (referring to individual attitudes) and macro-level (referring to the responses to (perceived) organisational behaviour) attitudes. This so-called methodological triangulation involved a combination of questions focusing on more qualitative aspects of the emergency services' intentions towards social media and their usage before, during and after an emergency at a micro-level, as well as more quantitative aspects to obtain a comprehensive picture of emergency services' attitudes towards social media within emergencies at a macro-level.

The survey was created using the open-source survey application LimeSurvey (https://www.limesurvey.org) in 2014 and SurveyMonkey (https://www.surveymonkey.com/) in 2017. The change of the tool was due to organisational reasons and did not influence the questions and the outcome. In both September 2014 and in October 2017 we sent out the link to the online survey to different networks of emergency services as well as to different national and international mailing lists. These included the Federation of the European Union Fire Officer Associations (FEU), European Emergency Number Association (EENA), Emergency Services Staff Network (ESSN), various fire and rescue units (e.g., Fire Brigade Dortmund and Ljubljana), Norwegian regional authorities and others.

3.3.1.2   Characteristics of Survey Participants

In 2014, about 696 of the emergency services staff responded to the survey. In 2017, we had a participation of 473 respondents. Although we did not focus on a particular group of agencies in 2014, most of the respondents came from fire departments, volunteer fire brigades and volunteer support agencies. In 2017, roughly seven times as many police staff responded compared to 2014. In terms of the participants' period of service and their positioning within the organisation, not too many differences were found between the datasets—they were almost equally distributed. Similar distributions were also observed concerning the participants' age. However, the proportional distribution of gender moved towards a higher number of female respondents, from 7.8% to 18%. Due to reasons of anonymity, we are not able to reconstruct if individuals participated in both surveys.

3.3.1.3 Analytical Instruments

3.3.1.3.1 Comparison of the 2014 and 2017 Datasets

In a first attempt to analyse the field of attitudes of emergency service staff in Europe, we start with comparing our dataset from 2014 with the new dataset from 2017. To do that, we weigh the two datasets in order to account for the discrepancies in the number of respondents. As weighting variables, we use the organisational background, age, gender and years of service, as these are possible dimensions in which the groups may show a base-line-bias. For the comparison we use the non-parametric Mann–Whitney test and treat the scale as ordinal. In addition, we conduct a t-test for the question sets "general attitude towards social media", "the current social media usage in the participant's organisation" and "the assessment of the future social media use of the organisation" (see Section 9.1.2.1) to verify the significance of the model.

3.3.1.3.2 Subgroup Analysis

Having completed the comparison, we analyse the relation between the given response and the demographic characteristics in order to pin down groups that are of interest for answering the research question.

Therefore, we perform a Spearman correlation for each item and an analysis of variances (ANOVAs) with the general social media attitudes of the participants as well as their opinions on current and future usage in the organisation. Thereby, the question sets are compared to the obtained demographic data, such as age, years of service, gender and the personal attitude. As gender is not measured in a metric or ordinal scale, we switched to a Mann–Whitney test for each individual item and a t-test for attitude-combined scores. Regarding the variable 'personal attitude towards social media', we could not perform an ANOVA. Instead, we used a Spearman correlation for each individual item and a Spearman correlation for a use-combined score to compare it to the current and future organisational use of social media. Although we need to weigh the variables due to the differences and therefore risk a decrease in the variance of the analysis, we are still able to extract a lot of significant outcomes. Another point for the interpretation is that the characteristics of the variables are reversed so that higher values are negative and low values are positive.

3.3.1.3.3 Structural Equation Model (SEM)

For a more in-depth analysis, we performed a structural equation model (SEM) (see Aichholzer, 2017) in order to visualise more complex correlations between the question-sets. We operationalised this in-depth analysis by performing two models with increasing complexity. The reason for using a SEM is that we thereby can display not only the simple item-based correlations with the data set but shed light on the depending structures within the dataset. Regarding its construction, an SEM is essentially a combination of a factor analysis3F[2] and a pathway analysis displaying causal relations between—in our case—opinions. In other terms, it shows how factor A causes the outcome of factor B. Furthermore, the model is able to show us moderating and mediating effects. Moderating effects in this context are factors that can further explain a dependency, meaning the inclusion of another factor (C) in the dependency form A and B, so that the interaction now goes from A to C to B. For example, you pay your taxes and if you want your tax returns, firstly you need to fill out the form requesting these taxes in order to get refunded. In this case, the moderating effect (C) is the filled-out form that improves the explanation of why you are getting the tax returns. The mediating effect is a factor that is just taking influence on the dependency from A to B: For example, sending a letter instead of an e-mail to the treasury department containing questions about your tax return, because you know that any other form of interaction with the department will fail. In this case we try to get a brief idea of how the factor 'private experience' causes the outcome of the attitudes to the social media usage of the staff's organisation.

Hence, the SEM is inspired by the theory of the sociology of knowledge by Berger and Luckmann (1967) and Knoblauch (2010). The main interest of this theory is how an individual processes and aggregates knowledge. Therefore, the theory focuses on the subject's surrounding environment and the subject's interactions with this self-constructed reality. More precisely, we focused on the theory of phenomenological knowledge sociology by Knoblauch (2010), which combines the concepts of Berger, Luckmann and Schütz (Berger & Luckmann, 1967; Schütz, 1932; Schütz & Luckmann, 2017). It states that individuals construct a

---

[2] The factor analysis, in this case the confirmatory analysis (CFA), is used to visualise latent variables in the dataset, such as norms and opinions. It is used for all of those variables that can't be measured directly in the field due to social acceptancy or unaware opinions. For performing such an analysis, you need at least two variables that are loading with at least .5 to the factor (possible range -1 to $+1$) (see Aichholzer, 2017, p. 74–85).

reality—based on their experience, knowledge and subjective interpretations of situations—which is altered and generated by every action. Following this theoretical concept, it is possible to make out four levels: (1) *experiences*, of which every individual has its very own set depending on age, gender, years of service, status in the service, type of organisation (e.g., police, fire brigade, technical relieve organisations, etc.) and cultural background (e.g. the individual's country of origin); (2) *meaning*, where the individual combines the experience-based knowledge with the situational context of structures of meaning. The individual is enabled to recognise and typecast the environment as well as to assign a certain relevance to the various parts. If those two levels are passed, the individual enters into level (3): the *action* level. Actions have to be planned for a future reality (Knoblauch, 2010), a reality that will be changed by the actions of the individual once again. Thus, individuals find themselves in a dynamic and subjective (4) *reality* in which they need to constantly alter their actions in accordance with the changing conditions.

To map the theory onto the survey and its structure, we use the already defined sections of the questionnaire leaving out Part I, i.e., the demographic details, because they were not compoundable into one or more factors. Furthermore, we do not work with level 4 of the theory, reality, mainly because our core interest is emergency services' staff' perception of reality. We transform the other Parts (II–IV) and theory levels (1–3) into factors, which did not require their alteration. In the end, the following 6 factors were aggregated:

- *Individual member side* (Theory: Experience (1)) (Survey part II): This factor describes the individual experiences of the staff in their daily lives.
- *Meaning-structuring factors* (Theory: Meaning (2)) (Survey part III): The factors reconstruct staff's latent structures of meaning on what information they would wish emergency service organisations to share (Factor 3) and how the organisations could improve their social media presence. The question-sets underlying the factors ask staff to draw from their experiences and apply these to think of possible improvements for their organisation's information sharing policy and workflow.
- *Individual organisational attitude* (Theory: Action (3)) (Survey part III–IV): These factors describe the opinion towards the actions taken by the organisations to use social media in the past and anticipated actions in the future.

Using this structure, we try to visualise the influence of both private usage and private experiences of the staff with respect to the other factors (i.e., factors 3–6). After the basic construction of this model, we analyse the correlation of private usage and private experiences with other factors in order to shed light on their direct influence. Moreover, we extend our model so that it fits the theoretical framework more precisely. Therefore, the meaning-structuring factors (factors 3–4) are treated as moderating effects in the model. This reflects our assumption, drawn from the sociology of knowledge by Knoblauch (2010), that private experiences do not necessarily influence opinions on the usage of social media in emergency organisations directly but are moderated by the meaning-structuring factors. In the models run to account for this, the private-use factor shows no significant influence on the other factors. Thus, the factor of how often someone uses social media applications appears to be unimportant. We therefore exclude the factor from the model to reduce complexity and improve the model fit. We trace the relative redundancy of this factor back to the question's composition, namely asking how often they use social media and how often their friends and relatives use such platforms. While in the absence of an emergency, the general frequency of using social media alone does not seem to shape people's opinions, experiences on social media platforms certainly shape their opinions in an emergency. Also, when performing the model with moderating effects on the factor of "opinion on an effective organisational social media usage", the numbers show that the factor has no significant influence on other factors, especially not with regard to the question of how the organisations will use social media in the future. Hence, the model was excluded from this analysis.

It needs to be noticed that the SEM is not performed for each year separately but for the merged dataset of 2014 and 2017. This was done due to the fact that in non-merged datasets the number of samples would have been too small to converge. Noticeable attention also needs to be drawn to the model fits and the general outcomes which are not strong overall but meet the criteria in order to be seen as a tendency to how the answers depend on private experiences.

3.3.2 Empirical Results I: Trends between 2014 and 2017

In the following we will first present the trends between 2014 and 2017 and then merged data results.

3.3.2.1   Attitudes towards the Use of Social Media for Private and Organisational Purposes (Q7)

Most of the emergency service staff used social media for private and/or organisational purposes. Overall, usage for both purposes increased from 2014 to 2017. Most emergency service staff used social media for private purposes. As can be seen in Figure 3.16, the proportions of staff agreeing with the statements slightly changed from 2014 to 2017. In 2014, 66% were using social media in their private life. In 2017, 71% were doing so. The share of emergency service staff who agreed with the statement that most of their friends were using social media to keep in touch increased significantly from 76% in 2014 to 83% in 2017.

However, a greater number of survey respondents (see Figure 3.16) thought that information provided on social media is not reliable (48%) in 2017 than in 2014 (17%). At the same time, a majority agreed with the statement that social media could be useful for keeping in touch with the public during emergencies (73%, 2017).

In 2014, the share of survey respondents who agreed with this statement was significantly smaller (68%). The majority of emergency service staff further agreed that social media platforms are an important tool for emergency services. The approval rating thus changed significantly from 59% in 2014 to 70% in 2017. The survey participants also agreed that social media could be useful for gaining situational awareness (78%, 2017), which is also an increase similar to the statement on keeping in touch with the public (68%, 2014). In 2017, nearly nine out of ten surveyed staff agreed that social media is useful for sharing information with citizens. The approval rating thus increased significantly from 83% in 2014 to 88% in 2017. Even though the majority of respondents agreed that social media could be useful for emergency services, 33% in 2017 and 27% in 2014 agreed that emergency services are too busy to use social media. This points to the gap between potential and reality discussed above: Although the potential usefulness is acknowledged and praised by staff, problems regarding the unreliability of citizen-generated content and the additional workload for agencies impede its realisation (Figure 3.17).

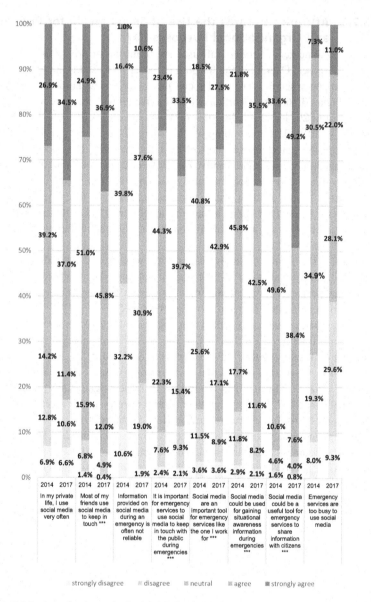

Figure 3.16 Attitudes towards Social Media for Private and Organisational Purposes. (Note. *** indicates p < 0.001, ** p < 0.01 and * p < 0.05 for further information see Table 9.1)

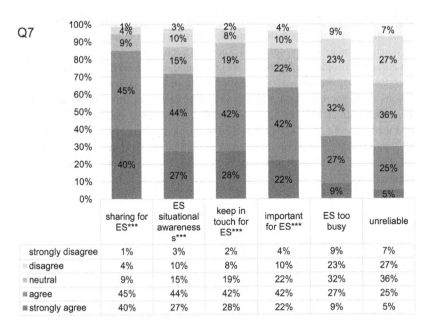

	sharing for ES***	ES situational awareness s***	keep in touch for ES***	important for ES***	ES too busy	unreliable
strongly disagree	1%	3%	2%	4%	9%	7%
disagree	4%	10%	8%	10%	23%	27%
neutral	9%	15%	19%	22%	32%	36%
agree	45%	44%	42%	42%	27%	25%
strongly agree	40%	27%	28%	22%	9%	5%

Figure 3.17 Please Indicate how Strongly you Agree or Disagree with the following Statements (Q7—Cumulative Results 2014 and 2017)

3.3.2.2 Opinion on the Current Organisational Usage of Social Media (Q9, Q11)

From the perspective of the emergency service staff, the organisations managed to increase their presence on social media. Yet it is important to note that information gathered cannot be used to extrapolate real changes in organisational behaviour. However, research made on actual organisational behaviour points into the same direction: Regarding the publishing and sharing of preventive information in 2014, only 16% of emergency service staff stated that relevant information was often publicised, whereas in 2017 almost 39% agreed with the statement. Furthermore, the emergency service staff perceive an increase in organisations' social media work not only before but also during emergencies. In 2014, only 10% in the five-point answer scale said that their organisation was often providing citizens with information on how to behave during an emergency, while over 37% indicated that their organisation did not pass information to the public. As for 2017, 24% reported that informing citizens is a frequently used tool for their organisations and slightly more than 19% claimed that it is never used.

When it comes to the communication between organisation and public, the percentage of people stating that two-way communication with the public is often used nearly doubled from 11% in 2014 to 21% in 2017. According to the organisations' staff, more organisations try to receive messages from the public during emergencies. In 2014, only 5% indicated that receiving messages is a frequently used method and 17% said that it is used occasionally. In contrast, 14% of staff in 2017 said that their organisations "are receiving messages during an emergency" and 20% said that their organisation is "receiving messages at least sometimes" (Figure 3.18).

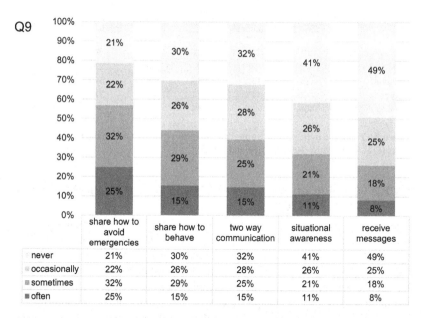

Q9	share how to avoid emergencies	share how to behave	two way communication	situational awareness	receive messages
never	21%	30%	32%	41%	49%
occasionally	22%	26%	28%	26%	25%
sometimes	32%	29%	25%	21%	18%
often	25%	15%	15%	11%	8%

Figure 3.18 Does your Organisation use Social Media? (Q9—Cumulative Results 2014 and 2017)

If we now focus on the use of social media content to raise situational awareness, we see that 8% of the emergency service staff in 2014 stated that it is used regularly and 18% that it is used sometimes. In 2017, 17% reported that their organisation is using it often, while 25% stated that their organisation is using it sometimes. Therefore, 16% of the emergency service staff in 2014 indicated that specific information, such as injuries and damages to property, would be very useful to their organisation, when asked which information is perceived to be useful to the organisation. In 2017, the percentage of emergency service staff stating that this specific information would be very useful to their organisation rose to 23% (p < 0.05). To summarise the development, we can identify a similar tendency to the set of questions in Section 3.3.2: Staff have the impression that not only would it be helpful for the organisations to use social media but that the organisations are already increasing the social media usage (Figure 3.19).

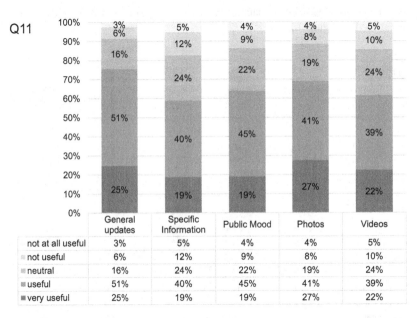

	General updates	Specific Information	Public Mood	Photos	Videos
not at all useful	3%	5%	4%	4%	5%
not useful	6%	12%	9%	8%	10%
neutral	16%	24%	22%	19%	24%
useful	51%	40%	45%	41%	39%
very useful	25%	19%	19%	27%	22%

Figure 3.19 Which of the following Types of Information Shared on Social Media by the Public Would you find Useful to Receive during an Emergency? (Q11—Cumulative Results 2014 and 2017)

3.3.2.3 Key Factors for more Effective Social Media Use by the Emergency Service Organisations (Q12)

Next, we examined the question of how to ensure a better use of social media content for the organisations. In 2014, 33% argued that it would be essential to have skilled emergency service staff working with social media. In 2017, 42% agreed with this statement. Furthermore, in 2014 28% indicated that it would be more important to change or develop the organisational culture towards enhanced use of social media. In 2017, 44% agreed with this statement. The staff also indicated that an expansion of equipment purchases for the departments dealing with social media is needed. Whereas 24% reported in 2014 that an expansion of such purchases is very important, 30% did so in 2017 (p < 0.05). Part of this expansion of purchases are better and more efficient software solutions to access social media. 23% stated in 2014 and 34% in 2017 that it would be very important to improve the software solutions. Hence, staff see the need to be educated better in using social media and demand proper technical solutions when working with social media (Figure 3.20).

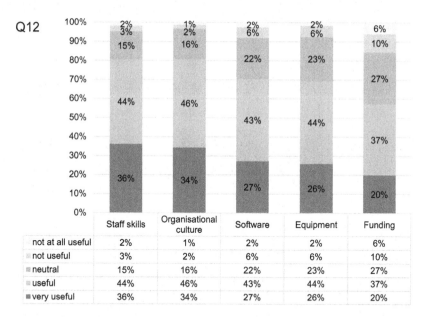

	Staff skills	Organisational culture	Software	Equipment	Funding
not at all useful	2%	1%	2%	2%	6%
not useful	3%	2%	6%	6%	10%
neutral	15%	16%	22%	23%	27%
useful	44%	46%	43%	44%	37%
very useful	36%	34%	27%	26%	20%

Figure 3.20 How Important do you Think are the following Factors to Ensure that Social Media is Widely Used by Emergency Services Like Yours? (Q12)

3.3.2.4 Opinion on the Future Use of Social Media in the Emergency Service Staff' Organisation (Q14)

As for the future, 37% of emergency service staff in 2014 and nearly 50% in 2017 believe that their respective emergency service organisation will continue to publish and share preventive information on how to avoid accidents. The staff increasingly believe that sharing information on social media during an emergency is a concept that needs to be continued or will become an important part of the organisation in the future (32% in 2014 and 42% in 2017). Equal rates of growth can be observed when evaluating the questions regarding communication. In 2014, 17% answered the question of whether the organisation will have two-way communication with the public with 'very likely'; in 2017 24% did. Concerning the question whether the organisation will receive and process messages from the public in an emergency, in 2014 16% responded with 'very likely', whereas 23% did so in 2017. If such messages from the public, or from social media in general, will be utilised to gain situational awareness is therefore questionable. In 2014, 27% did not know if this was going to be implemented

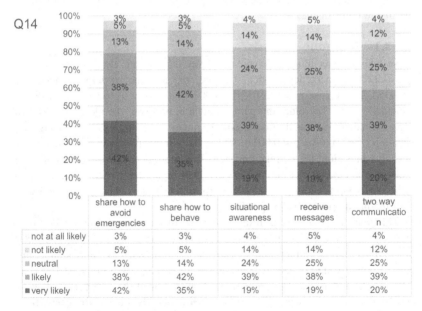

Q14	share how to avoid emergencies	share how to behave	situational awareness	receive messages	two way communication
not at all likely	3%	3%	4%	5%	4%
not likely	5%	5%	14%	14%	12%
neutral	13%	14%	24%	25%	25%
likely	38%	42%	39%	38%	39%
very likely	42%	35%	19%	19%	20%

Figure 3.21 Please Indicate the Extent to which you Expect your Organisation to Increase its use of Social Media in Future (Q14)

and only 17% indicated that using social media for gaining situational awareness is 'very likely'. In 2017, however, 23% thought that usage of social media to gain situational awareness is likely to occur, while only 18% remained neutral to the question.

This shows that the staff of the emergency service organisations believe in the usefulness of social media and are under the impression that more and more is done in their organisation and will be done in the near and distant future. Yet it is immanent that without an increase of more efficient technical solutions and a more sufficient education this expansion is not manageable (Figure 3.21).

3.3.3 Empirical Results II: Merged Data Results

In terms of the data, we decided to merge the datasets from 2014 and 2017 to fit the size criteria for our subgroup analysis and gain, due to larger variance, a deeper understanding of the emergency service staff's attitudes. Albeit the fact that there is a time span of three years between data points, we could not detect much difference with respect to demographic factors, which would have made the merge unjustifiable.

3.3.3.1 Subgroup Analysis

If we take a closer look at the age of survey participants, the data implies that the older the emergency service staff are, the less the participants and their friend(s) ($r = 0.251$; $r = 0.280$ ($p < 0.001$)) are likely to use social media in their daily lives. The older the participants are, however, the more they tend to perceive social media as useful for gaining situational awareness in an emergency situation ($r = -0.091$ ($p < 0.005$)). As for the current state of social media usage in the organisation, the correlations show that the older the participants are, the higher the likelihood that they believe that their organisation uses social media to raise situational awareness ($r = -0.104$ ($p < 0.005$)) and actively communicates with the public ($r = -0.073$ ($p < 0.05$)).

This tendency is reflected in the evaluation of questions asking which information could be useful to the emergency service staff's organisation. The older the staff are, the more they find specific information (such as injuries and damages to properties) to be useful to the organisation ($r = -0.085$ ($p < 0.01$)). They further believe that visual information such as videos of the emergency situation can be helpful ($r = -0.075$ ($p < 0.05$)). However, the older participants indicated that processing such data streams, leading to a more effective social media usage, would require an increased amount of time in order to train the general use of social media ($r = -0.180$ ($p < 0.001$)) as well as a proper software ($r = -0.085$ ($p < 0.01$)). The older participants further believe that emergency service staff need to be trained to extend their skills in terms of using social media ($r = -0.067 p < 0.05$). When asked about the future use of social media in the organisation, the younger respondents assumed that the organisations will shift towards both preventive publishing (e.g. to avoid accidents ($r = 0.081$ ($p < 0.01$)) and active two-way communication ($r = 0.074$ ($p < 0.05$)). By contrast, the older emergency service staff assumed that the organisations will focus on emergency operations in terms of how to behave ($r = -0.110$ ($p < 0.001$)) and how to receive information ($r = -0.109$ ($p < 0.001$)).

Examining these findings, one is left with the impression that older survey participants have a more positive attitude towards social media in general. However, that does not mean that the younger generations in the emergency organisations are less convinced of social media usage.

3.3.3.2 Structural Equation Model (SEM)

For performing an SEM, an initial factor analysis is needed. The results of this analysis show that in every factor at least four variable loads are over 0.60 and can therefore be considered as a valuable influence on the factor. However, as already mentioned, factor 1 does not fit the criteria but is also not in use for the further analysis and thus can be neglected (Table 3.1).

The rudimentary SEM shows that private experiences tend to have a positive influence on all other factors and that the model fit is satisfying (Figure 3.22). Not surprisingly, the model indicates that the factors measuring how frequently social media is used influence the experiences made with social media platforms. The private experiences of staff have a strong influence on the expectations of and opinions on information distribution in social media as well as the organisations' operational handling of social media presence.

The strongest influences on private experience are found in the expectations of how the public should be informed, followed by the opinion on future use of social media in the organisation. The more positive experiences the participants have made with social media, the more likely they are to agree with or even demand greater use of social media in emergency service organisations. The opinion on the current organisational usage of social media, however, shows a relatively weak influence regarding private experiences of the emergency service staff.

In a next step (Figure 3.23), we use the information expectation factor as a moderating effect towards the factor of current usage of social media in the

Table 3.1   Structural Equation Model

Factor	Load in the Factor	Variable
Individual member side (Theory: Experience (1)) (Survey part II)		
Factor 1: "Private use of social media"	0.9	Q7.1
	0.57	Q7.2
Factor 2: Private experience	0.8	Q7.4
	0.73	Q7.5
	0.72	Q7.6
	0.71	Q7.7
Meaning-structuring factors (Theory: Meaning (2)) (Survey part III)		
Factor 3: "information expectations from social media platforms in case of an emergency"	0.67	Q11.1
	0.69	Q11.2
	0.57	Q11.3
	0.62	Q11.4
	0.61	Q11.5
Factor 4: "Opinion on an effective organisational social media usage"	0.77	Q12.1
	0.79	Q12.2
	0.61	Q12.3
	0.57	Q12.4
	0.66	Q12.5
Individual organisational attitude (Theory: Action (3)) (Survey part III–IV)		
Factor 5: "Opinion on the current organisational social media usage"	0.69	Q9.1
	0.74	Q9.2
	0.76	Q9.3
	0.7	Q9.4
	0.68	Q9.5
Factor 6: "Opinion on future social media usage in the organisation"	0.55	Q14.1
	0.67	Q14.2
	0.68	Q14.3
	0.69	Q14.4
	0.73	Q14.5

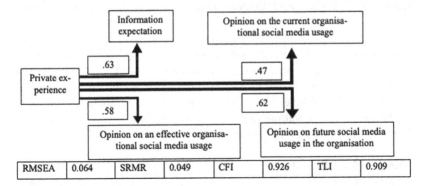

Figure 3.22 Simple SEM on Private Experience towards the Attitudes (Description of the Fit Values in the Section 9.1.2.2)

organisation, the factor of how to ensure a more effective use of social media and the factor of future developments in organisational social media usage.

The moderating effects of private expectations towards information publishing tend to have a rather weak influence on the other factors. The moderating effects, however, do have an influence on the factor "opinion on an effective organisational social media usage". This means that the experiences the staff make in their private lives shape their expectations towards being informed of social media channels. This again influences their thoughts on how to develop an adequate and sufficient social media usage strategy.

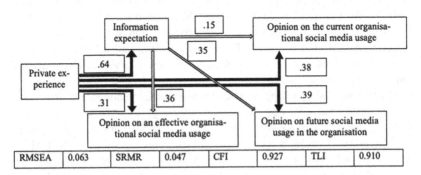

Figure 3.23 SEM with the Moderator "Information expectations" (Description of the Fit Values in Section 9.1.2.2)

3.3.4   Discussion and Conclusion

In our comparative survey, we conducted two opinion-based surveys in 2014 and 2017, asking emergency service staff about their opinion towards social media in private life and in relation to their organisation. In total, we received 1,169 answers: In 2014, 696 persons responded to the survey and in 2017, 473 persons participated. The resulting discrepancies were balanced by applying weights to the datasets. The respondents came from a variety of European countries and different types of emergency service organisations.

3.3.4.1   Main Results

We began this analysis by performing a descriptive comparison of results from 2014 and 2017. The comparison revealed an *increasingly positive attitude* towards social media. Furthermore, a growing number of participants indicated that they themselves and their friends are using social media. They also confirmed that social media is of increasing importance to them and their organisations. More-over, the emergency service staff in 2017 believed more strongly in the advantages of communicating with the public via social media. At the same time, more emer-gency service staff nonetheless question the reliability of information gained from social media platforms, as compared to 2014. Arguing that citizen-generated con-tent needs to be treated with caution, they further point to the fact that emergency service organisations are too busy to properly manage a social media presence.

Despite the personal point of view of emergency service staff towards the reliability of information gleaned from social media, a growing number of staff opine that the organisation in fact uses social media before, during, and after an emergency more frequently—not only to inform the public but also to receive messages from citizens. To further support the usage of social media, the partic-ipants think that the training of staff and a reorientation of the organisation are essential. A growing percentage of emergency service staff believe that the use of social media platforms can be increased if those key factors can be integrated into the organisations' culture.

Furthermore, when taking a closer look at the correlations, we discovered that *especially the older and more experienced staff are a driving force for an increased use of social media* albeit the fact that they do not use social media in their private lives on a daily basis (also see Feldman et al. (2016)). Here, age corresponds with service time and rank, meaning that the older emergency service staff are the more time they have spent in the organisation and hence are likely to occupy higher positions in the organisation's hierarchy. Those two correlation variables, i.e., 'age' and 'time working in the service', show quite exact the same correlation coefficient when they are put in relation to questions concerning the current and future use of social media in the organisation. Even though the younger participants seem to use social media on a more frequent basis, they are not as related to the topic of using social media in emergency situations.

It is also important to note that overall, correlations are not very strong or highly valid, but in sum show a tendency towards the older and more experienced staff being more positive about their organisation's information sharing practices. This is probably due to the likelihood of them occupying higher positions where questions of organisational social media usage are more important than in daily work.

Another important note is that those results are staff attitudes and do not reflect the actual organisational use of social media. By performing a structural equation model, we showed that particularly their private experiences with social media are a driving factor for their answers to the question of how the organisation uses social media in the present and how it will utilise social media platforms in the future.

3.3.4.2 Relationship with Related Work

In distinction to most existing qualitative surveys on social media use by emergency services (Flizikowski et al., 2014; Plotnick et al., 2015; San et al., 2013), our study centres on a descriptive comparison of results from 2014 and 2017. Thus, we were able to confirm the positive attitude towards social media shown in existing studies and identify an increase of perceived importance, e.g., for citizen interaction, information sharing and situational awareness. Similar to Flizikowski et al. (2014), however, the reliability of citizen-generated content was perceived to be an issue for social media use. Although the recurring International Association of Chiefs of Police studies allow annual comparisons of results, e.g. 2015 (International Association of Chiefs of Police, 2015) or 2010 (International Association of Chiefs of Police, 2010), they examine American police departments in contrast to our European multi-organisational focus. Still, in both cases an increase in social media use was observed. While the IACP studies examined the use of specific social media platforms (e.g., Facebook, Twitter or YouTube), our study focused on application (Q9) and the expected future increase of social media usage (Q14). Therefore, our study contributes to a wider perspective within the discussion of social media usage in emergency organisations in general, while opening up this field to a European viewpoint.

3.3.4.3   Limitations and Outlook

Nevertheless, there are limitations to this analysis, mainly the large size difference between the two surveys. To address this issue, the authors needed to weight the 2017 dataset to make it comparable to the dataset of 2014. We also examined a particularly European point of view. Hence, individual perspectives of organisations and countries (such as environmental details and locational specifics) are not taken into account. However, the focus of this survey lies in finding common ground regarding the social media presence of emergency service organisations in the European Union in general. Choosing a theoretical perspective based on Berger and Luckmann (1967) as well as Knoblauch (2010) allowed us to design a structural equation model incorporating assumptions of individual usage and particularly experiences influencing views on organisational use, mediated by individuals' information expectations. Still, in future research it may prove plausible to include other potential factors, such as experience with local policies or type of area (countryside vs. city), in order to comprehend emergency staff's reasoning more accurately.

This chapter shows emergency organisations how staff perceive their social media presence as well as what they expect from emergency organisations in the future. Based on this information, the organisations are able to tackle the challenges described by Hiltz et al. (2014), develop guidelines and system solutions with their operators 'on the ground' and ensure an effective utilisation of social media before, during, and after emergency events (Kaewkitipong et al., 2012). Although we did not analyse samples that are representative in terms of age, gender, country of origin, role and type of organisation, it is noteworthy that the perceived unreliability of social media increased from 43% (2014) to 48% (2017). Thus, there is a need to further investigate the decrease in perceived reliability of social media qualitatively and quantitatively, such as the potential impact of the recent discussion of fake news (Tandoc Jr. et al., 2018). In addition, research suggests that social media guidelines may avoid chaotic use of social media during emergency events by both authorities and citizens as consumers or producers (Kaufhold et al., 2018a). Furthermore, artificial intelligence algorithms may assist in overcoming issues of information credibility, reliability or overload by the classification, clustering, summarisation and quality assessment of information (Imran et al., 2018; Kaufhold et al., 2020a).

However, as emergency mangers need to make sense of algorithmically computed data, usable interfaces are required that support the actionability of information, i.e. provide the right information at the right time in the right form to the right audience (Zade et al., 2018). One promising approach is the application of visual analytics to deliver solutions that are tailorable with regard to role-specific interests (Onorati et al., 2018). We envision that the combination of tailorable and usable algorithms and interfaces will help to counter the increasing perception of emergency services being too busy to monitor social media (33% in 2017 vs. 27% in 2014). Furthermore, despite the perceived usefulness of photos and videos by emergency services, the vast majority of studies focus on textual content (Alam et al., 2018b). Thus, the design of systems supporting multimodal content analysis (integrating text, video and photo processing) both on algorithm and interface level is a direction for future research. In a long-term perspective, improved crisis information management, including a social media presence and information extracted from social media (Rossi et al., 2018) and processed by emergency staff, can lead to a more prepared and better-informed civil population in emergency situations. Of course, this survey can only be a first framework for implementing a social media presence as pointed out. Further research needs to be done to meet the preferences of various countries and emergency service organisations across Europe.

3.4 Summary and Next Steps

This study outlines that (1) emergency service personnel in Europe have the opinion that social media in emergency service organisations is of increasing importance in terms of preventive and situational communication, (2) more experienced staff believe more strongly in the usefulness of social media in the context of an emergency service organisation and (3) the private usage of social media is a driving force in shaping the opinion on organisational use.

Nevertheless, successful use of social media in emergencies does not just depend on emergency services, their attitudes and actual use, but of course also on citizens themselves. Therefore, the next chapter will focus on citizens' perceptions. This can help to identify synergies in the perception and actual use of social media in emergencies between the population and emergency services, but also to uncover possible areas of tension in relation to unrealisable expectations or insurmountable obstacles.

Citizens' Perception of Social Media in Emergencies in Europe

Social media is increasingly being used during emergencies. Most available studies focus on how citizens and/or authorities use social media during specific events. However, larger quantitative studies with significant results on citizens' attitudes, needs, and future plans in such events are not available—especially such of a comparative nature related to emergency services. This chapter first presents the findings of a survey of 1,034 citizens across 30 European countries conducted between February and June 2015 to explore citizens' attitudes towards the use of social media for private purposes and specifically in emergency situations. The work briefly compares these findings with a second survey conducted with 761 emergency service staff across 32 European countries from September to December 2014.

Based on these findings, and assuming that social media usage during emergencies and respective perceptions varies across countries we then present the results of our representative survey of 7,071 citizens in Europe (the Netherlands, Germany, Italy, and the United Kingdom). It shows differences of current use of social media in emergencies, expectations towards authorities monitoring social media, intensity of perceived barriers regarding the use, as well as variances concerning the (likelihood of future) use of mobile apps. While German and British participants' frequency of use of social media is medium and low, respectively, Italian and Dutch respondents use social media relatively frequently. Our comparison of the four countries allows for an interpretation of divergent behaviour across countries with respect to risk cultures as well as expanding the respective model to social media contexts. Concerning social media usage, our findings

Supplementary Information The online version contains supplementary material available at https://doi.org/10.1007/978-3-658-39720-3_4.

© The Author(s), under exclusive license to Springer Fachmedien Wiesbaden GmbH, part of Springer Nature 2022
C. Reuter, *A European Perspective on Crisis Informatics*,
https://doi.org/10.1007/978-3-658-39720-3_4

stress that across the four European countries participants assessed similar advantages, such as dissemination of information, and barriers, such as false rumours. Distributed equally across nations, age, and gender, the study showed significant relationships with social media usage which, among other findings, suggests being helpful for effective implementation of management structures using new technologies.

*This chapter has been published as two articles: "**Towards Social Resilience: A Quantitative and Qualitative Survey on Citizens' Perception of Social Media in Emergencies in Europe**" by Christian Reuter and Thomas Spielhofer in the International Technological Forecasting and Social Change (TFSC) (Reuter & Spielhofer, 2017) [Paper D] as well as "**The Impact of Risk Cultures: Citizens' Perception of Social Media Use in Emergencies across Europe**" by Christian Reuter, Marc-André Kaufhold, Stefka Schmid, Thomas Spielhofer and Anna-Sophie Hahne also in TFSC (Reuter et al., 2019b) [Paper E]. The introduction contains content from both papers, related work mainly from Paper D. Section 4.2 has been published as Paper D, and Section 4.3 as Paper E.*

4.1   Related Work

Very few quantitative studies have been conducted where citizens have been asked about their perception of using social media in emergencies. Three in particular, however, are worth mentioning. This includes a comparative study with over 1,000 participants conducted by the Canadian Red Cross (2012), which aimed to identify to what extent Canadian citizens use social media and mobile devices in crisis communication and what they expect from the emergency services both currently and in future. This study emphasises the requirement of trained social media personnel and pointed to the credibility issues of citizen-generated content. It also, however, shows the benefits of reassurance for citizens, providing situational information and monitoring. Social media was seen as a support for existing channels, but not as a replacement for them. It is noteworthy that the Canadian Red Cross employs "trusted volunteers" to support official response via social media.

Secondly, the American Red Cross (2012) also studied citizens' use of social media during emergencies, with 1,017 online and 1,018 telephone survey respondents. According to the study, 12% of the general public, and respectively 22% of high school graduates, have used social media to share or obtain information during emergencies and disasters or in severe weather conditions. Users were most likely to seek information about weather, traffic, damage caused and information on how other people were coping. Beyond that, users shared not only weather information, safety reassurances and their feelings about the emergency but also their location, and eyewitness information. In terms of trustworthiness, friends, family, news media (or reporters) and local emergency officials were the most trusted sources, while unknown people in the general vicinity of the emergency were the least trusted.

Thirdly, Flizikowski et al. (2014) present a survey within Europe, conducted among citizens (317 respondents) and emergency services (130 respondents). The study focuses on the identification of user needs concerning crisis management with the support of social media and mobile devices. The main goal of the study was to identify the possibilities and challenges of social media integration into crisis response management. Generally, the participants had a positive attitude towards social media. During the study, both citizens and emergency services identified the same challenges, such as a lack of knowledge, personnel issues, uniform terms of use, credibility of citizen-generated content and accessibility for older generations. Although this quantitative study examined a cross-cultural sample, cultural differences affecting social media use during emergencies were not investigated rigorously. To address this issue, the notion of risk cultures offers an interesting theoretical framing, proposing an alternative to individualistic models of risk perception (Lee et al., 2013).

Even though we know that many citizens use social media in emergencies, there is very little evidence exploring what proportion and types of citizens currently do so. Most existing quantitative studies focus on emergency services only or study the attitudes of citizens in North America only (American Red Cross, 2012b; Canadian Red Cross, 2012). We still know relatively little about the situation in Europe, which might be very different. Flizikowski et al. (2014) did focus on Europe although the study is relatively small scale (based on 317 respondents) and is primarily dependent on open-ended qualitative questions. Our study sought, therefore, to add to existing knowledge by providing a combined analysis of qualitative and quantitative survey questions with 1,034 respondents across Europe both in respect of the present situation and in terms of perspectives for the future. In particular, we intended to shed light on how social media can be used to foster social resilience to deal with disasters.

4.2   Citizens' Perception of Social Media in Emergencies in Europe

In recent years, the use of social media has increased substantially and at the same time the nature of that use has shifted towards a more collaborative model. Based on the broader definition of *resilience* as the "ability of a system, community or society exposed to hazards to resist, absorb, accommodate to and recover from the effects of a hazard in a timely and efficient manner, including through the preservation and restoration of its essential basic structures and functions" (United Nations, 2009), more specific terms with overlapping meanings emerged: "*cooperative resilience*" (Reuter et al., 2016d) as the ability to overcome crises of cooperation with the help of adaptability to modified realities by means of cooperation technology, or *social resilience* as the "capacity of social groups and communities to recover from, or respond positively to, crises" (Maguire & Hagan, 2007). Social media can be understood as a key element for accomplishing social resilience. However, although we have a developing body of research which analyses use cases with regard to the use of social media during emergencies, there is less work which deals with attitudinal factors, especially with regard to the attitudes of citizens in such contexts.

In this chapter, then, we seek to explore the attitudes of European citizens towards the use of social media in emergency situations. We describe the methodology of our survey (Section 4.2.1) and present its quantitative as well as qualitative results (Section 4.2.2). Following this, the findings are compared to a previously published survey on emergency service staff attitudes towards social media. The conclusion discusses social resilience as it pertains to social media in emergencies (Section 4.2.3).

4.2.1   Methodology

This section presents our methodology. It has been adopted from a related study (Reuter et al., 2016b), which focused on the attitudes of emergency service personnel only. We first present the survey design (4.2.1.1), including questions, technical realisation and channels of distribution. Then we present a characterisation of our participants (4.2.1.2), followed by a description of our quantitative (4.2.1.3) and qualitative (4.2.1.4) analysis design.

4.2.1.1 Survey Design

The survey aimed to identify the attitudes of citizens towards the use of social media and was conducted as part of the EU funded project "EmerGent". It was designed with the aim of collecting a mixture of quantitative and qualitative evidence. In some parts, we aimed to gain statistical results, in some others we were interested in the reasons for answers. Therefore, quantitative as well as qualitative methods were used. The survey consisted of two parts (see Section 9.1.1 for details), as follows:

- Part I: Demographic details of survey participants (age, gender, country of origin, role, type of organisation) to explore any differences in responses depending on the characteristics of participants.
- Part II: Attitudes towards social media especially in emergencies—a combination of closed questions (using Likert scales (Likert, 1932), asking participants to rate on a scale of 1 to 5 how much they agree with a series of statements) and open-ended questions.

We designed the survey based on a strategy aimed at triangulation. This methodological triangulation involved a combination of questions that focus on more qualitative aspects of citizens' intentions towards social media and their usage before, during and after an emergency at micro-level as well as more quantitative aspects to obtain a comprehensive picture of citizens' attitudes towards social media within emergencies at a macro-level.

In the beginning of February 2015, project partners sent out a link to the online survey in English, Polish, Italian, German and Slovenian to friends, colleagues, professional and social contacts as well as via their own social media channels and websites (snowball sample). This means that the sample of citizens responding to this survey cannot be assumed to be fully representative of citizens across Europe.

4.2.1.2 Characteristics of Survey Participants

The survey responses of 1,034 citizens (including 195 working or volunteering for an emergency service—excluded from the main analysis) were received from citizens across 30 countries, with the largest number of respondents coming from Poland (306), followed by Slovenia (169), Germany (164), the United Kingdom (146), Italy (72), Greece (43) and Norway (39) (Q2) (Figure 4.1). It has to be noted that the sample is not representative for each country or for the whole of Europe. Respondents included roughly equal proportions of women and men (Q3), and a broad selection of citizens from different age groups—although the largest proportion (33%) were between 21 and 29 years old and only 4% were aged 60 or older (Q4) (Figure 4.2). Around one in five (19%) of survey participants were working or volunteering for an emergency service (Q5)—these were excluded from the main findings reported on in this summary report, as they were significantly more likely to use social media than other citizens and to express positive views about its use during emergencies.

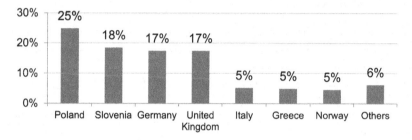

Figure 4.1 Countries

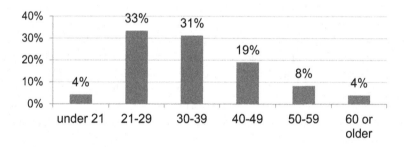

Figure 4.2 Age

4.2.1.3 Quantitative Analysis

For the quantitative analysis, the survey data was extracted and analysed using SPSS, a software package for analysing quantitative data (IBM, 2014). Furthermore, Excel was used for qualitative coding. The analysis consisted of three key steps:

Exploring basic frequencies for each question and *using cross-tabulations* to explore any significant differences across different types of respondents.

Factor-analysis of the 12 Likert scale questions (see above) on participants' attitudes towards social media. To measure respondents' attitudes towards the use of social media for both private and organisational purposes, we used the statistical technique of factor analysis. Factor analysis is a technique used in research to identify groups or clusters of variables, which, taken together, represent an underlying construct or variable of interest in the study (Field, 2009). The analysis identified two factors: the first measured participants' use of social media in general, while the second measured their attitudes towards using social media in emergency situations. Both of these factors had high reliability with Cronbach alpha scores, used to indicate reliability of the scale, of $\alpha = .725$ and $\alpha = .774$ (Cronbach, 1951), respectively.

One-way Analysis of Variance—ANOVA (Field, 2009) was then used to measure any significant differences between the types of respondents in relation to these two factors.

4.2.1.4 Qualitative Analysis

The analysis of our free-text survey questions was based on the inductive approach of *grounded theory* (Strauss, 1987). We used *open coding* associated with grounded theory to derive categories from the more qualitative free-text answers by careful reading and aggregating of categories.

The first step was to extract the entire dataset from the survey platform into an Excel (*.xls) output file. Accordingly, a second sheet was added which contained only the qualitative results including the response identifier and original language identifier. As the survey had been distributed all over Europe, responses made by citizens were in different languages and there was a need for translation. For each question, two columns for translation and categorisation were added. Thereafter, each response was read manually and translated into English, if required. The translation was performed by native speakers of the respective languages. Where possible, translations were performed by translation services, such as Google Translate and supplemented with dictionaries, if single words could not be translated automatically or the translations needed manual adjustment for better intelligibility. The need for translating the results might be highlighted as a limitation of the study, however we aimed to ask people from different countries in their language, to lower the barrier to participate in our study.

To be able to use the grounded theory-oriented method, the open-ended questions were coded openly, and participants' statements were divided into categories. Each response was then assigned to one or multiple categories to achieve a quick overview of the interesting and relevant topics. The previously acquired knowledge from the literature review and quantitative analysis was used to increase theoretical sensitivity. In the next section, we only present those responses that show identifiably positive or negative perceptions of social media and its use by emergency services from an organisational as well as individual perspective. Each quotation is referenced with the participants' response identifier (e.g., EN146).

4.2.2 Empirical Results

In the following sections, we present the results of our survey. First, we present results regarding personal attitudes towards the use of social media (Section 4.2.2.1). We then elaborate the results on receiving information (Section 4.2.2.2), information sharing (Section 4.2.2.3), expectations from emergency services (Section 4.2.2.4) as well as open question responses on what would encourage increased social media use in future (Section 4.2.2.5) and on the way social media was used in emergencies. Finally, we present results relating to participants' awareness of social media safety services (Section 4.2.2.6) and on their use of smartphone apps (Section 4.2.2.7).

4.2.2.1 Use of Social Media (Q8–10)

Initially, participants were asked about their use of social media in general (Figure 4.3, Q8). The results show that most participants use Facebook on a regular basis (73% answered "often" or "sometimes"). Many participants also use YouTube at least sometimes (69%). However, the majority also stated that they never use Twitter (62%) or Instagram (73%).

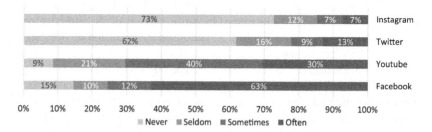

Figure 4.3 Current use of Social Media (Q8)

Most participants agreed with the statement that they use social media very often in their private lives (63%) and that they have many friends using social

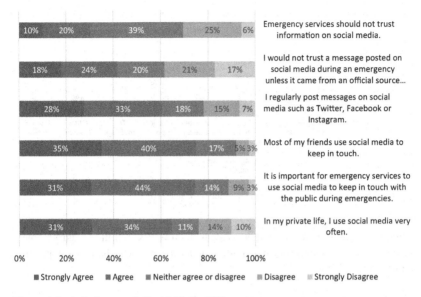

Figure 4.4   Attitude towards Social Media (Q9)

media to keep in touch (73%). 60% of the participants also stated that they regularly post messages on social media. While 73% of the participants thought that it is important for emergency services to use social media, 38% remarked that they would not trust messages on social media, apart from those from official sources. Moreover, about one third (30%) answered that emergency services should not trust information on social media (Figure 4.4, Q9).

When asked, which communication channels they have used to get information about an emergency, most participants indicated that they had used TV (86%) and online news (80%), followed by local radio (54%) and social media (42%). Furthermore, a smaller proportion of participants said that they had used online sites (31%) and mobile apps and text messages (22%). Only few people specified that they used other channels or none of them (Figure 4.5).

There are significant differences in the general use of social media among different groups of citizens—young people (F (5, 813) = 11.530, p<0.001) and women (F (1, 813) = 26.527, p<0.001) are far more likely to use it than other citizens. Overall, 13% of citizens currently do not use a smartphone—this rises to 29% of those aged 50 or above. The level of social media use decreased with increasing age of participants in an almost linear fashion. Women displayed a

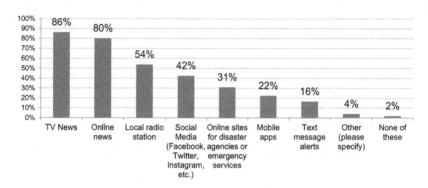

Figure 4.5 Current Communication Channels in Use (Q10)

significantly more positive attitude towards the use of social media during emergencies—similarly, citizens with children under the age of 18 had a more positive attitude towards this.

4.2.2.2 Searching Information (Q14–16+21)

When asked whether they have used social media to find out information in an emergency, 43% of the people said they had used social media for this purpose, while a similar proportion (49%) reported that they had not (Figure 4.6).

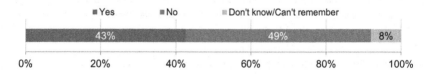

Figure 4.6 Current Use of Social Media for Information Gathering in Emergency situations (Q14)

Of those who had looked for information on social media relating to an emergency, most participants reported that they had looked for information about the weather (78%), road or traffic conditions (70%) or damage caused by an event (63%). Many participants also reported that they had used social media in the past to look for eyewitness videos or photographs (60%). Some also used it to find out the location or status of friends or family (41%) and information about how others were coping with the disaster (38%). Only a third (33%), said that they had looked for information about "what to do to keep yourself safe" (Figure 4.7).

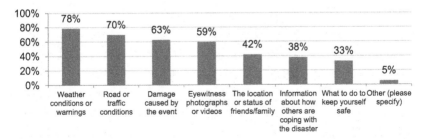

Figure 4.7 Current use of Social Media for Information Gathering in Emergency Situations (Q15)

More than half (58%) of participants indicated that it was either quite or very likely that they would use social media in the future to look for information. In contrast, just under a quarter (23%) thought it was unlikely they would do so (Figure 4.8).

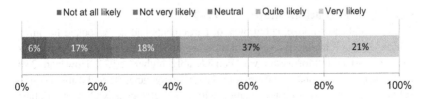

Figure 4.8 Future use of Social Media for Information Gathering in Emergency Situations (Q16)

We furthermore asked participants questions about the possible reasons for using social media as an information source. As can be seen in Figure 4.9, 54% of citizens thought that information provided on social media sites during emergencies is more accessible than information provided via more traditional media channels such as TV, radio or media websites. Similarly, 77% indicated that information provided on social media is made available faster during emergencies than via traditional media channels. However, only 13% contended that information provided on social media is more accurate than information provided via

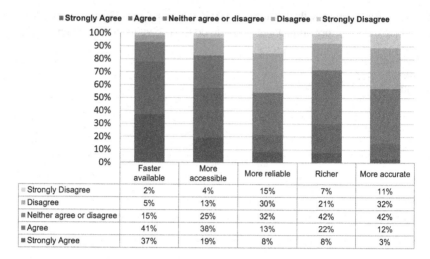

■Strongly Agree ■Agree ■Neither agree or disagree ■Disagree Strongly Disagree

	Faster available	More accessible	More reliable	Richer	More accurate
Strongly Disagree	2%	4%	15%	7%	11%
Disagree	5%	13%	30%	21%	32%
Neither agree or disagree	15%	25%	32%	42%	42%
Agree	41%	38%	13%	22%	12%
Strongly Agree	37%	19%	8%	8%	3%

Figure 4.9   Attitude towards Social Media as Information Source (Q21)

traditional media channels—in contrast, almost half (44%) disagreed with this statement.

4.2.2.3 Information Sharing (Q17–19)

While, as indicated above, about 50% of participants had never looked for information on social media as a result of an emergency, the proportion of those who had never shared information was considerably higher (67%). However, 27% stated that they had shared information about emergencies in social media—this is likely to include sharing information with other citizens as well as with emergency services or authorities (C2A) (Figure 4.10, Q17). Women were significantly more likely ($\chi^2(1) = 17.926$, p<0.001) to have done so (33%) than men (only 20% had done so).

Of those who had shared information on social media, this was most likely to have involved information on weather conditions or warnings (66%), road or traffic conditions (64%) or uploaded eyewitness photographs (53%). In contrast, only 22% had shared an eyewitness video on social media. A complete overview is given in Figure 4.11.

Asked whether they might be inclined to use social media in future to share information with others, 48% of the participants said that they thought it was

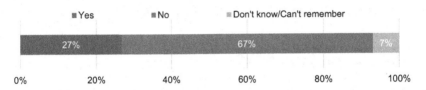

Figure 4.10 Current use of Social Media for Sharing Information Regarding Emergency Situations (Q17)

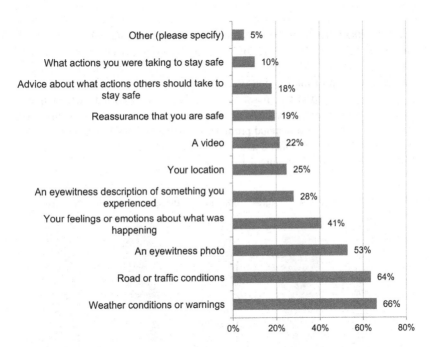

Figure 4.11 Current use of Social Media for Sharing Information regarding Emergency situations (Q18)

likely they would do so; in contrast, as can be seen in Figure 4.12, 28% indicated it was unlikely.

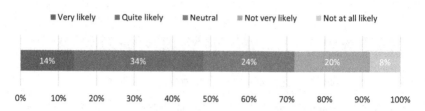

Figure 4.12 Future use of Social Media for Sharing Information Regarding Emergency Situations (Q19)

4.2.2.4 Expectations from Emergency Services (Q22)

The survey also included a series of questions exploring citizens' expectations of how emergency response organisations would or should react to a citizen posting a request for help or information on their social media site. It showed that 41% of citizens would expect a response within an hour if they posted such a request, while 69% agreed that emergency services should regularly monitor their social media sites to be able to respond promptly to such a request. In contrast, 56% of participants thought that emergency services were too busy during an emergency to monitor social media (Figure 4.13).

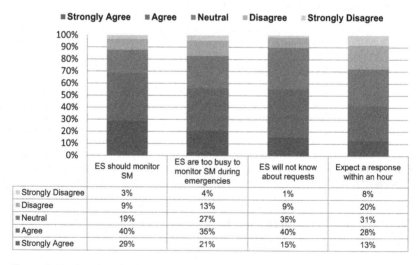

Figure 4.13 Perceived Social Media Integration of Emergency Services (Q22)

4.2.2.5   Encouraging Citizens to use Social Media More Widely in Future (Q20)

The survey contained an open question, asking participants what would make them more likely to use social media to share information with others in future to which 485 participants provided at least one response. The answers indicated that the main ways of encouraging such more widespread use of social media in emergencies included:

- The need for a clearer purpose for sharing information, in particular that emergency services would definitely make use of such information (185 responses fell into this category): *"If I had something to tell them that I thought was relevant." (EN05); "To know in what ways it might be helpful. To be more aware of how the emergency services would use this information" (EN10).*
- More confidence in the quality and data security of information shared on social media (157 responses): *"Impossible to say, there's so much guff on social media sites that you'd never could be 100% that a disaster is truly a disaster as opposed to 'banter'." (EN112); "Including organisations (firefighters, police, civil protection) into social networks with beneficial up-to-date information, regular publishing on their web sites, also during peace times, when there are no natural or other accidents"* (SL95, translated)
- The provision of improved or more user-friendly applications to share and access such information (64 responses): *"Something very easy to use and already integrated in the apps I currently use" (EN08); "Validating Information. Performant selecting algorithms. Geo referenced data supply." (EN146)*
- Better guidelines and encouragement from authorities on the best ways of sharing information during emergencies (27 responses): *"Didn't know where to look for information and advice. Felt the authorities should at least have had advice on the front of their websites." (EN34); "Change in form, now social media is used for any other purpose. The state would have to announce a new form of transmission of such information." (PL71, translated).* Unsurprisingly, there are some guidelines for emergencies available, which have emerged from the recent EU projects ISAR+(Simão et al., 2015) and COSMIC (Helsloot et al., 2015). However, there is little or no evidence to suggest that awareness of such guidelines is particularly high among citizens across Europe.

Other participants (98 responses) made comments which did not fall into specific categories. This included answers like "Nothing" (45 responses), or "I don't use social media (for this purpose)" (22 responses) as well as "I don't know" (21 responses).

4.2.2.6 Awareness about Social Media Safety Services (Q23)

There is generally low awareness among citizens of existing social media safety services provided on Twitter and Facebook—thus, only 6% of citizens said they were 'very aware' of Twitter Alerts, while only 3% were very aware of Facebook Safety Checks (Figure 4.14). However, awareness of Twitter Alerts is considerably higher among those using Twitter on a regular basis—32% of citizen who say they use Twitter 'often' are aware of this service. This contrasts with only 4% of regular Facebook users (that use it 'often') who say they are aware of Facebook Safety Checks.

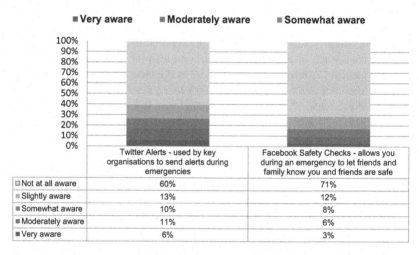

	Twitter Alerts - used by key organisations to send alerts during emergencies	Facebook Safety Checks - allows you during an emergency to let friends and family know you and friends are safe
▢ Not at all aware	60%	71%
▪ Slightly aware	13%	12%
▪ Somewhat aware	10%	8%
▪ Moderately aware	11%	6%
▪ Very aware	6%	3%

Figure 4.14 Knowledge about Social Media Services (Q23)

4.2.2.7 Use of Emergency Smartphone Apps (Q11–13)

The majority of participants (71%) reported that they had never downloaded a smartphone app for emergencies or disasters, while 22% said that they had done so (Q11). 208 people answered the open question what kind of apps they had downloaded (Q12). The most popular apps were Warning apps (49 mentions), followed by Weather apps (28 mentions) and First Aid apps (16 mentions). Moreover, several people named Emergency Call apps (14 mentions), News apps (11 mentions) and Earthquake apps (10 mentions) (Table 4.1). Apropos of the separate apps in the different countries, the App *Regionalny System Ostrzegania* (RSO), which is named 21 times by Polish people, is eye-catching. Furthermore,

German survey participants mentioned *Katwarn* 13 times. Both apps are warning apps developed by the government and are open to the whole population. No other apps were named by more than five respondents.

Table 4.1 App-Categories and the Frequencies of Mentions (Q12)

App-categories	Mentions	App-categories	Mentions	App-categories	Mentions
Warning App	49	Traffic (Jam) App	8	Twitter App	4
Weather App	28	Location App	5	Safety App	4
First Aid App	16	Red Cross App	5	Breakdown App	3
Emergency Call App	14	Maps App	5	Fire App	3
News App	11	Lifesaver App	5	Flashlight App	3
Earthquake App	10	Hazardous Material App	4	Others	15

While only a relatively small proportion of participants had previously downloaded an app, most (60%) thought that it was either very or quite likely that they would download an app to share information with, or receive information from, emergency services in an appropriate situation. Only 21% stated that it was not likely they would do so (Q13) (Figure 4.15).

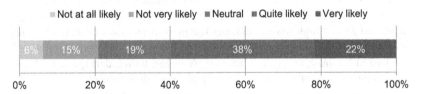

Figure 4.15 caption legend: ▪ Not at all likely ▪ Not very likely ▪ Neutral ▪ Quite likely ▪ Very likely

Bar values: 6% | 15% | 19% | 38% | 22%

Axis: 0% 20% 40% 60% 80% 100%

Figure 4.15 Future use of Apps for Information Exchange in Emergency Situations (Q13)

4.2.3 Discussion and Conclusion

Recently "the role held by members of the public in disasters [...] is becoming more visible, active, and in possession of greater reach than ever seen before" (Palen & Liu, 2007). Social media has enabled many of these possibilities and may foster social resilience. Many studies are available that cover the use of social media during specific events, but some large studies also try to focus on citizens' perception (American Red Cross, 2012b; Canadian Red Cross, 2012). However, it is doubtful whether findings from America can be assumed to be transferable to Europe. Only one study was found which sheds some light on the comparative situation in Europe, as discussed above, but it included only a relatively small number of respondents (Flizikowski et al., 2014). This chapter has therefore sought to provide recent evidence of how European citizens are disposed towards the use of social media in emergencies.

Figure 4.16 summarises some of the main results and points to selected facts

This study has shown that many citizens across Europe are already using social media to share and look for information during emergencies and that they expect their usage to increase in future. In particular, around a quarter (27%) of citizens said that they had used social media for information sharing (Fact 1 in Figure 4.16, Q17) and 43% had used it to look for information during an emergency. The most popular shared topics were weather conditions or warnings (66%) and road or traffic conditions (64%) (Figure 4.16: Fact 3). Furthermore, the survey suggests that citizens expected to increase their use of social media for such purposes in future. This includes 48% of participants who thought it was likely that they would share emergency information on social media platforms in future (Figure 4.16: Fact 7) and 58% who thought that they would use social media to look for information. The main positive reasons for using social media as an information source included that it was seen as faster (76%) and more accessible (54%) than conventional media. The levels of use of social media were considerably higher than found in previous studies, including a study in the USA in 2012 (American Red Cross, 2012) which found that 12% of the general public and 22% of high school graduates had used social media to share or obtain information during emergencies and disasters. The types of information shared and looked for most frequently, however, (weather, traffic, damage caused and information on how other people were coping) were very similar.

The survey also showed that use of social media for private purposes and in emergencies was not uniform demographically and that particular types of citizens are more likely to do so than others. This means that younger citizens and women are significantly more likely to use social media both to look for and share information, while men and those aged 50 or above are significantly less likely to use social media for this purpose (Figure 4.16: Facts 2 and 4). As the results of the survey showed, this was exacerbated by the fact that almost a third (29%) of those aged 50 or above do not use a smartphone which is a necessary prerequisite for using social media while not at home. The implications of this are that while social media use is widespread and increasing, some groups are

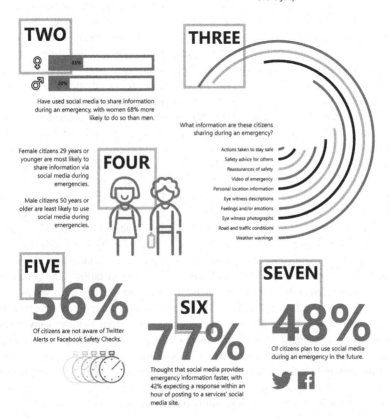

Figure 4.16 Infographic of Selected Survey Results

in danger of being excluded from any support, advice or instructions provided via social media before, during or after emergencies from emergency services or other citizens. This could mean that those most vulnerable in an emergency—older or disabled citizens—may be least likely to benefit from an increased use of social media by emergency services.

The study revealed that citizens' awareness of Twitter Alerts and Facebook Safety Checks was generally low—about 56% have never heard of at least one of them (Figure 4.16: Fact 5). Sixty percent of participants were not at all aware of Twitter Alerts and 68% were not at all aware of Facebook Safety Checks. Likewise, 71% have never downloaded a smartphone app for emergencies—in contrast, most participants (60%) indicated it was likely that they would download an app in future for an information exchange with emergency services in an appropriate situation. It seems that the general awareness of such tools depends on the frequency of emergencies someone is confronted with—something other studies also suggest (Reuter, 2014a). In other cases, it is likely that such tools are just used if they are integrated in daily used media, such as Facebook.

The current study has also shown that accompanying many citizens' increased use of social media in emergencies is a growing expectation for emergency services to communicate with citizens via social media and to make use of information shared by citizens via social media. Thus, the majority (69%) of citizens agreed that emergency services should regularly monitor their social media sites, and 41% expected a response within an hour (Figure 4.16: Fact 6). This is higher than in the Canadian study where 63% of participants thought that emergency responders should be prepared to respond to calls for help posted on social media. This could be explained by the fact that the Canadian study was conducted over three years ago and could suggest that our study reflects an increased awareness among citizens of social media and how it can be used during emergencies—with greater demands made to emergency services to use and be responsive to social media in disaster situations. However, a recent survey conducted in the same project (Reuter et al., 2016b) has shown that even though many emergency services sometimes use social media to share information with the public, only very few often make use of data on social media during emergencies. This reality was reflected in citizens' responses, as part of which 56% thought that emergency services were currently too busy during an emergency to respond to a request for help or information. Furthermore, many of those responding to an open-ended question asking participants to explain what would encourage them to share information via social media said that this depended on a clearer purpose for sharing information, in particular that emergency services would definitely make use of such information. This suggests that citizens' perception of the behaviour of emergency services does not match their expectations of how they would like them to behave in relation to social media.

The before mentioned gap between citizens' perception and emergency services behaviour means that the potential of social media aiding the social resilience of citizens during emergencies is not yet fully realised (Boin et al., 2010; Maguire & Hagan, 2007) and that both emergency services and citizens need further support and encouragement to find ways of using social media more effectively and cooperatively. If supported in this way, such a concept of resilience could be seen as linking with other related concepts of *resistance* (to prevent damages), *recovery* (to fix damages quickly) and *creativity* (to learn from losses and improve the system in future). Thus, the emergence of so-called *emergent citizen groups* (Stallings & Quarantelli, 1985) is today often initiated by social media, based on the activities of *digital volunteers* (Starbird & Palen, 2011). Technologies supporting collaboration not just within a planned frame, but that allow emergent collaboration, the "need for spontaneous collaboration in novel and changing structures", such as ad hoc participation, are needed (Reuter, 2014b). This would suggest that increasing cooperation could increase social resilience via a complex web of (collaborating) actors on social media. One contribution of this chapter is to outline the perception of citizens in Europe, which is a necessary prerequisite for approaches addressing the issue.

The survey has also revealed that citizens were more likely to use Facebook (73%) and YouTube (69%) rather than Twitter (21%) for private purposes. This is of particular interest given the fact that many international studies on the role and use of social media in emergencies rely on the analysis of Twitter only, as it is more accessible for research purposes (Kaufhold & Reuter, 2016). It means though that a lot of citizen activity on social media during emergencies remains under-researched. This has been one of the limitations of the current study—that we have not explored differences in the use of different types of social media platforms during emergencies. It is hoped that future studies will fill this gap. It is also worth noting that almost all participants of the Canadian Red Cross (2012) study were Facebook users (97%). This might suggest that our sample was more representative of the whole population, including older people who on average use social media much less. Furthermore, about three quarters of the respondents are from the countries Poland, Slovenia, Germany and the United Kingdom. Therefore, we cannot necessarily draw conclusions for the whole of Europe. A representative study among selected countries in Europe might help to fill this gap. However, the answers did not differ by country a lot. The participants from Slovenia use Facebook more often (91% "very often") than survey participants overall (60%); and in the UK, Twitter is used more often (30%

"very often") compared with survey participants overall (12%, Q8). Furthermore, most people in Germany said that they used the local radio as an information channel during an emergency (81%) while the average reported use across the whole sample was 54% (Q10). Otherwise, there were no significant differences between countries or the number of responses from countries were too small to make any valid comparisons.

Finally, our study identified very similar barriers to the increased use of social media as found in the only other study of citizens' attitudes in Europe (Flizikowski et al., 2014). The previous study found that both citizens and emergency services identified the same challenges, such as a lack of knowledge, personnel issues, uniform terms of use, credibility of citizen-generated content and accessibility for older generations. In comparison, our study mainly identified 'mistrust' as well as the perceived lack of a clear purpose for using social media in emergencies. These points can be addressed if citizens gain awareness that the value of the information being provided fits their expectations and needs.

4.3   The Impact of Risk Cultures in Social Media Use in Emergencies

Social media is used across the world. However, the use of these media differs across several factors such as age but also across nation states. Comparing general social media use in the United Kingdom (UK), Germany (GER), the Netherlands (NL) and Italy (IT), the latter makes the least use of them, with 40% (37 million) of the Italian population active. The UK (59%, 39 m), Germany (55%, 45 m) and the Netherlands (57%, 9.74 m) are almost equal (Statista, 2017) at the point in time this study has been conducted. Based on the fact that mobile devices are very often used to communicate via social media, not least because they are always ready to hand, it is not surprising that social media is also used in emergencies (Reuter et al., 2018b). However, there is a lack of robust quantitative and comparative findings on citizens' perceptions of social media use in emergencies across different countries. Focusing on four European countries, we present and compare representative survey results with the aim of grasping similarities and differences in social media use during emergencies. Referring to situations of disaster, previous research indicated varying risk cultures in European countries to shape populations' behaviour (Dressel, 2015; Dressel & Pfeil, 2017).

Research into emergencies has become more common in Human Computer Interaction (HCI) (Ludwig et al., 2017; Reuter et al., 2018b). It is important to gain a deep understanding of social media use in emergencies as it poses various advantages which are yet to be fully exploited. Social media offers a more effective way of knowledge management, as it brings together important information by various actors, contributes to situational awareness in crises and allows for crowdsourcing (Gao et al., 2011; Hughes & Palen, 2009; Lim et al., 2011; Vieweg et al., 2010; Yates & Paquette, 2011). As a vast body of literature has shown, we can assume risk perception not to be independent from individuals' various contexts (Coppola, 2006; Dressel & Pfeil, 2017; Renn & Rohrmann, 2000). Thus, a cross-cultural comparison allows to focus on culture-specific encounters of risks and actual situations of emergencies, offering useful insights for the application of emergency management procedures (Coppola, 2006; Renn & Rohrmann, 2000; Viklund, 2003). Therefore, it seems worthwhile examining cultural differences in terms of use of social media in emergencies, proposing an explanation of individuals' behaviour. Referring to models of risk culture, we contribute to the respective discourse by shedding light on attitudes and behaviour towards and within social media channels. Our comparison proposes varying degrees of social media usage and openness towards its current and future use during emergencies, pointing out to the importance of individuals' willingness to use social media and its collaborative value (Chang et al., 2015).

Our chapter introduces findings on the perception of social media use in emergencies in four European countries: Italy, Germany, the Netherlands and the UK by presenting a representative survey of 7,071 participants and offering a respective analysis of its results. Our research questions are as follows: *(R1) How do citizens of Italy, Germany, the Netherlands and the UK use social media during emergencies? (R2) What are their expectations towards emergency services, (R3) what are perceived barriers, and (R4) what is their attitude towards mobile emergency apps?*

Presenting answers to our first question (R1), we focus on current use and participants' reasonings behind it. Findings regarding the following three questions (R2-R4) help to complement our task pointing out to important aspects of citizens' perception and use of social media during emergencies. Our work proves valuable not only with respect of providing scientific input based on a large, representative, and comparative sample but also yields relevant findings regarding future practice of disaster and emergency management, implying implementation of social media channels.

In answering these questions, similarities and differences across the four countries become apparent. Our findings show that 45% of the citizens have already used social media during emergencies, and that social media is used more to search for information than to share. Citizens expect emergency services to monitor social media (most in Germany) and to respond within an hour (most in Italy); rumours and unreliable information are considered as important barriers—while barriers are most seen in Germany, less in UK and Italy and least in the Netherlands. Especially Italian participants suggest being open for social media use during emergencies while showing high expectations with regards to authorities' performance. Contrasting in use and attitude towards managing emergencies via social media, the British case points out to perceiving future crisis management and communication via social media to be unnecessary.

The section is structured as follows: First, we shed light on findings of related work and our theoretical framing (Section 4.3.1). In the following, we present method (Section 4.3.2) and quantitative as well as qualitative results of the surveys (Section 4.3.3). Discussing our findings, we propose an interpretation of main results and indicate limitations and outlook (Section 4.3.4).

4.3.1 Theoretical Framing

Since 2001, the use of social media in emergencies, such as natural hazards (e.g., tsunamis, hurricanes, earthquakes, floods) and human-induced disasters (e.g., accidents, shootings, terror attacks, political uprisings) (Reuter et al., 2017b), has increased considerably, and a number of trends have been identified. This seems to be the case regardless of the scale of the emergency (Reuter et al., 2018b). Accordingly, crisis informatics (Palen et al., 2007) research examines opportunities and challenges of social media in emergencies by both authorities, such as emergency services (Reuter et al., 2016b), and citizens (Pipek et al., 2014). Published studies have tended to focus on the examination of social media data in the English language, often on Twitter (Hughes et al., 2016), and the study of US-based events, complemented by a recent trend of non-US case studies (Gaspar et al., 2014). Mark and Semaan (2008) focus on continually disruptive environments and technologies as a resource, examining the cases of Iraq and Israel while various studies concentrate on incidents in China and other Asian countries (Acar & Muraki, 2011; Huang et al., 2010; Qu et al., 2011) as well as dedicating special attention on events of the Arab spring (Kavanaugh et al., 2011b). Al-Saggaf and Simmons (2015) examine social media use and its potentials in times of natural disasters in Saudi-Arabia. Reuter et al. study emergency services' attitudes towards the use of social media, thereby focusing on another relevant group of actors in emergency-related contexts (Reuter et al.,

2016b). Generally, we follow the definition of social media by Kaplan and Haenlein (2010); yet, with respect to citizens' attitudes towards emergency apps, we assumed participants' to not differentiate greatly between social network sites, instant messengers and mobile apps created for (local) communication, finding and sharing of information.

Contrasting prior work focusing on bigger disasters (Federal Emergency Management Agency, 2018; UN Office for Disaster Risk Reduction, 2016; Western Cape Government, 2015; Whittaker et al., 2015; World Health Organization, 2002), we choose a broad definition (Haddow et al., 2007; Perry et al., 2001) of emergencies, referring not only to academically conceptualised emergencies and disasters (UN Office for Disaster Risk Reduction, 2016) but also emergency situations in which only a few individuals may be affected and call upon emergency services' standard procedures for help (e.g., burglary). Communication via social media may prove effective in each scenario. Aware that individual incidents differ in scope and individuals may pursue actions via social media differently, citizens may want to contact emergency services or have high expectations towards authorities independent from the type of emergency. Assuming a broad understanding of an emergency takes into consideration that various participants define emergency based on their experiences and conventional usage of the term; the common understanding forming the basis of individual action and defining circumstances at which social media may aim.

In contrast to other studies focusing, e.g., only on perceptions of directly involved individuals, we defined individuals to use social media during emergencies even when they were not directly involved as primary sources of information as this may prove interesting results as well.

4.3.1.1 Risk Cultures as a Theoretical Framing of Social Media Use in Emergencies

As each society may deal differently with risks and our work focuses on behaviour of populations during emergencies including respective attitudes, theoretical work regarding so-called risk cultures proves helpful in interpreting our survey results (Cornia et al., 2016; Gierlach et al., 2010; Hewitt, 2012; Marris et al., 1998). Choosing this relational approach allows for an analysis based on already conceptualised types (Cornia et al., 2016), at the same time testing the potential of the respective theoretical framework. Alternatively, one may assume socioeconomic or demographic factors to impact social media use in emergencies. Even though GDP per capita varies across the four European countries, survey results did not implicate any related causality, while neither income nor distribution of age groups did vary heavily (while social media usage did) (Economics,

2019; index mundi, 2019). Additionally, our cases suggested everyday internet or social media use being relatively constant across our cases (Internet World Stats, 2019). Thus, we followed the framework of risk cultures, which poses a plausible starting point for an analysis of perception, which is influenced by a community's use of language and non-verbal behaviour. While the risk culture approach concentrates on individuals' behaviour in and attitudes towards emergency situations, including populations' perception of traditional media, it does not take "new" social media into account. The work of Cornia et al. (2016), proposing a conceptualisation of risk cultures and an analysis of seven European countries, forms our point of reference in interpreting perceptions regarding and actions within social media channels, this focus being disregarded in the prior risk culture debate. Referring to the work of Douglas and Wildavsky (1983), they follow a traditional understanding of risk cultures (Cornia et al., 2016; Dressel, 2015). The three types identified as well as the respective classification of cases, along the criteria of *framing* incidents, *trust* towards authorities and target of *blaming*, prove useful here. Thus, risk culture grasps the ways in which collectives perceive a disruptive event, show trust towards involved authorities, and ascribe responsibility of (consequences of) the event. We follow the conceptualisation of Germany as a state-oriented risk culture, the Netherlands as an individualistic one and Italy as a fatalistic risk culture (Cornia et al., 2016), as it matches satisfactorily our analysis, even though Italy suggests change towards an individualistic risk culture. We include the UK in our study, constituting a first analysis of this case from the chosen risk culture perspective. In light of our findings, we classify it as a fatalistic risk culture, although our results suggest a higher level of trust than its fatalistic ideal type indicates. Interestingly recent studies also found that "residents of capital cities do indeed have significantly less trust in their local administration than residents of secondary cities. It was also shown that satisfaction with the extent to which high and low expectations are met does significantly influence the trust in the local administration" (de Vries & Sobis, 2018).

In *state-oriented risk cultures* people assume that prevention of disasters is generally possible, often framing disasters as events which are not solely in nature's hand but also determined by human environment. Trust in state authorities is high and they are expected to prevent and manage emergencies. Generally, one can identify high trust in mass media and high compliance with authorities' instructions while citizens show little knowledge and awareness of coping mechanisms and low confidence of their respective individual capabilities (Cornia et al., 2016). *Individualistic risk cultures* assume similarly that disaster risk prevention is possible while negative consequences can be minimised as well;

thus, disaster is framed as an incident humankind can generally manage and control. While trust towards authorities is not particularly low, citizens still feel that they individually share responsibilities of being informed, prepared, aware with respect to risks, showing relatively high knowledge of coping mechanisms (Cornia et al., 2016). Roughly, risk cultures have been characterised on a continuum of individualism and collectivism (Gierlach et al., 2010; Zheng, 2017). A *fatalistic risk culture* perceives hazards as "unpredictable and unavoidable", implying nature's or a Godly power over the human population (Cornia et al., 2016). Trust in authorities is low due to prior inefficacy as is trust towards mass media which is often perceived as subjective and clientelistic. Furthermore, individuals have low confidence in their respective problem-solving potentials. Disillusioned, they still generally expect the state to act during emergencies while not taking state communications (e.g., warnings) seriously (Cornia et al., 2016). Defining risk culture as a configuration of the variables *framing, trust* and *blaming*, our study allowed for an operationalisation of risk cultures with respect to social media (see Table 9.3).

Following Cornia et al. (2016), we consider citizens' perception of efficacy of management structures to stabilise or change risk cultures with a fatalistic risk culture evolving when authorities' actions are considered inefficient and strengthening state-oriented risk cultures when society perceives management structures to be successful. Additionally, we suggest frequency of emergencies, also with respect to certain types of incidents (small- vs. large-scale events), to count as relevant factors strengthening perceptions of (lacking) efficiency of management structures, thus, determining citizens' perception regarding necessity of change.

4.3.1.2 Research Gaps

Much research on social media in emergencies focused on the Anglo-Saxon discourse, US-based events and Twitter. There are some studies on national differences of social media use although not focusing on emergencies. Furthermore, there are not many studies on citizens' perceptions of social media use in emergencies providing any comparison across countries (first gap). Moreover, opportunity-based samples largely form the basis of most studies. The number of participants might be high, but they do not ensure representativeness in relation to age, education, income, gender and region. From a methodological perspective this restricts, to some extent, the reliability of these studies regarding generalisable statements (second gap). These gaps point out to the necessity of quantitative work, which may enable to triangulate against more qualitative studies. Regarding explanatory factors of divergent behaviour with respect to social media use during emergencies, our work poses a first attempt to transfer models of risk culture to the sphere of social media, allowing for an interpretation of usage patterns (third gap).

4.3.2 Methodology

We decided to commission representative online surveys to collect more robust data and up-to-date information on citizens' attitudes towards the use of social media in emergency situations in Europe. We chose to compare countries that (a) differ in risk cultures and (b) in the general use of social media (Dressel, 2015; Dressel & Pfeil, 2017). We conducted four representative studies in Germany, Italy, the Netherlands and the UK.

4.3.2.1 Case Selection

Our study constitutes the first cross-country comparison focusing on Europe. To account for differences in outcome, i.e., diverging behaviour of and attitudes towards social media use during emergencies, deriving from variation of risk cultures, we chose four countries which are relatively similar with respect to demographic factors as well as internet access and service conditions (OECD, 2018b; 2018c; 2018a). The latter, paired with socialisation of social media use through similar products (e.g., Facebook, iPhone) across these countries, may account for similar outcomes. At the same time, all four democratic countries are part of the European Union, thus, following same supranational regulations of disaster management and the Internet while sharing membership of the European organisation since its offspring. Diverging with respect to risk culture, implying concrete formations of state-society relations and self-evaluations of subjects embedded in respective social and cultural contexts, the cases allow for approaching the independent variables' effect on social media use during emergencies. Each country represents a certain configuration of the variables *framing, trust* and *blaming*, defining the respective risk culture regarding social media (see Table 9.3).

4.3.2.2 Survey Questions

The survey consisted of nine questions, with the first eight in closed-ended form using five-point Likert rating scales (Q4, Q5 and Q8) and multiple-choice items (Q1, Q2, Q3, Q6 and Q7). The endpoints of the three rating scales were 'Strongly agree' and 'Strongly disagree', 'This would definitely put me off' and 'Would definitely not put me off' as well as 'Very likely' and 'Not at all likely' (see

Section 9.1.2). First, participants were asked about frequency of use of social media (Q1), their previous usage of social media in emergencies (Q2) and, if applicable, the kinds of information shared (Q3). Regarding the latter, participants could choose more than one option among the most typical types of information shared on social media (Reuter & Kaufhold, 2018), including various kinds of social media usage patterns applicable to various situations of different degrees of involvement. Then, we requested the expected responsiveness of emergency services to messages posted via social media (Q4) and regarded opinions about discouraging factors for using social media in emergencies (Q5). We also considered previously downloaded apps for emergencies (Q6) and specifications concerning the types of emergency-related apps the participants had already downloaded (Q7). We also wanted to know about future usage of apps in emergencies for exemplified purposes (Q8). Finally, the last question was open-ended and covered experiences with social media in emergencies (Q9). The questions were derived from our interest in answering the research questions (R1–R4). Asking for usage patterns regarding social media channels and smartphone applications made it possible to approach the countries' respective risk cultures reflected by social media behaviour and attitude (e.g., relatively high interest towards use). At the same time, it became also clear which activities cannot be easily traced back to a specific type of risk culture. Referring to participants' expectations towards authorities' responsiveness allowed us to reflect on citizens' targets of potential blaming depending on the type of risk culture. Focusing on discouraging factors also allowed us to focus on individualistic, state-oriented and fatalistic risk cultures' related attitudes indicating levels of trust.

4.3.2.3 Data Collection

The surveys in Italy, the Netherlands and the UK were conducted by Opinium (http://opinium.co.uk), also co-working with London School of Economics[1]. The survey in Germany was carried out by the ISO-certified[2] market and social research agency GapFish (https://gapfish.com/). All participants of the online surveys were paid a small amount of money, with the sample selected from a pool of volunteers. A study solely based on the German sample has already been published (Reuter et al., 2017b). All surveys were conducted between October 2016 and March 2017. Both research agencies offered robust samples, allowing for generalisation. The surveys in Italy, the Netherlands and the UK were

---

[1] https://www.opinium.co.uk/case_study/london-school-of-economics/

[2] https://gapfish.com/gapfish-is-again-iso-certified/

weighted to be in line with population statistics. The German survey was strati-fied according to gender and age to achieve representative responses from citizens and therefore did not need to be weighted for these variables. Furthermore, we ensured a wide spread of the survey sample in terms of income, education and region. Attempts at weighting it regarding the income of survey participants were not possible due to lack of access to nationally representative data for this vari-able. The Dutch survey was weighted regarding gender, age, household income, working status and region. National statistics were used from the Dutch Central Bureau of Statistic (https://www.cbs.nl/en-gb). The UK survey was weighted to be in line with population statistics regarding gender, age, region, working status and social grade. Population statistics were derived from the Office for National Statistics (https://www.ons.gov.uk). Italy has a much lower proportion of inter-net users, 66% compared to around 90% in the other three countries (http://data. un.or). Thus, in addition to gender, age, region, working status and household income, the data of the Italian survey was also weighted by Facebook and smart-phone use as there was a risk of bias towards internet users. National information about demographic statistics was used from the Italian National Institute of Statis-tics (http://www.istat.it/en), and information of Facebook and smartphone use was taken from a recent *We Are Social* survey on internet and social media use across the world (Kemp, 2017).

4.3.2.4 Data Analysis

The quantitative analysis of all surveys was carried out using IBM SPSS Statis-tics 23. Tables and figures were created in Microsoft Excel. The analysis involved calculation of frequencies regarding all questions. To test for differences between the countries, various significance tests were used depending on the level of measurement. Chi-Square tests were used for categorical variables and Kruskal-Wallis tests for ordinal variables. Kruskal-Wallis test is a non-parametric test for independent samples with more than two groups. Because of the multiple-comparison problem, the Bonferroni correction ($\alpha' = 1 - (1-\alpha)1/k$) was used to control for the increased type I errors. The original significance level of .05 was reduced to .0015. Figures are used to display results across countries. In order to present results comprehensible, figures simplify responses to the three rating scale questions. The combined results consider that sample size is much lower in Germany (1069) than in Italy, the Netherlands and the UK (2001, 2001 and 2000, respectively) so each country's results were determined in equal measure. Addi-tionally, gender (categories: female, male) and age (categories: 18–24, 25–34, 35–44, 45–54, 55–64, 65+) were used to perform subgroup analysis.

Our open question "Please provide any additional details of your experience of using social media in emergencies or what might encourage you to do so in future" (Q9) provided several interesting results. We used open coding (Strauss & Corbin, 1998) by developing codes abductively, performing a qualitative data analysis (Hickey & Kipping, 1996). Codes were derived from thorough reading of answers to open-ended questions as well as from code categories grasping our research interest. Throughout the coding process, codes were jointly defined and checked. Each open-ended response was then assigned to one or multiple categories to achieve an overview of the relevant topics. For each country, the code categories *experience, perceived barriers* and *assessed advantages* were used, the two latter aggregating any codes connoting social media characteristics combined with negatively and positively associated signifiers, respectively, while the former term includes usage-related phrases with respect to frequency and diversity of use; thus, all of the three categories constitute end results of an open process, aiming at offering insights with respect to our research questions. While regarding the Netherlands, the UK and Italy, conditions of use, reflecting perceived barriers, could be made out, German participants did not formulate demands for improvements but still presented sceptic attitudes. The three code categories were derived from 21 codes in total (see Table 9.4). Codes of both the categories of *perceived barriers* as well as *advantages* constitute indicators for the independent variables *trust* and *framing*, respectively. *Experience* as a code category serves as an indicator for the dependent variable of social media use in emergencies (see Table 9.3). In all surveys, a few responses were unusable or incomprehensible. The previously acquired knowledge from the literature review and quantitative analysis was used to increase analytical sensitivity. Each quotation is referenced with the participants' response identifier.

4.3.3   Empirical Results

This section reports the quantitative and qualitative findings from four representative online surveys, exploring citizens' attitudes towards and use of social media in emergencies, conducted in four European countries (N = 7,071): Germany, Italy, the Netherlands and the UK (Figure 4.17).

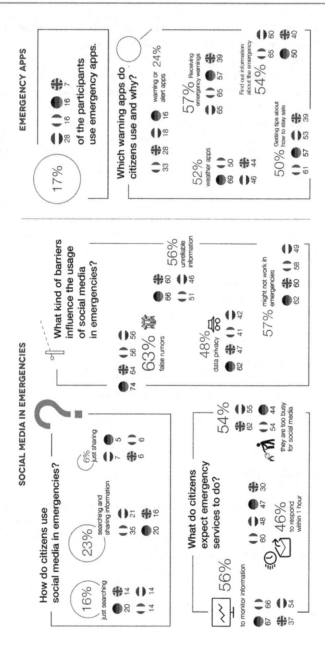

Figure 4.17 Infographic of Statistical Results of the European Survey

4.3.3.1   Finding/Sharing Information on Social Media during Emergencies

Analysis of the survey showed that almost half (45%) of citizens across the four countries have used social media during an emergency. However, as can be seen in Figure 4.18, there are significant differences in the level of use across the four countries[3]. Italy represents the country with the highest proportion of citizens that have used social media during an emergency. More than half of the Italian population (54%) have used social media during emergencies, with 41% using it to share information. Qualitative analysis revealed that not only Italian, but participants from all four countries, independent of their cultural background, considered the flow of information as advantageous. Further, improved communication and up-to-date and immediate transfer of news were rated as positive features of social media use, traditional media being a point of reference. German and Dutch participants pointed out to social media as an alternative in comparison to overloaded phone networks, while the latter group also thought of preventing such a situation. German participants raised awareness regarding the prevention of panics by emergency services' monitoring via social media. Italian participants named prevention as advantageous as well. Only British participants did not refer to prevention. Furthermore, the lowest usage is reported in the UK, where only

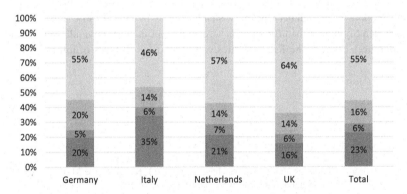

Figure 4.18   Use of Social Media during an Emergency (Q2) (Note: N = 6723 (excluding 348 participants choosing 'Don't know/Can't remember')

---

[3] (χ^2(9, N = 6723) = 239.57, p < 0.001, Cramer's V = .11).

36% of citizens had used social media in the past to share and/or to find out information about an emergency.

This is backed by qualitative analysis of answers of the open-ended question. UK participants revealed to be most inexperienced regarding social media use in emergencies (54%), followed by Germany (46%), while the Netherlands (22%) and Italy (12%) have considerably less respondents who do not use social media, do not have a smartphone or have never experienced an emergency. UK respondents' answers did not suggest any explicit interest or opinion with respect to (future) use of social media during emergencies. Some Italian participants pointed out that the thought of using social media during an emergency had just not occurred, not necessarily indicating that they were generally reluctant to use it.

4.3.3.2 Types of Information Shared

Across all countries, citizens are most likely to share weather conditions or warnings via social media in emergencies (Figure 4.19). This is especially the case in Germany, where nearly two thirds (63%) chose to do so. In contrast, only 33% of citizens in the Netherlands have shared this type of information. The second most likely information to share is feelings or emotions. Nearly half of German participants (46%) have shared feelings or emotions and 31% of British citizens have shared this type of information. Another noticeable finding is that the proportion of Italians who have shared photos or videos (40% and 38%) is considerably higher than for citizens across the four countries overall. Significant differences between the four countries were found for all types of information[4].

---

[4] weather conditions or warnings: $\chi^2(3, N = 1983) = 70.07$, p < 0.001, Cramer's V = .188; Road and traffic conditions: $\chi^2(3, N = 1982) = 97.91$, p < 0.001, Cramer's V = .222; Your feelings or emotions about what was happening: $\chi^2(3, N = 1982) = 21.43$, p < 0.001, Cramer's V = .104; What actions you were taking to stay safe: $\chi^2(3, N = 1981) = 20.72$, p < 0.001, Cramer's V = .102; An eyewitness description of something you experienced: $\chi^2(3, N = 1981) = 32.13$, p < 0.001, Cramer's V = .127; An eyewitness photo: $\chi^2(3, N = 1983) = 183.84$, p < 0.001, Cramer's V = .304; A video: $\chi^2(3, N = 1983) = 76.01$, p < 0.001, Cramer's V = .196; Other: $\chi^2(3, N = 1983) = 22.41$, p < 0.001, Cramer's V = .106), besides 'Reassurance that you are safe' ($\chi^2(3, N = 1982) = 7.01$, p = 0.072, Cramer's V = .059), 'Your location' ($\chi^2(3, N = 1981) = 10.71$, p = 0.013, Cramer's V = .074) and 'Advice about what actions others should take to stay safe' ($\chi^2(3, N = 1983) = 4.23$, p = 0.237, Cramer's V = .046).

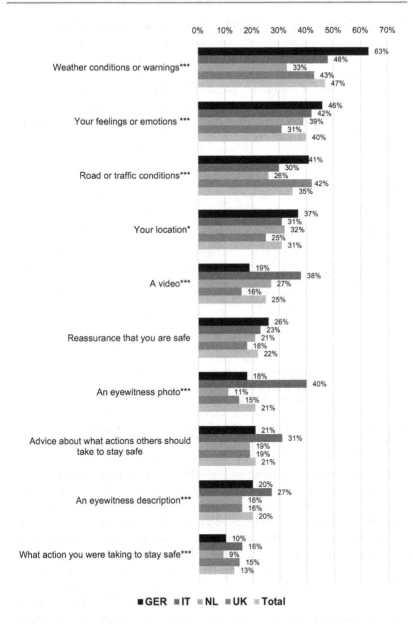

Figure 4.19 Types of Information Shared (Q3). (Note. N = 1983, *** indicates p < .001, ** p < .01 and * p<.05.)

4.3.3.3 Barriers to use Social Media during Emergencies

The majority of citizens across countries had not shared information during an emergency but had either only used social media to find information or not been active on them at all. They might had done this deliberately or they may not have had the possibility or need to use social media during an emergency. Therefore, it may prove substantial to track down barriers keeping people from using social media during emergencies. Figure 4.20 displays the main reasons why citizens would rather not use social media during an emergency.

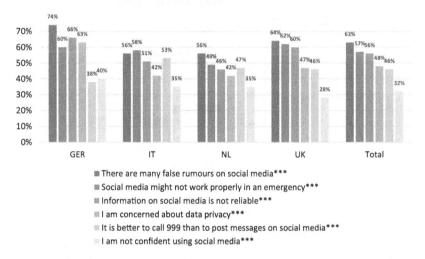

Figure 4.20 Reasons for not Using Social Media during an Emergency (Q5; This would [definitely] put me off). Note. N = 7071, *** indicates p < .001

Reasons include concerns about credibility of social media content (such as false rumours or that information on social media are not reliable), technical concerns (that social media might not work in an emergency), as well as data privacy concerns, low confidence regarding one's own ability to use social media, and the opinion that it is better to make an emergency phone call than to use social media. Across all countries, the biggest concern of citizens is that there are many false rumours on social media (63%). This fear is not unjustified as in the aftermath of the May 2017 Manchester suicide bombing, photos of supposedly missing people were posted on social media (ProspectMagazine, 2017) or regarding the 2016 Brussels bombing, where photos of another attack were shared. This is particularly a concern for German citizens, with 74% indicating that false rumours might put them off using social media during an emergency[5]. The second biggest concern (57% of citizens overall) related to technical issues of using social media in emergencies. Only Dutch citizens seem to be less worried with 49% expressing doubt of functionality as a reason for not using social media in an emergency[6]. Answers to the open-ended questions were mostly supportive of statistical distributions. British, Dutch and Italian participants often stated that they would use social media in emergencies but only under certain conditions. Many Italians (20%) mentioned several conditions making the use of social media more likely. Dutch people (12%) do not generally reject usage of social media in emergencies but still have some concerns, e.g., with respect to data security, reliability and the flood of information. If these aspects were improved, they would consider using social media in emergency situations. British participants perceived social media use during time-critical situations only to be necessary "if it was quicker than 999" or "if it was the only way to contact [...]" (#630). Several Dutch respondents (16%) reject the use of social media in dangerous situations as they prefer traditional media or do not trust social networks regarding efficiency. German (11%), British (9%) and Italian (8%) respondents also expressed various doubts about social media use but less than the Dutch.

Reasons include concerns about credibility of social media content (such as false rumours or that information on social media are not reliable), technical concerns (that social media might not work in an emergency), as well as data privacy concerns, low confidence regarding one's own ability to use social media, and the opinion that it is better to make an emergency phone call than to use social media. Across all countries, the biggest concern of citizens is that there are many false rumours on social media (63%). This fear is not unjustified as in the aftermath of the May 2017 Manchester suicide bombing, photos of supposedly missing people were posted on social media (ProspectMagazine, 2017) or regarding the 2016 Brussels bombing, where photos of another attack were shared. This is particularly a concern for German citizens, with 74% indicating that false rumours might put them off using social media during an emergency[7]. The second biggest concern (57% of citizens overall) related to technical issues of using social media in emergencies. Only Dutch citizens seem to be less worried with 49% expressing doubt of functionality as a reason for not using social media in an emergency[8].

---

[5] $(\chi^2(3) = 156.62, p < 0.001)$
[6] $(\chi^2(3) = 111.15, p < 0.001)$
[7] $(\chi^2(3) = 156.62, p < 0.001)$
[8] $(\chi^2(3) = 111.15, p < 0.001)$

Answers to the open-ended questions were mostly supportive of statistical distributions. British, Dutch and Italian participants often stated that they would use social media in emergencies but only under certain conditions. Many Italians (20%) mentioned several conditions making the use of social media more likely. Dutch people (12%) do not generally reject usage of social media in emergencies but still have some concerns, e.g., with respect to data security, reliability and the flood of information. If these aspects were improved, they would consider using social media in emergency situations. British participants perceived social media use during time-critical situations only to be necessary "if it was quicker than 999" or "if it was the only way to contact […]" (#630). Several Dutch respondents (16%) reject the use of social media in dangerous situations as they prefer traditional media or do not trust social networks regarding efficiency. German (11%), British (9%) and Italian (8%) respondents also expressed various doubts about social media use but less than the Dutch.

4.3.3.4 Expected Responsiveness of Emergency Services

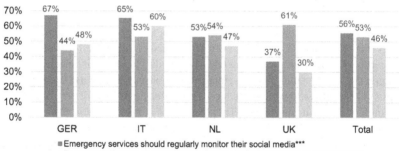

Figure 4.21 Expected Responsiveness of Emergency Services to Messages Posted via Social Media (Q4; Strongly agree, Agree). Note. N = 7071, *** indicates p < .001

Considering the importance of citizens' willingness to cooperate with authorities during emergencies, it is reasonable to ask whether there are specific expectations towards emergency services with respect to potential use of communicated data or responses to any requests. The survey showed that there is considerable variation between citizens' attitudes in the four countries (Figure 4.21). More than two thirds of German citizens expect their emergency services to regularly monitor social media, while in the UK only 37% of citizens share this expectation[9]. Similarly, while 60% of Italian citizens think that emergency services should reply to any request for help sent via social media within an hour, in the UK the proportion was only 30%[10]. This, combined with findings reported above, indicates that at the time of the survey most citizens in the UK did not expect emergency services to access information shared with them or others during an emergency, contrasting with the other countries' respective results.

4.3.3.5 Downloading and Using Emergency Apps

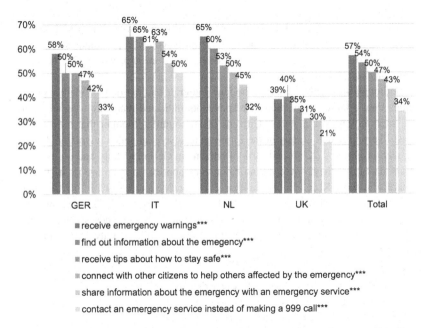

Figure 4.22 Likelihood of Using an App in the Future for Different Purposes (Q8; Very likely, Quite likely). Note. N = 7071, *** indicates p < .001, ** p < .01 and * p < .05

The survey shows that the use of relevant apps during emergencies is still in its infancy in most European countries—except for the Netherlands where 28% of citizens had downloaded such an app (Q6). In contrast, only 7% of citizens

---

[9] $(\chi^2(3) = 462.21, p<.001)$
[10] $(\chi^2(3) = 391.49, p<.001)$

in the UK and 16% in Germany and Italy, respectively, had done so[11]. There are several types of apps that could be helpful during an emergency, e.g., weather, warning, first aid and emergency call apps. Across all countries, weather apps (52%) were the most popular apps citizens had downloaded. This proportion was especially high in Germany (69%) and lowest in the UK with 44%[12]. In the Netherlands warning apps were most common with 53% having downloaded such an app, with an average across all four countries of 42%[13]. Downloading of emergency calls apps was more common in Italy (33%) and the UK (28%) than in the Netherlands (18%) and Germany (16%)[14]. Only the proportion of citizens that had downloaded a First Aid app did not vary significantly between the countries[15].

There is a significant relationship between downloading an app and gender (towards male participants[16]) and age (towards younger participants[17]). Only 8% of the oldest age group (65+) had downloaded an app, while 23% of those younger than 25 had done so.

Although most citizens across the four countries had not downloaded an emergency app, a larger proportion of respondents indicated that they were likely to use such an app in the future. Citizens of all countries thought that they would most likely use such an app in the future to receive emergency warnings. As can be seen in Figure 4.22 around 60% of citizens in Germany, Italy and the Netherlands stated that they would use an emergency app for this purpose in the future, whereas in the UK the proportion was considerably lower (39%)[18]. Differences between the countries were also found for all other reasons[19]. The least popular reason for using an app in the future is to contact an emergency service. In the UK, only 21% would use an app for this purpose while in Italy 50% said they would do so.

---

[11] ($\chi^2(6, N = 7071) = 406.11, p<0.001$, Cramer's V $= .17$)

[12] ($\chi^2(3, N = 1065) = 29.38, p<0.001$, Cramer's V $= .159$)

[13] ($\chi^2(3, N = 1067) = 23.63, p<0.001$, Cramer's V $= .142$)

[14] ($\chi^2(3, N = 1066) = 30.29, p<0.001$, Cramer's V $= .161$)

[15] ($\chi^2(3, N = 1065) = 6.84, p = 0.077$, Cramer's V $= .077$)

[16] ($\chi^2(2, N = 7071) = 23.95, p<.001$, Cramer's V $= .058$)

[17] ($\chi^2(10, N = 7070) = 272.64, p<.001$, Cramer's V $= .14$)

[18] ($\chi^2(3) = 514.44, p<0.001$)

[19] ('find out information about the emergency': $\chi^2(3) = 381.54, p < 0.001$; 'receive tips about how to stay safe': $\chi^2(3) = 367.37, p<0.001$; 'connect with other citizens to help others affected by the emergency': $\chi^2(3) = 447.00, p<0.001$; 'contact an emergency service instead of making a 999 call': $\chi^2(3) = 417.40, p<0.001$; 'share information about the emergency with an emergency service': $\chi^2(3) = 345.83, p<0.001$)

4.3.4   Discussion and Conclusion

Our surveys with 7,071 participants from Germany, Italy, the Netherlands and the UK showed that almost half (45%) of citizens across the four countries have used social media during an emergency. We visualised the results of the statistical analysis (see Section 4.3.3). The main results are interpreted and discussed referring to the framework of risk cultures, section 4.3.4. gives an overview of the four countries in comparison, presenting configurations of risk culture and variations in use of social media in emergencies.

4.3.4.1   Interpretation of Main Results
The interpretation of main results is structured by our research questions. Here, it is not only possible to present relevant findings but also to reflect upon limitations of the theoretical framework, thereby pointing out to potentials of future research.

4.3.4.1.1 How do Citizens use Social Media during Emergencies (R1)?
Twenty-three percent in total use social media both to find out and share information, with Italy (35%) having the largest proportion in comparison and the UK (16%) presenting the smallest share. Italy, being the forerunner of social media use during emergencies but usually depicted as a fatalistic risk culture indicating little individual action (Cornia et al., 2016), seems to undertake a social change towards an individualistic risk culture, pushed by relatively frequent occurrences of emergencies, which may affect communities collectively (Benessia & De Marchi, 2017; Mysiak et al., 2013; Schelfaut et al., 2011).

Regarding the types of shared information, weather conditions or warnings are most likely to be shared as well as feelings or emotions across the four countries, with the Netherlands and the UK sharing less often respective information while Germany (regarding weather-related content) and especially Italy were more active. Note that behaviour of German respondents may be explained by occurrences of a specific kind of emergency happening (e.g., thunderstorms) and otherwise low incentives of state-oriented participants. Studies during COVID-19 in Germany in February 2021 "demonstrate that people who trust traditional media and official bodies in Covid-19 reporting also have a high specific trust in politics—in contrast to those who tend to believe alternative internet sources" (Jäckle & Wagschal, 2022). A systemic perspective on crisis management in Germany concluded "is generally favourable of the ability of the German politico-administrative system to master challenging crises" (Behnke & Eckhard, 2022).

Again, Italy may have experienced more large-scale emergencies (e.g., floods, earthquakes and avalanches) preceding the timing of this survey, making inefficiency of conventional management structures obvious (Schelfaut et al., 2011). There is no coherent explanation based on the risk culture approach when it comes to the low percentages of Dutch participants sharing videos or eyewitness pictures. Yet, it might be worth to consider that in the light of already effective conventional disaster management structures, Dutch citizens do not perceive expanded usage of social media to be necessary (Kievik & Gutteling, 2011; Wachinger et al., 2013). When reflecting on (overall) UK results, it is suggested that self-reliant activities via social media are blocked by a similar, yet rather pessimistic perception. This is backed by qualitative results regarding the open-ended question with British participants pointing out to non-confidence and social media communication being unnecessary.

In sum, there are significant relationships with age[20] and gender[21] regarding attitudes and behaviour, independent from national and cultural context. Across all countries and respective risk cultures, younger people were more likely to have used social media during an emergency. Only 28% of the youngest age group (below 25) have not used social media during an emergency, whereas 77% of those aged 65 or older have not used it. Similarly, women are significantly more likely to have used social media in an emergency (47%) than men (42%), independent from their home location. As age and gender is distributed equally across the four countries, these factors apply for similar cross-national behaviour.

4.3.4.1.2 What are Citizens' Expectations towards Emergency Services (R2)?

On the one hand, emergency services are clearly expected to monitor social media by 56%, which is mostly expected by Germans (67%) and Italians (66%). Moreover, they are expected to respond within an hour by 46% in total and in a high proportion by Italians (60%). These two points correlate significantly. On the other hand, they are perceived as too busy to monitor social media by 54% in total, especially by British respondents (62%).

Low expectations of the British may be explained by ranking social media communication of emergency services low on their list of priorities, i.e., by evolving disinterest or fatalism. At the same time, low percentages regarding the need of social media monitoring by emergency services may point out to a more individualistic risk culture with less accounting responsibilities to state actors (Cornia

---

[20] ($\chi^2(15, N = 6724) = 967.32$, $p<.001$, Cramer's V $= .22$)
[21] ($\chi^2(3, N = 6724) = 18.88$, $p<.001$, Cramer's V $= .053$)

et al., 2016). Grand expectations of German emergency services match the state-oriented risk culture as well as Italy's strong focus on state responsibilities despite mistrust towards authorities (Cornia et al., 2016). The latter is stressed by Italian respondents referring to the state's responsibility to control communication via social media according to privacy rights, reliability and validity when answering the open-ended question. Imran et al. (2017) suggests that by combining the understanding of data processing, surveillance, and the socio-technical to privacy can address the many issues involved in processing crisis data. The Netherlands poses again a coherent example for an individualistic, self-reliant risk culture with comparatively lower expectations towards authorities (Cornia et al., 2016).

4.3.4.1.3 What are Citizens' perceived Main Barriers of Social Media during Emergencies (R3)?

Main barriers of using social media mentioned are false rumours by 63% in total, with Germans (74%) and British (64%) being most sceptical; unreliable information by 56% in total, representing a similar distribution of scepticism by Germans (66%) and British (60%); data privacy by 48% in total, largely by Germans (62%); and the possibility that social media might not work properly in an emergency by 57% whereby Dutch (49%) indicated the least scepticism.

Germany's trust in state authorities as well as towards traditional mass media is reflected by the highest distrust regarding information spread via social media, comparing among the countries and the respective risk cultures. As the state is regarded to be the central actor (Cornia et al., 2016), it is persuasive that in the light of social media being dominated by non-state actors and a relatively great number of sources which are not credited or used as references by state actors, including private individuals spreading information, Germans perceive social media to be unreliable in a strong way. This also points out to the UK having similarly high trust issues (i.e., false rumours or data privacy). The UK results surprise, having in mind the country's neoliberal turn as well as diverse use of smartphones in the British population's everyday lives (Fortunati & Taipale, 2014). The Netherlands, with an individualistic understanding of risk management and lower expectations towards state actors are more likely to trust corporate and individual sources. The numbers again suggest a change of Italy's risk culture from fatalistic to individualistic.

However, two results are striking. Aware of Italy's comparatively disappointing management structures (Alpaslan & Gianni, 2012; Mysiak et al., 2013) which led to the establishment of a fatalistic risk culture, having mistrust towards state institutions, blaming them in cases of mismanagement while feeling individually powerless (Cornia et al., 2016), it is interesting that Italian participants rated highest regarding the statement of rather calling emergency phone numbers than communicating via social media. The respective number was lower across all other countries, with Germany showing the lowest percentage. Second, it should be noted that privacy concerns are high regardless of risk culture; thus, further elaboration and analysis of populations' attitudes towards social media (companies) may be useful. Regarding responses to the open-ended question which were qualitatively analysed, perceived barriers like privacy issues, usability as well as assessed benefits like effective information flow, immediate communication, were named across all four countries, independent from risk culture or disruptive incidents. This suggests factors like human-computer interaction, habits, and perception of media (social vs. traditional) to be helpful in explaining the choice of similar parameters of evaluation when it comes to social media use during emergencies.

4.3.4.1.4 What are Citizens' Attitudes towards Mobile Emergency Apps (R4)?

They are only used by 17% in total, but in larger proportions in the Netherlands (28%), with a significant relationship with gender towards male participants, and age towards younger participants. The most downloaded apps are weather apps by 42% in total, mostly by Germans (69%), and warning or alert apps by 42% in total with a visibly higher proportion in the Netherlands (33%). For future use, the most likely opportunities mentioned (for details see (Reuter & Spielhofer, 2017)) were receiving emergency warnings by 57% in total, UK (39%) having the least expectations, and tips about how to stay safe by 50% in total, whereby Italians (61%) expressed the highest expectations. Finally, finding out information about the emergency was mentioned by 54% in total.

The individualistic nature of the Dutch risk culture can explain the proactive measure of downloading emergency apps. Further analysis of decisive factors regarding the choice of specific app categories needs to be done as it is not sure whether the types of emergencies have influenced the choices of app categories, with German participants having downloaded weather apps significantly more than British respondents. Referring to their individualistic risk culture, Dutch behaviour can only partly be explained, noting that the frequency of downloading warning apps was considerably higher than of emergency call apps when comparing.

As an alternative to apps, *cell broadcast* is a method of sending messages to multiple mobile telephone users in a defined area at the same time. One important remark with regard to the low number of warning apps in the Netherlands is that NL-Alert, a cell broadcast alarm system is already available and used since 2012, while other countries such as UK and Italy have introduced this technology in 2021 (UK-Alert and IT-Alert) and Germany has just established the legal basis for the use of cell broadcast for warning in 2021. Uniform European solutions might be desirable here, but in the sense of multilevel governance (Benz et al., 2021) competences are distributed and include the level of the district, the federal state, the country, rarely the EU, depending on the extent and type of the incident, emergency, crisis or conflict.

Across countries, rankings for reasons to use respective apps in the future were nearly identical. Still, Italy's comparatively high ranking of justifying future use with reference to social connections which might prove helpful to others contrasts with the other countries' results. The latter may be due to their relative collectivist nature (Bontempo et al., 1997; Gierlach et al., 2010; Statman, 2008). A collectivist nature, compared to the Netherlands and the UK (Statman, 2008), became also prevalent regarding German participants' relatively higher interest in sharing information, as answers to the open-ended question suggested. Greater willingness among Italians of using emergency apps prospectively does not surprise keeping in mind changing attitudes towards more individual engagement. Still having a strong sense of blaming state authorities, 50% of Italian participants potentially prefer contacting services via emergency apps over phone calls, contradicted by highest results when it comes to favouring calling emergencies via telephone instead of using social media (cf. main barriers). This suggests that participants may have divergent attitudes towards social media and emergency apps.

4.3.4.2 Relevant Characteristics and Implications

An analysis of the four European countries revealed several interesting findings which may prove fruitful not only for the scientific debate but also regarding the implementation of emergency management structures via social media. Especially with respect to citizens' expectations towards authorities' monitoring (R2) and attitudes towards the use of mobile emergency apps (R4) our findings match with prior research referring to risk cultures (Cornia et al., 2016; Dressel & Pfeil, 2017). Furthermore, intensity of perceived barriers (R3) varies according to risk culture, with German participants being more sceptical about (citizen-generated) social media content (Reuter & Spielhofer, 2017). Yet, current risk culture approaches exclude frequency and types of emergencies as contextual factors, even though both variables may have an impact on citizens' perception of the respective efficacy of management structures (R1).

Our findings suggest Italian citizens to rely relatively strongly on social media which may be due to frequency of disruptive events affecting a larger proportion of the collective (e.g., natural disasters). Departing from a rather fatalistic risk culture, as framed in prior work (Dressel, 2015; Dressel & Pfeil, 2017), thus, showing signs of readiness regarding individual action, Italian participants seem to be open towards an improvement of authorities' monitoring of emergencies via social media. This implies that in practice social media use in emergencies should be especially useful to populations potentially relying on it due to strongly perceived need of improving management structures.

Contrasting answers were given by British respondents who had used social media less frequently in emergencies, were above-average sceptical towards it and perceived (future) use rather unnecessary. As the UK has not been classified as a specific model of risk culture, our findings may contribute to this process by pointing out to an evolving fatalistic attitude towards disruptive events.

Regarding more specific actions of social media use, a small part of it could be interpreted to be of either collectivistic or individualistic nature, following the traditional division of such approaches (Bontempo et al., 1997; Statman, 2008; Zheng, 2017). Yet, our analysis made clear that common assumptions of risk cultures fail to incorporate for example concrete content-sharing behaviour into their theories.

Age was shown to be strongly correlated with the use of social media during emergencies[22] and the availability of an emergency app[23] as indicated by large effect sizes. Apart from age, gender correlated with some of the answers. These categories are distributed equally across the four countries, thus, applying for similar attitudes and behaviour. Especially habitual use of social media by younger people should be taken into consideration when managing emergencies as well as less frequent use by older generations by aiming for addressing them sufficiently through "multimodal warnings" and tighter linkages between public authorities, press and social media, keeping in mind growing ageing populations (Righi et al., 2017; Wendling et al., 2013).

Focusing on risk culture-specific use of social media yields relevant consequences. It sheds light on the importance to factor cultural embeddedness into an understanding of risk perception, individuals' actions as well as emergency and disaster management procedures. Our work suggests this context, created through specific ways of framing, trust and blaming, not to be restricted to the offline world. Crisis informatics focuses on the potential of interactive systems in times of disruptive events; this chapter tries to grasp individuals' perceptions and behaviours, both influencing cooperation efforts. As other scholars insist

---

[22] (Q2, $\chi^2(15, N = 6724) = 967.32, p<.001$, Cramer's V $= .22$)
[23] (Q6, $\chi^2(10, N = 7070) = 272.64, p<.001$, Cramer's V $= .14$)

(Alexander, 2013; Lo & Chan, 2017; White, 2011), incorporating social media into emergency management implies various advantages with respect to collaborative work. At the same time, it is necessary in times of frequent use of social media, especially when expectations towards authorities are high and fatalism in risk perception is evolving (Lo & Chan, 2017; Wendling et al., 2013). Additionally, examining risk cultures, respective perceptions and behaviour during emergencies may prove useful in light of disaster management in countries facing rather more than less climate change enhanced hazards in the nearest future (Lo & Chan, 2017).

Our work allows for deriving policy implications focusing on crisis communication. Generally, we follow Dressel and Pfeil (2017) by supporting the view of the need to centre individuals' attention in state-oriented risk cultures on potentially helpful proactiveness while individuals embedded in individualistic risk cultures should be assured of state authorities' responsiveness to avoid fatalistic tendencies. Crisis communication in fatalistic risk cultures should work in both directions while a framing of emergencies as un-manageable incidents and failure of foresight at its initial stage may be omitted or counteracted, respectively (Constantinides, 2013). Our focus on social media behaviour opens further possibilities, pointing out to the necessity of authorities to present themselves to be approachable and efficient via social media. Our findings on perceived barriers stress the importance of transparency, reduction of rumours, and privacy in risk and crisis communication, supporting other research (Wendling et al., 2013). One may also keep in mind that certain kinds of emergency apps may be more helpful in some contexts than in others. Crisis communication agendas may also include optimising communication to the population about reliability of social media correspondence, enhancing trust regarding cooperation between citizens and authorities and offering information which may prove necessary.

4.3.4.3   Limitations and Outlook

Of course, this study has limitations. The online survey's results might be biased due to possible self-selection of volunteering individuals. Our findings are based on individuals' answers and not observation of actual behaviour. However, citizens' perceptions were our focus and, as such, the study provides valuable results, not at least with respect to potential further implementation of management structures via social media, a process relying on the respective addressees' attitudes. Depending on the type of smartphone used, it may have been perceived necessary to download weather apps for general use and the multiple-choice questionnaire might have pre-limited the choice of answers to the open-ended question. We restricted our study to four cases, controlling various variables while focusing on risk culture induced divergences. Future research may complement our work by including other (European) countries. The validity of the findings' interpretation is limited due to rough and non-examination of actual frequency of (certain types of) emergencies as well as conventional and digital implemented risk management structures, respectively. Nevertheless, taking frequency and types of emergencies as influencing factors into account poses a starting point for future research. Our choice to restrict cultural spaces along national borders may be complemented by regional, sub-national studies, which may, for example, represent earthquake-prone communities, locations close to the sea or metropolitan areas with a higher risk of human-induced emergencies. Such comparisons of different emergency contexts may reveal a respective effect regarding behaviour. Analysis on state-level may still prove inadequate, as a comparison between respondents from Bavaria and North Rhine-Westphalia reveals no significant results[24]. As we proposed British passive behaviour towards social media use in emergencies and scepticism towards authorities' performance, it is certainly interesting to examine the UK populations' culture of dealing with risks more accurately. Adapting the framework of risk cultures to social media and offering an interpretation of variances of use of social media in situations of emergency, we proposed an argument regarding the frequency of use, and implicitly the diversity of usage patterns. Future research may engage with findings of the media sciences and psychology regarding human-computer interaction, perceptions of social (vs. traditional) media and habits, thereby grasping cross-cultural similarities of behaviour and attitudes as well as diverging behaviour when it comes to specific actions taken via social media. We offer first insights into social media use during emergencies from a risk culture perspective; in future work, it may prove valuable, especially with respect to the design of emergency apps, to focus on specific settings of emergencies. Further, as we chose to dichotomise originally Likert-scaled answers to simplify the interpretation, it may prove fruitful to have a more nuanced look at participants who opted for "extreme" answers, their risk culture as well as other potential factors.

---

[24] There was no statistically significant difference of the use (i.e., share/find info) of social media during emergencies between respondents living in Bavaria and respondents living in NRW ($\chi2$ (4, N = 257) = 3.361, p >.05). Only with respect to expectations towards emergencies, the test revealed significant correlations between answers and state (p>.05). Yet, the differences between the two states are very small. Bavaria was assumed to pose a more provincial state and NRW, as a highly densely populated area, a metropolitan region with potentially rather small-scale emergencies (in contrast to foregrounding natural disasters). Yet, the results indicate that observation on the state-level is still not accurate enough.

Regarding the risk culture framework, future research could examine in which way ICT, such as social media and mobile emergency apps, potentially support citizens from two perspectives. Firstly, since it is a desirable condition that both authorities and citizens are prepared for emergencies, ICT might assist in (1) *complementing the weaknesses* of specific risk cultures. Thus, state-oriented risk cultures should be supported in terms of individual proactive behaviour and individual-oriented risk cultures assured of their authorities' capabilities and responsibilities, while fatalistic risk cultures potentially benefit from both approaches. Secondly, ICT might support in (2) *utilising the strengths* of specific risk cultures. Since trust in authorities is high in state-oriented risk cultures, citizens expect authorities to communicate, or *push*, emergency-relevant information, i.e., by disseminating accurate and relevant information across different channels. On the other hand, individual-oriented risk cultures, which emphasise citizens' responsibilities, should be provided with information resources that they can use, or *pull*, on demand, i.e., by providing relevant information on how to behave before, during and after emergencies via emergency crisis apps. Although both ways cannot be considered as strengths of a fatalistic risk culture, our results on Italians' use and intended future use of social media and mobile emergency apps suggest a change from fatalistic to individual-oriented risk culture, making it worthwhile to examine the transformative potential of ICT on risk culture in future studies.

4.4   Summary and Next Steps

Complementing the view of emergency services (Chapter 3), this chapter studied citizens' perceptions and showed that (1) 40% have already used social media in emergencies, however only 17% have used warning apps, (2) there are high expectations of authorities, especially that they monitor social media (56%), and (3) the main obstacles to the use of social media are false rumours (63%).

Comparing citizen's perceptions with emergency services' views, it turns out that they see most value in "preventive and situational communication", so authorities to citizen (A2C) communication, while citizens express high expectations in citizen to authorities (C2A) communication, which sets different priorities—precisely those that have the best cost-benefit ratio for the respective group.

It might be the case, that this is also related to a lack of awareness about applications to ease situation assessment with social media. In order to research this, chapter 5 focuses on concrete ways of assessing the situation with social media, e.g., to support emergency forces. Chapter 6 then shifts the focus to the self-organisation of volunteers in social media.

Tailorable Situation Assessment with Social Media

5

The amount of available data is rapidly increasing. Based on the technological advances with mobile and ubiquitous computing, the use of social media is increasingly becoming a normal part of daily life and extraordinary situations, such as crises. Not surprisingly, this increasing use is one reason why data on the internet is also developing so quickly. In 2022, more than 4 billion people use the internet and the majority is also registered with social media platforms, such as Facebook or Twitter. While processing this kind of data by the majority of non-technical users, concepts of End-User Development (EUD) are important. This chapter researches how concepts of EUD might be applied to handle social big data. Based on foundations and an empirical pre-study, we explore how EUD can support the gathering and assessment process of social media. In this context, we investigate how end-users can articulate their personal quality criteria appropriately and how the selection of relevant data can be supported by EUD approaches. We present a tailorable social media gathering service and quality assessment service for social media content, which has been implemented and integrated into an application for both volunteers and the emergency services.

*This chapter has been published as two articles "**End-User Development and Social Big Data—Towards Tailorable Situation Assessment with Social Media**" by Christian Reuter, Marc-André Kaufhold and Thomas Ludwig in the book New Perspectives in End-User Development (Reuter et al., 2017a) [Paper F] as well as: "**Social-QAS: Tailorable Quality Assessment Service for Social Media Content**" by Christian Reuter, Thomas Ludwig, Michael Ritzkatis and Volkmar Pipek in the Proceedings of the International Symposium on End-User Development (IS-EUD) (Reuter et al., 2015c) [Paper*

Supplementary Information The online version contains supplementary material available at https://doi.org/10.1007/978-3-658-39720-3_5.

© The Author(s), under exclusive license to Springer Fachmedien Wiesbaden GmbH, part of Springer Nature 2022
C. Reuter, *A European Perspective on Crisis Informatics*,
https://doi.org/10.1007/978-3-658-39720-3_5

G]. The whole chapter has been published as Paper F, only Section 5.2 has been published as part of Paper G.

5.1   Related Work

The amount of data has experienced exponential growth—data generation has been estimated at 2.5 Exabytes (=2.500.000 Terabytes) per day. The sources are manifold and include not only technical sensors, but also social sensors, such as posts on social media such as Facebook or Twitter. To handle this big data, new applications, frameworks and methodologies arose that allow efficient data mining and information fusion from social media and new applications and frameworks (Bello-Orgaz et al., 2016). Usually, the data is called user-generated content, which is according to the definition of the Organisation for Economic Co-operation and Development (OECD) (2007), "content that has been made publicly available via the internet".

Not only in daily life but also in recent emergencies, such as the 2012 hurricane Sandy or the 2013 European floods, both the people affected and volunteers alike used social media to communicate with each other and to coordinate private relief activities (Kaufhold & Reuter, 2016). Since the involvement of citizens is, still, mostly uncoordinated and the content is therefore not necessarily created in a structured way, a vast amount of resulting data has to be analysed. Appropriate methods of valuation are essential for the analysis, whereby a consistent evaluation of the quality of information can be complex (Friberg et al., 2010). Especially in cases where a selection, whether by emergency managers or citizen volunteers, has to be made from a variety of information sources and formats under time-critical constraints, it is helpful if the evaluation can be simplified by applying situationally relevant quality criteria. Thus, our research question is how the concepts of EUD can be applied to support individuals in extracting relevant social media information in the extraordinary and unique settings of emergencies.

This chapter explores the challenges arising from the integration of citizen-generated content and the analysis of information from social media focusing on EUD. Based on a review of related work in big data analysis, social media and EUD, we present a design case study (Wulf et al., 2011) on social media use in emergencies and its assessment by the tailorable weighting of information quality criteria. Accordingly, an empirical study (Section 5.2) on the use of citizen-generated content and social media by emergency services and the challenges, focusing on individual and dynamic quality assessments of social media data, informed the implementation of tools for platform-independent social media gathering (Social Media API) and quality assessment (Social-QAS) (Section 5.3). Furthermore, we have prototypically integrated and evaluated Social-QAS in two reference applications (Section 5.4). Finally, we draw conclusions (Section 5.5).

5.1.1 Big Data, Social Media and Data Analysis

Although—or because—big data is a buzzword, there is no unified definition of the term big data across various origins (Ward & Barker, 2013). According to the Gartner IT Glossary, big data is "high-volume, high-velocity and high-variety information assets that demand cost-effective, innovative forms of information processing for enhanced insight and decision making". Dijcks (2012) distinguishes between different types of data: traditional enterprise data, machine-generated/sensor data and finally social data, which are also known as *social big data*: it "will be based on the analysis of vast amounts of data that could come from multiple distributed sources but with a strong focus on social media" (Bello-Orgaz et al., 2016). Reviewing current literature, Olshannikova et al. (2017) contribute with the definition of social big data as "any high-volume, high-velocity, high-variety and/or highly semantic data that is generated from technology-mediated social interactions and actions in digital realm, and which can be collected and analysed to model social interactions and behaviour". Ward and Barker (2013) explicitly research for a definition of big data and suggest that it: "is a term describing the storage and analysis of large and/or complex data sets using a series of techniques including, but not limited to: NoSQL, MapReduce and machine learning". An important attempt is to deal with biases in the data. A study found that analysts fail to successfully debias data, even when biases are detected (Paulus et al., 2022).

Garnis and Kohikar (2012) consider that most big data is from social media: "Where is all of this big data coming from? It's produced within the many social media applications by a wide variety of sources (people, companies, advertisers, etc.)". Additionally, Basset (2015) outlines that the existence of social media as big data was underplayed in the past, and, to bridge the gap to the domain of emergency management, Watson et al. (2017) exemplify promising benefits of big data to support situational awareness and decision making especially before and during emergencies.

Data from social media contains complex dependencies and relationships within itself and this, combined with its—not to mention the characteristics of crises and emergencies—heterogeneous nature, imposes strong limitations on the data models that can be used as well as on the scope of information that can be discovered. In the case of current social media, the amount of data is increasing steadily as the data set is constantly supplemented. Data analysis or mining in the context of social media must continuously transform raw social media data into a processable form by selectively using specific characteristics needed for the upcoming analysis process. In the following, we will specify characteristics for the analysis process.

- *Big Data Paradox:* Social media data has a huge amount of records consisting of different data types, like profiles, posts, groups, relationships and other. Therefore, enormous computing and storage capacities are required to process the data (Batrinca & Treleaven, 2014). However, little data exists for individuals, and conventional data mining techniques do not process relationships between profiles.
- *Obtaining Sufficient Samples:* A wide range of data is accessible so that trends, indicators and patterns can be detected based on statistical information (Zafarani et al., 2014). However, collecting data from social media has several limitations. In many cases one gets only a limited amount of data in a restricted period of time (Reuter & Scholl, 2014).
- *Context and User Dependency:* A large part of data from social media is generated and consumed by users and, from the interactions between different actors and the environment, new metadata such as time, location, groups, hashtags and other variables arise. When analysing data, it is important to mention that the data that is being processed originates from a variety of sources (e.g. third-party applications) which have their own use context and purpose (Mislove et al., 2007).
- *Structured and Unstructured Data:* Profile data, the number of likes or retweets are structured data and can easily be compared with each other. In contrast, user-generated text is usually in an unstructured form and varies in quality and quantity (Stieglitz et al., 2014). This is a challenge because data mining requires the identification of *high-quality* information in the large data sets (Agichtein et al., 2008).
- *Importance of Metadata:* Metadata represent an essential part of the social media's information content. They provide the interaction context of users such as a specification of time and location. Because a large set of metadata is available in almost any situation, it may be possible to draw conclusions on the user intention and situation. The in-situ context influences user behaviour significantly and is formed by activities, time, place and conversations of the respective user (Church & Oliver, 2011).

- *Historicity of Data:* The historicity of data can be represented not only by the data and metadata itself but also through the interactions between social media. A snapshot can be created in the virtual space of social media including all dependencies. Here it is vital that the collected data is stored persistently because the access to data from social media such as Twitter is volatile, particularly at high-traffic events such as crises.
- *Type of Content:* Social media is strongly characterised by the use of images, videos and sounds and by text comments and annotations from users and therefore important contextual information may be present. Hence, data mining of social media usually includes natural language processing (NLP). A major problem with NLP on social media is non-standard language (Ritter et al., 2011; Xu et al., 2013). Social media reports frequently contain non-standard grammar (punctuation, capitalisation, syntax) and vocabulary (including non-standard spelling) (Eisenstein, 2013).

5.1.2 The End-User Development Perspective in Data Analysis

Referring to situation assessment during emergencies, it is important to have information available at the right time, the right place and in the right format (Ley et al., 2012). Endsley (1995) makes a distinction between *situation awareness* as a "state of knowledge" and *situation assessment* as the "process of achieving, acquiring, or maintaining" that knowledge; he defines information gathering as a selection procedure which results in the construction of a mental model pursuant to individual goals. Since several emergencies are extraordinary and time-critical, they require a demand for unpredictable information. It is therefore essential to have instantaneous access to as many sources as possible. Still, it is not easy to dispose of all the necessary information (Turoff et al., 2004). Simultaneously, it is very important to prevent a possible information overload so that the decision making is not affected (Hiltz & Plotnick, 2013).

In crisis management, situation assessment and decision making are supported by information systems (van de Walle & Turoff, 2008). Of course, it can come to difficulties, particularly when dealing with seldom used technologies within emergencies and while assessing social media. Adjustments of these technologies and especially of the considered information are essential and play a big role at 'use-time' (Fischer & Scharff, 2000; Pipek & Wulf, 2009; Stevens et al., 2009).

EUD supports flexible adjustments by making it possible for end-users to tailor and rearrange information systems independently (Lieberman et al., 2006). EUD can be defined as all "methods, techniques, and tools that allow users of software systems, who are acting as non-professional software developers, at some point to create modify or extend a software artefact" (Lieberman et al., 2006). One essential part of EUD, with regard to the change of a "stable" aspect of an artefact, is adapting (Henderson & Kyng, 1991). Nonetheless, for some people it is 'tailoring', for others it is 'use'. An essential part of software with regard to its establishment in practice definitely is tailorability. EUD uses mashups to combine services or information from various sources (Cappiello et al., 2011). The metaphor of a "bazaar" has therefore been used (Doerner et al., 2009). While component-based architectures in software engineering enable tailorable systems (Won et al., 2006), intuitive notions as well as interaction designs are needed to support end-user articulations (Hess et al., 2012). Pipek (2005) argues that tailoring might lead towards appropriation support to support the users.

5.1.3 Existing Approaches in EUD and Emergency Management

There are existing approaches and models (Costabile et al., 2007; Doll & Torkzadeh, 1988; Grammel, 2009) to deal with data analysis using EUD: Wand and Hong (2007) argue that there is "a tremendous amount of web content available today, but it is not always in a form that supports end-users' needs". Addressing this, their EUD tool enables end-users to create mash-ups that re-purpose and combine existing web content and service. In the domain of social networks, Heer and Boyd (2005) present a case study of the design of Vizster, an interactive visualisation system for end-user exploration of online social networks. Resulting techniques include connectivity, highlighting and linkage views for viewing network context, X-ray mode and profile search for exploring member profile data as well as visualisation of inferred community structures. Coutaz and Crowley (2016) present their "lived-with" experience with an EUD prototype deployed at their home.

Considering the domain of visual programming, Borges and Macías (2010) present a visual language and a functional prototype, called VISQUE, providing an easy-to-use mechanism to create SQL queries for non-programmer professionals, such as engineers, scientists and freelancers. With VISQUE the users can build the queries through a web-based visual interface to explore and analyse data without the need of SQL skills. Ardito et al. (2014) conducted a study to identify end-user requirements for accessing and customising web-services and

APIs. Based on their findings, the authors present a prototype, which enables people without programming skills to create a dashboard of widgets. With the help of a wizard the users can create a widget to combine data from different services and APIs and choose a visualisation format. In addition, FaceMashup (Massa & Spano, 2015) is an EUD environment that "empowers social network users, supporting them in creating their own procedures for inspecting and controlling their data".

Taking the case of emergency management, where social media is used for about 15 years (Reuter & Kaufhold, 2018), in addition to information that is provided automatically (meteorological data, water levels, etc.), there are two other kinds of information sources provided by people: emergency services in the field from whom information can be requested (Ludwig et al., 2013) and other individuals and organisations not actively dealing with the emergency. In the case of a house coal for example, the (target) number of residents can be requested from the registration office, but the estimation of the fire's size and of the (actual) number of affected people can only be performed on-site. Unlike sensor data, information provided by citizens is not always objective. Sometimes citizen-generated content is accurate—illustrated at a comparison of Wikipedia and Britannica encyclopaedia articles (Giles, 2005). In some cases, however, the subjectivity of citizen-provided reports can generate some sort of vigilantism (Rizza et al., 2013). Additionally, the misinterpretation of a situation—whether deliberate or not—can lead to potential misinformation; this can result from the reporter paying too little attention to some aspects of the situation or from an incorrect representation of the facts (Thomson et al., 2012). However, some information cannot be obtained from other sources (Zagel, 2012). This subjectivity makes data analysis rather complex.

There are approaches concerning the selection and use of data from social media; these, however, do not support a complete quality assessment (Reuter et al., 2015c): *Twitcident* (Terpstra et al., 2012) allows the user to select tweets by keywords, message types or users and to display them on a map. Nevertheless, quality assessment based on meta-information such as the time of creation is not possible. *Alert.io*[1] offers individual trainable tonality analyses and thus first approaches to the integration of machine learning in the form of a learning process to be carried out by the end-user. *HootSuite*[2] emphasises the design of the analysis by adapting and extending software artifacts. *Tweet4act* (Chowdhury et al., 2013) enables the tracing and classification of information on Twitter

---

[1] https://mention.com/en/

[2] www.hootsuite.com.

by matching every Tweet against an emergency-specific dictionary to classify them into emergency periods. With *TwitInfo* (Marcus et al., 2011) information concerning a specific event can be collected, classified and visualised graphically including additional information about the (not adaptable) quality of the actual information. *Netvizz* is a "data collection and extraction application that allows researchers to export data in standard file formats from different sections of the Facebook social networking service" (Rieder, 2013) to allow quantitative and qualitative research in the application, mainly based on pre-defined categories. *Ushahidi* (McClendon & Robinson, 2012) enables citizens to exchange information. Additionally, emergency services can get access to the information. The direct communication and the spread of unfiltered information can cause an information overload, which forces the user to evaluate the information manually according to its quality.

To sum up, one can say that many studies and approaches about citizen-generated content exist, but concerning EUD in quality assessment of social big data, they are missing a tailorable tool for assessing social media information.

5.2   Social Media Assessment by Emergency Services

To gain a deeper understanding of the impact citizen-generated content has on social media within emergencies, we analysed the data from a previous empirical study on the current work practices of the emergency services (focus on fire departments and police) in two different regions of Germany with regard to social media assessment by emergency services. The results of this pre-study have already been published (Ludwig et al., 2015a; Reuter & Ritzkatis, 2014) and we aggregate the main results within this chapter.

5.2.1   Methodology

The bases for the data analysis were the results of multiple empirical studies from 2010 to 2012 (Reuter, 2014b). The studies were embedded in a scenario framework describing a storm with many minor and connected incidents and energy breakdowns, which had been developed together with actors from the police and fire departments, county administration and an ENO. The purpose of the scenario was to be able to create a common understanding of an occurring emergency quickly and therefore it helped to increase validity and comparability in our interviews.

First, we conducted observations in order to acquire knowledge regarding the practical work in inter-organisational crisis management. The observations took place in a control centre on a normal working day (observation time: 9 hours); in the crisis management group and the operations management during a crisis communication practice course (4 hours); as well as at a major cultural event with about 400,000 visitors (6 hours). In addition to observations, we conducted 5 inter-organisational group discussions (W1-W5, each 4 hours with about 10 participants respectively) to understand the communication methods of inter-organisational crisis management. Furthermore, we conducted 22 individual interviews with actors from the participating organisations (I01-I24). Each interview lasted between 1 and 2 hours and followed a guideline, which was separated into three parts. The first part focused on the participants' role, qualification, tasks and work activities under normal conditions. The second part covered the participants' tasks during emergencies in our developed scenario framework. The third part covered applied information and communication systems and perceived problems with these tools. To study mobile collaboration practices more closely, also in regard to the creation, exchange and use of information by the response teams and the control centre, an additional 5, partially structured, interviews were conducted (IM1–5; each 1 hour).

Group discussions and interviews were audio recorded and later transcribed for subsequent data analysis. The analysis of the data material was based on the inductive approach found in *grounded theory* approach (Strauss, 1987). We chose this systematic methodology to discover insights about the work practices through the analysis of data. To be able to use this methodology, the transcripts were coded openly and the agents' statements were divided into text modules and later into categories. The knowledge previously acquired in the literature study was used to heighten *theoretical sensitivity* (Strauss, 1987).

5.2.2 Results I: Use of Citizen-Generated Content for Situation Assessment

Generally, it is not possible to base a situation assessment solely on the information gathered from one's own organisation. External information can improve the information basis (W3). In addition to textual data, pictures provided by citizens are often used. These pictures enable better assessment of how the emergency was caused and what the actual situation looks like:

"If you look at information during demonstrations or other events, you can see that it is often provided faster via Twitter than we can manage on police radio or mobile phone [...]. When events are taking place, they can also often be found on the internet, accompanied by pictures and videos. We will have a lot more to do with that in the future; I am pretty sure about that." (I02).

One example is the debriefing of an event: *"Our investigators like to use fire pictures because obviously, our criminal investigation is not on-site when the fire starts. Of course, they depend [on them] [...] to see the fire behaviour."* (I02).

But information is not always necessarily helpful: *"Information is only helpful when it affects my behaviour. Any information that does not affect my behaviour is a sensory overload"* (I06). An attempt is therefore made to gather only that information which is relevant: *"We try to obtain information from each and every caller"* (I15). Even in emergency situations, people on-site are becoming involved in supporting the emergency services: *"There are many special cases where you need basic skills or previous knowledge but there are also cases in which you can fall back on knowledge and skills provided by citizens"* (I11). Regardless of the large amount of information, the time factor exerts considerable pressure on the emergency services. Due to this, it is always important that each operation is executed promptly. There is *"no time to deal with strangers additionally"* (I02). The fact still remains that citizen-generated content may be defective and therefore requires information assessment.

5.2.3 Results II: Selection and Quality Assessment of Social Media Content

The question: *"Who is going to evaluate this now [...] and is it really going to help us to assess the situation?"* (I03) often appears in emergency situations. The sheer amount of citizen-generated content makes its use especially difficult: *"Above all, 290 [messages] of 300 are trash. You can only get something from ten reports"* (I02). The mass of information quickly raises the problem of how to handle it: *"You have to read them all. Of course, it would be helpful if there was a preselection"* (I02).

For this reason, automatic selection is recommendable: *"It would be nice if there were a selection that separates the important from the unimportant"* (I03). Nevertheless, information has to appear in a certain quantity to render it trustworthy for the emergency services: *"It's a problem if I only have one source. It is certainly more reliable to have five sources than just one"* (I15). External sources are especially susceptible to providing misinformation (I14, I15) and have to be verified (I15) because of this: You *"have to be careful with the content because it does not always reflect reality"* (I14)—*"In such cases it becomes obvious that someone is trying to lead us up the garden path [...] and we have to evaluate the information for ourselves"* (I02). In these cases, misinformation is not always intended; potentially it can result from the subjective perception of the situation which can appear very different to a neutral observer. In conclusion, the use of citizen-generated content from social media fails because of the need for assessment by the emergency services: *"There is simply a bottleneck which we cannot overcome"* (I02).

Overall, it is noticeable that *"the more precise information, the more relevant it is"* (I02). This kind of precision can be achieved by assessment. There has to be some form of guarantee that the selected information is useful for the emergency services (I02, I03). Global selection also proves to be difficult because *"it does not seem possible to me that we can select in advance what is important for the section leader. He might need the same information as the chief of operations—or not"* (IM01). This therefore necessitates the possibility of flexible assessment criteria (I19). Due to the time-critical aspect of emergency situations, it is imperative that the personal selection of information be supported since every member of the emergency team has to decide *"relatively quickly between the important and the unimportant"* (I19).

The first impression has to include some amount of significance and has to be helpful for the situation assessment: *"If someone he takes a photo of a window, I know that he was really there. But where is that window exactly?"* (I16). This shows that pictures need additional meta-information just as normal textual information does. Pictures can be especially helpful for assessing crowds of people at huge events: *"If someone had noticed that a relevant number of people were congregating in certain areas, you could have closed the entrance immediately with the help of the security"* (I06). Even though this entails gathering a lot of information, *"most people [...] do not [know] what counts and what kind of information we need"* (I02). There is therefore a risk that the information has no additional value and cannot be used in the emergency situation: *"I do not believe that who is not connected in some way to the police or the fire service is capable of providing useful information in these stress situations"* (I02). It is unusual for an untrained citizen to have knowledge of this sort. *"You have to be very careful with this kind of information"* (I14).

5.2.4   Results III: Responsibility and Decision Making

Ultimately, it is a member of the emergency team who has to take responsibility
for actions taken and who also has to decide if the information is used or not
(I15). Misinterpretation is possible both by humans as well as through computer
support. It does not matter how good the assessment mechanism is: there *"remains a risk and the person in charge has to bear it, it is as simple as that"* (I15).
That is the reason why the emergency services are so careful when using external
information. In conclusion, it can be stated that *"assessing information, assessing
it correctly and dealing with it [...] is a challenging task"* (I15). Every single piece
of information is an input to evaluate the whole situation: *"You add more and
more flesh to the skeleton you start off with, so that in the end, you have a picture;
not just a silhouette but a whole figure and any actions executed by the police are
mostly based on that figure"* (I16). Situation assessment influences the actions
which in return influence the situation. However, it does not always make sense
just to increase the amount of information. Because as the American political sci-
entist Simon has early stated in 1971, the higher the amount of information, the
higher the consumption of information, which in turn creates a "poverty of attention and a need to allocate that attention efficiently among the overabundance of
information sources that might consume it" (Simon, 1971).

5.3   EUD in Social Big Data Gathering and Assessment

Based on the results of our literature review, an empirical pre-study and further
analysis, we developed two tailorable services processing social media content.
This section introduces the "Social Media API" (SMA), which allows end-users
to gather, process, store and re-access social media content and it serves as a foundation of the "Social Quality Assessment Service" (Social-QAS) that facilitates
the assessment of social media content by the tailorable weighting of information
quality criteria.

5.3.1   EUD in Social Big Data Gathering

Before assessing any social media data, ways of gathering relevant information must be established with the flexibility to support EUD applications, such
as Social-QAS (section 3.3). Thus, the "Social Media API" (SMA) allows its
users to gather, process, store and re-query social media data (Reuter et al.,

2016c). Although it was developed as enabling technology for emergency management applications initially, its implementation enables the support of a variety of use cases in different fields of application, e.g. it allows its users to examine the impact of a product image within the field of market research (Reuter et al., 2016c). Because it serves as the foundation of Social-QAS, we discuss its key challenges and concepts, implementation and tailorability in the following sections.

5.3.1.1 Key Challenges and Concept

To enable access to social big data and allow subsequent analysis, our first step was to specify a service for gathering and processing social media content. During the analysis, we agreed upon the following requirements, which are partly derived from section 2.2 and enriched with considerations from conceptual and implementation viewpoints.

- *Multi-Platform Support:* Relevant data during emergencies is spread across different social media services. Furthermore, depending on the participants, different services are used. As a result, it is required that a request allows access to multiple platforms. To obtain sufficient samples and reach most users, a further requirement is therefore to allow the gathering and posting of citizen-generated information spread widely on social media services.
- *Extensible and Unified Data Format:* Both the multi-platform support and cross-platform usage imply the requirement of a standardised data format that is capable of mapping the diverse attributes, whether structured or unstructured content, of different social media content and providers. The possible emergence or relevance of new attributes, which define the activity's and users' context, requires the extensibility of the data format.
- *Gathering Service*: The historicity and volatility of social media content require the continuous capturing of citizen-generated information in nearly real time in order to accumulate a rich representation and allow post-analysis of the emergency. We therefore need to specify a service that constantly gathers the data over a defined period of time.
- *Integration of Rich Metadata:* Literature not only identifies textual content but also images, sounds and videos as important information carriers during emergencies. Furthermore, location- and time-based information are very important metadata, because they provide interesting context-data to the information itself. Therefore, a requirement is that location- and time-based data are provided with the information itself.

- *Flexible Query of Data:* Not only in the acquisition but also in the retrieval of already gathered data from database, sufficient filtering parameters are required to enable situated data analysis and provide a high degree of flexibility to support tailorable client applications or services.

5.3.1.2 Implementation of a Cross-Platform Social Media API

To gather and process social media content, we developed a REST web service called "Social Media API". With *gathering* we refer to the ability to uniquely or continuously collect social media activities (e.g., messages, photos, videos) from different platforms (Facebook, Instagram, Flickr, Reddit, Thumblr, Twitter, YouTube, as well as Google + before it was discontinued) in a unified manner using multiple search or filter criteria. *Processing* means that the API is capable of accessing, disseminating, enriching, manipulating and storing social media activities. The SMA is realised as a service following the paradigm of a web-based, service-oriented architecture (SOA). It is a Java Tomcat application using the Jersey Framework for REST services and the MongoDB database for document-oriented data management. Several libraries facilitate the integration of social media platform APIs such as Facebook Graph API or Twitter Search API. All gathered social media entities are processed and stored according to the ActivityStreams 2.0 specification (World Wide Web Consortium, 2016) in JSON format (JavaScript Object Notation). The SMA uses service interfaces, allowing a standardised implementation of further social media if its APIs provides suitable access to their data.

It comprises four main services, each providing a multitude of service functions: The *Gathering Service* comprises endpoints for gathering and loading social media activities. The main components are the Search service, enabling onetime search requests, and Crawl Service, which continuously queries new social media activities across a specified timeframe. Using the *Enrichment Service*, gathered social media activities are enriched with further computed and valuable metadata. Moreover, the *Dissemination Service* is a unified endpoint for publishing, replying to or deleting (multiple) social media activities (simultaneously). The *Data Service* provides structured database management operations. For instance, it encapsulates remote MongoDB operations to insert, load, update or delete data.

While working with SMA, based on the available type of social media, different data attributes are accessible (Table 5.1).

The implementation or support of different attributes depends on the individual policies of social media providers. For instance, while it is certainly possible to add the age to a Facebook user account, the Facebook Graph API, which provides

Table 5.1   Excerpt of Source-Based Data Attributes

Attributes	Facebook	Google + (until 2019)	Instagram	Twitter	YouTube
Date, Time	✓	✓	✓	✓	✓
Sender	✓	✓	✓	✓	✓
Age	✗	✓ (Age Range)	✗	✗	✓ (Age Range)
Location	✓	✓	✗	✓	✓
Real name	✓	✓	✓	✓	✓
Title	✗	✓	✓ (Caption)	✗	✓
Tags	✗	✗	✓	✗	✓
Replies	✓ (Comments)	✓ (Replies)	✓ (Comments)	✗	✓ (Google +)
Content	✓	✓	✓ (Caption)	✓	✓ (Description)
Mentions	✓	✗	✗	✓	✗
Views	✗	✗	✗	✗	✓
Likes	✓ (Likes)	✓ (Plusoners)	✓ (Likes)	✗	✓ (Likes)
Dislikes	✗	✗	✗	✗	✓ (Dislikes)
Retweets	✗	✗	✗	✓	✗
Shares	✓	✓ (Resharers)	✗	✗	✗

applications and developers access to Facebook data, does not allow retrieving the age of Facebook users. On the one hand, the flexibility of the document-oriented approach allows the social media users to store distinct structured documents with different numbers of attributes. Using ActivityStreams 2.0, the majority of attributes is stored according to a standardised specification. On the other hand, in terms of divergent metadata, the comparability and therefore analysis of social media activities is restricted. Therefore, it is not possible to apply all quality assessment methods in the same way. Also, because not all attributes can be mapped to the ActivityStreams 2.0 specification, we needed to add a custom property when mapping our special metadata. Furthermore, as already discussed in Section 5.3.1.2, during implementation some technical and business-oriented limitations became apparent (Reuter & Scholl, 2014): Quota limits restricted the access to social media data and most data is publicly available for a limited time only. Consequently, especially with non-expensive approaches, it is possible to capture and process merely small portions of the high-volume social data. Concerning the historicity of data, another challenge arose: As social media activities are likely to be updated regarding, for instance, the number of comments, number of likes or the content itself, inconsistencies between the online data and the stored data occur.

Besides the available data, there are two kinds of additional valuable data: First, some data is only available in certain social media, but computable for others. For instance, embedded hyperlinks, mentions or tags can be extracted from activities to get a comparable amount of data from each social media. Second, some required data regarding the assessment of quality is not available in any social media. Therefore, the SMA computes classification attributes (negative sentiment, positive sentiment, emoticon conversion, slang conversion), content attributes (number of characters, number of words, average length of words, words-to-sentences ratio, number of punctuation signs, number of syllables per word, entropy) and metadata attributes (hyperlinks, language, location, media files, tags) manually.

5.3.1.3 Tailorability: Filtering Data during Gathering and Post-Processing

A key challenge of a tailorable SMA is the provision of suitable service endpoints with sufficient filter parameters that behave consistently over heterogeneous social media. Table 5.2 summarises our implemented filter parameters of the *Crawl* and *Search* services.

The flexibility of filtering depends on the providing APIs to a certain degree: While some social media APIs support location (Twitter, YouTube) and temporal (Facebook, Twitter, YouTube) filtering, it has to be realised manually for the other ones. However, given the quota limitations of social media, manual filtering always implies the prior gathering of results that do not match the filter criteria and is therefore less efficient than using native filter parameters. Another issue is the keyword parameter, because social media processes keywords differently and supports various types and notations of logical query operators (e.g., and, or, not, or similar phrases). Here, the need for a unified query language and layer becomes apparent, which translates the unified query parameters into the platform-specific parameters.

After data is gathered and stored into the database, the access becomes an important factor to allow loading and post-processing of data. Given the job id, social media activities of past crawl or search jobs can be loaded and filtered by count (amount of data returned) and offset (position of the first result to be returned) parameters. Alternatively, a list of activity ids allows loading the desired social media activities explicitly. However, to enhance the tailorability of SMA in order to increase the flexibility for consuming client applications, the implementation of additional parameters is planned, e.g., keyword, platform, location and time-based filtering, or language. In this case, the efficiency and flexibility of filtering is dependent on the underlying database management solution. Based on the SMA, the application Social Data Service has been implemented, which aims to allow the generation of data sets (Reuter et al., 2016c).

Table 5.2 Parameters for Social Media Search

Parameter	Type	Description
Keywords	String	Required. The search term.
platforms	String	Required. A csv-list (Facebook, Google +, Instagram, Twitter, YouTube).
since	Long	Search Service. Lower bound of the searched timeframe (Unix time).
until	Long	Search Service. Upper bound of the searched timeframe (Unix time).
start	String	Crawl Service. Starting point of the crawl job (Unix time, default: now).
end	String	Crawl Service. Termination of the crawl job (Unix time, default: null).
latitude	Double	Latitude for geo search (decimal degree).
longitude	Double	Longitude for geo search (decimal degree).
radius	Double	Radius for geo search (km).

5.3.2   EUD in Social Big Data Assessment

As our literature review suggests, citizens may provide emergency-relevant information via social media, but challenges regarding the quality of information, especially under time-critical constraints, persist. Moreover, our pre-study and further literature report on the relevance of quality-relevant metadata during emergencies, e.g., author reputation, location and time. That is why the "Social Quality Assessment Service" (Social-QAS) aims on facilitating the assessment of social media content by the tailorable weighting of information quality criteria. This section refers to content that has already been published in a research paper

(Reuter et al., 2015c), but is required to introduce the application's concept, depict its evaluation and elaborate the chapter's discussion.

5.3.2.1 Key Challenges and Concept

Our literature review and the empirical study have proven that the quality assessment of mass information and extractions of relevant information is a great challenge. Of course, various circumstances call for various assessment methods. That is why the possibility to combine these methods could help to improve the quality assessment practice (Ludwig et al., 2015). Our concept allows the assessment of (social media) content with 15 assessment methods (Table 5.3), which are subdivided into four categories pursuant to their technical execution:

1. The *rating of metadata* consists of five assessment methods (author frequency, temporal proximity, local proximity, number of followers/likes, amount of metadata), in which either the discrepancy from the entered research criteria or the absolute appearance is defined by rating the difference.
2. The *rating based on the content* allocates two assessment methods (frequency of search keyword, stop words), which identify the occurrence of particular words (or their synonyms) from a list.
3. The *rating based on the classification of the message* supplies six assessment methods (sentiment analysis, fear factor, happiness factor, named entity recognition, emoticon, slang), which determine the occurrence of words applying word lists. Thus, information is sorted in different categories.
4. The *rating based on scientific methods* provides two assessment methods (Shannon Information Theory (Entropy), term frequency, inverse document frequency).

A subjective quality of information can be defined if the (non-specified) end-user of an application based on Social-QAS has the option to select various assessment methods. In addition to that, this selection and the classification enable further use of the quality assessment service within several scenarios. Generally speaking: Initially, the individual messages are analysed absolutely regarding the specific method. Then the score of each message is determined. The message with the highest absolute score is rated with "1.0" (100%), the one with the lowest absolute score gets a "0.0" (0%). After that, an overall score is received by weighting the single scores. Further, to address both the requirements of querying multiple sources and enabling the subjectivity of quality assessment, the individual user gets the option to choose the desired social media sources.

Table 5.3 Implemented Quality Assessment Methods (Reuter et al., 2015c)

#	Method / Criterion	Description
A	**Assessment of metadata**	
1	Author Frequency (Reputation)	Number of messages from the same author in the message set. The level of knowledge about the situation depends on the number of messages an author writes.
2	Temporal Proximity (Currency)	Temporal proximity of the messages to the centre of the search period. The information's importance depends on the proximity to the search moment.
3	Local Proximity	Distance between the place where the message was created and the incident's place. Short distance stands for higher probability that the message is about the current disaster.
4	Followers / Likes (Credibility)	It is assumed that credibility and the number of likes/followers conferred on a particular message/author grow proportionally.
5	Metadata (Pictures/Links)	It can be helpful to complement textual information with an image or other media material. With this assessment criterion the amount of data can be ascertained.
B	**Assessment based on content**	
6	Frequency of search keyword (Interpretability)	The keyword indicates the issue; it does not appear randomly in the message. The message is also searched for synonyms.
7	Stop words	Stop words such as "so" do not allocate any information as long as they do not increase the validity of the message. That is why the decrease of stop words increases message utility.
C	**Assessment based on classification of the message**	
8	Sentiment Analysis (Impartiality)	The message is analysed concerning its emotional property. Emotional content, especially fear, can falsify the meaning.

(continued)

Table 5.3 (continued)

#	Method / Criterion	Description
9	Negative Sentiment (Fear Factor)	Words that are related to the subject of fear are identified in the message; The Fear Factor determines the degree of expression of fear.
10	Positive Sentiment (Happiness Factor)	Words that are related to the subject of joy are identified in the message; The Happiness Factor determines the degree of expression of joy.
11	Named Entity Recognition (NER)	Number of entities in the message. The relation between the information's content and another information source is indicated by an entity. The more entities, the higher the information quality.
12	Emoticon Conversion	The possibility to make a message readable for different audiences by converting emoticons into language expressions.
13	Slang Conversion	The possibility to make a message readable for different audiences by converting slang words into standard language.
D	**Assessment based on scientific methods**	
14	tf-Idf (term frequency—Inverse document frequency)	The appearance of individual search keywords (term frequency) with the frequency of appearance in all messages (inverse document frequency). Helpful if more than one single keyword is used since the occurrence of a fragment of the whole term, which only appears frequently in few documents, is weighted higher than the occurrence of a fragment, which appears in many documents but less frequently. $tf(t,d) = \frac{f(t,d)}{\max\{f(w,d):w\in d\}}$
15	Shannon Information Theory (Entropy)	Shannon theory of information. The average amount of information contained in each message received. $I(p_x) = \log_a\left(\frac{1}{p_x}\right) = -\log_a(p_x)$

5.3.2.2 Implementation of Social-QAS

The actual quality assessment service is conceived as a service that follows the paradigms of a web-based, service-oriented architecture (SOA). The use of such architecture enables a central rating and makes it possible to integrate it into various applications by allocating assessment results with the original data in JSON format (JavaScript Object Notation). The interface is called "via HTTP-GET" and the URL is complemented with query parameters, which are separated by "&". The client's processing load is supposed to decrease by the server-sided information rating. Via SMA, as illustrated in Figure 5.1, the APIs of the particular social network providers are used to extract data from the social networks (Reuter & Scholl, 2014). In this context, especially Twitter and Facebook appear to be essential APIs: these APIs allocate many possibilities to both export and import data concerning the related social network.

To collect the semantic content of the message, one can apply a Named Entity Recognizer (NER) (No.11). The Stanford NER[3] is available as Java library for free. The corpus "deWac generalised classifier" was used for the NER because it works exceptionally well with German messages from social networks. The library Classifier[4] was utilised for the creation of a Bayes Classifier (No. 8) that enables the division of information into various categories since it can be skilled with lists of words. The list of synonyms (No. 6) was created by applying the Open Thesaurus web services[5]. One requires a geographical reference in order to visualise the information; however, in many cases the information does not contain any geographical metadata so that it has to be geocoded. The Gisgraphy Geocoder[6] is usable by web services and geocodes location information for any map material. To accelerate the process, there is a list of locations which have already been geolocated and whereof the coordinates can be defined without geolocation. GSON[7] is used for conversion since it allocates an automatic generation of a JSON object based on a java object model.

5.3.2.3 Tailorability: Integration of Social-QAS into a web Application

To test the implemented service, we have integrated Social-QAS into a web-based application specified for emergency services as well as a Facebook-app "XHELP"

---

[3] http://nlp.stanford.edu/software/CRF-NER.shtml.

[4] http://classifier4j.sourceforge.net/

[5] http://www.openthesaurus.de/

[6] http://www.gisgraphy.com/

[7] https://code.google.com/p/google-gson/

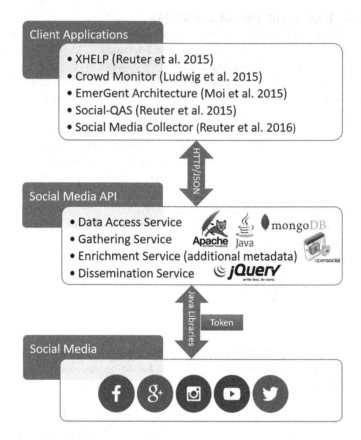

Figure 5.1 Overall Architecture of Client Applications such as Social-QAS that use the Social Media API to Access Different Social Media over a Unified Interface

to support volunteer moderators during disasters. In the following we will out-line prototypically the implementation into XHELP, which allows information to be both acquired and distributed cross-media and cross-channel (Reuter et al., 2015b).

Inside this application, it is possible to search for information by using differ-ent quality parameters in order to perform a quality assessment (Figure 5.2). For this, the user chooses an assessment criterion with the help of a slider. Integrating the user in this way meets the requirements for a flexible and manageable quality assessment, as identified in the pre-study.

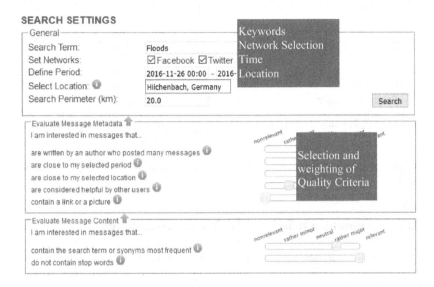

Figure 5.2 Quality Assessment Service Integrated into an Application

The search results are presented in a table and on a visual situation map. An abundance of meta-information such as the degree of completion of particular methods is illustrated as tool tips in the table. Simultaneously, the situation map makes it possible to directly determine the proximity of the information to the search location (Figure 5.3). Thus, the user may select one mode in which s/he wishes to view the results; this method improves the flexibility of the application. This user interface is only one of several possibilities how Social-QAS can be applied.

To sum up, Social-QAS unifies the following functionalities (Reuter et al., 2015c): Assessment takes place on the basis of metadata as well as on the basis of content. The user decides upon the weighting of each method. When all the assessments of every method have been combined, the subjective quality of a message develops. Social-QAS is very flexible since it makes it possible to expand the sources and assessment methods very easily. Due to the SOA-based implementation it is possible to integrate it and use it in other applications.

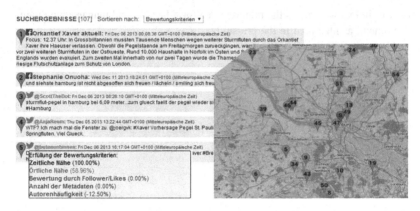

Figure 5.3   Search Results (left), Degree of Completion (Lower Left) and Map Presentation (Right)

5.4   Evaluation: Tailorable Quality Assessment

To answer the question how tailorable assessment services can be provided to users properly and how users can articulate the assessment criteria appropriately, Social-QAS has been evaluated by potential end-users.

5.4.1   Methodology

The philosophy behind the evaluation process was derived from the notion of "situated evaluation" (Twidale et al., 1994), in which qualitative methods are applied to draw conclusions about real-world use of a technology using domain experts. The purpose is to derive subjective views from experts about how useful and relevant the technology might be in use instead of measuring the relationship between evaluation goals and outcomes.

In order to obtain as much knowledge as possible about the potential of the service and the quality assessment of citizen-generated information, the evaluation consisted of a scenario-based walkthrough with a subsequent semi-structured interview. The participants were directed to tell us their thoughts according to the think-aloud protocol (Nielsen, 1993), enabling underlying reasoning and subjective impressions to be gathered. Each evaluation took about 45 minutes and was performed with 20 people in all (E1-E20). Besides general knowledge on the use of social media, 15 participants were skilled technology experts, four partici-pants had been initiators and moderators of Facebook pages during the European floods in 2013, and one was member of a voluntary fire brigade. Any participant who was not a volunteer using social media very actively had a role defini-tion introduced to them, enabling them to place themselves in the position of a volunteer.

The scenario was supposed to show the participants a disaster's character and what volunteers do in crises (unless the participant was already an experienced volunteer). They worked on the basis of hurricane Xaver, which destroyed big parts of the German coast in December 2013. The participants got a general role description in order to know how to deal with the information demands of affected citizens with the help of Social-QAS embedded in XHELP (see Section 5.3.2.3). After that, the participants had the chance to get to know the application by solving a concrete problem: they were supposed to filter and search specific information about water levels. An evaluation mode was added to the search function for this purpose. The results of the search were assumed before-hand on preselected data records in order to be sure that the participants' results were comparable. In the following, semi-structured interviews were meant to support reflection on the evaluation process, on handling and the overall appli-cation's value. The questions were specialised in overall impressions concerning quality assessment, the advantages and disadvantages of Social-QAS, coverage of information demands, influence on information flow, potential overload and problems of cross-platform information acquisition. The interviews were evalu-ated and classified systematically. "Open" coding was employed, i.e., distributing data into adequate categories to reflect the issues raised by respondents relying on repeated readings of the data and its grouping into "similar" statements. The most remarkable classifications will be presented in the following.

5.4.2   Results I: How much Tailoring? Quality Assessment Criteria

Many users considered the number of assessment criteria to be too high for effective use under the time-critical constraints of emergencies (E09, E07, E19). Nonetheless, the respondents agreed with the opinion that different situations require different assessment criteria (E12, E13, E08); and that a certain adjust-ment of the criteria to the situation is necessary: *There are many criteria, but I think that this is important, because different questions require different search key-words* (E13). Accordingly, the suggestion was made that the assessment criteria could be adjusted in such a way that allows the goal to be achieved more quickly (E12). Furthermore, other possibilities—for example the opportunity to search for a hyponym (E19)—were requested in addition to the various settings. The evaluation demonstrated that the biggest challenge to be overcome is the identification of criteria of appropriate quality. Although currency was an important criterion for all respondents, only a few understood the meaning of coordinate quality. The explanation of coordinate quality as a measure for the local proximity helped them to understand its meaning. One participant raised the question of the correlation between the author's number of subscribers and his reputation (E4).

5.4.3   Results II: Broad Information Basis and Information Overload

In order to achieve a situational overview of an emergency setting, users especially regarded the opportunity to consider different information sources simultaneously to be an added value (E19, E15, E18): *"Because public networks are used such a lot, it is much better to relate them to each other. That could really help to meet the information need"* (E17). The number of sources should be steadily supplemented with further useful sources. What is more, not only social networks but also e.g., news sites should be taken into consideration. Furthermore, the interviewed persons were afraid of being confronted by a flood of information while searching for information in social networks during a large-scale emergency (E16, E19). This fear was soon quelled by sorting the results in Social-QAS. Most users did not want to go through the entire list of search results, but preferred to only look at the first few results on the list. Still, it should remain possible for the user to see the additional results at will since some scenarios potentially require an inspection of the additional results.

5.4.4   Results III: Automatic and Tailorable Quality Assessment Necessary

The quality assessment of information proceeds automatically. Users accept this automatism as they have the possibility to control the assessment and are able to comprehend why something was assessed in a particular way (E08, E11). *"As always, when something is evaluated, that does not replace your own opinion"* (E10). Yet the general possibility to combine criteria was considered a benefit:

"The default settings do not matter. That means if I do nothing, my search results will not change" (E13). *"As a consequence, diverse combinations are possible, of course, which seems to me to be helpful"* (E07). To counter negative impacts on actions, manual post-processing should be implemented, allowing the correction or recognition of defective entries.

Considering the possibilities and suggestions for improvement shown (E13, E19, E14), there is potential to improve the information flow in emergency situations. This could especially be realised by the classification of emergency situations and a preset of weightings based on this. Crucial temporal and organisational bottlenecks could be avoided by collecting information from local people (real volunteers) or the internet (digital volunteers) (Reuter et al., 2013) (E07, E16): *"The benefits are that I can find things quickly, [...] because it is possible to search specifically for something and that is really displayed on the different platforms, just how I want it. And I can weight very easily using the assessment criteria"* (E18).

5.5   Design Requirements and Social Media Observatory

From the perspective of EUD, many systems for analysing social media offer more or less customisation possibilities and are aimed at end-users who have little or no technical knowledge. However, the adaptability is largely limited to visualisation elements, e.g., in form of a central dashboard. There, the presented figures are prepared in such a way that the end-user can scale and analyse along fixed dimensions. At another level of customisation, there are systems such as HootSuite, which provide strong software extensibility by providing their own SDK. Expert users are able to create new functionalities available to all end-users. These extensions do not affect the design of the analysis process; thus, the end-user cannot tailor it to the individual preferences. The system alert.io with the structure of a learning process of tonality analysis shows approaches to such extensibility. An end-user trains this component based on his or her own situation understanding so that the machine learning algorithm can work independently on new data from a certain size of the experience data base. However, crisis management needs to "adjust and adapt its performance to fit the demands of an ever-changing physical, engineered, and social environment" (Comfort, 2007).

This chapter demonstrates how it is possible to combine EUD and social big data. It discusses how situation assessment practices of crisis management actors, namely emergency services (Ludwig et al., 2015a) and informal volunteers (Reuter et al., 2015b), can be encouraged by tailorable quality assessment of citizen-generated information from social media. At the beginning, the results of an empirical study involving emergency services concerning the use of citizen-generated content and social media within their current work practices are summarised. With the help of literature and empirical findings we identified the need for different quality criteria and applied them on information from social media. We implemented our own Social Media API and a quality assessment service.

We come to three results that extend the current state of the art:

(1) An analysis of dealing with citizen-generated content in emergencies by means of an empirical study, which emphasises the range and quality assessment of citizen-generated content in emergencies (Reuter & Ritzkatis, 2014).

(2) A concept for a tailorable social media gathering (Section 5.3.1.1) and quality assessment service (Section 5.3.2.1) for social media as well as a running implementation which is SOA-oriented, tailorable and can be applied in various applications (Reuter et al., 2015c; Reuter et al., 2016c).

(3) A reference implementation of the gathering service (Section 5.3.1.2) as well as quality assessment service (Section 5.3.2.2) inside an existing web-based application for emergency services (Ludwig et al., 2015a) and an existing web-app for volunteers (Reuter et al., 2015b) (Section 5.3.2.3).

The contribution of this chapter is to show the process from data selection to use from an EUD perspective including pre-study, design, implementation and evaluation in order to generate findings to the field.

To sum up, it is useful to be flexible by tailoring options for source platform selection and quality assessment criteria since situation assessment revealed itself to be very subjective. Consequently, personal feelings, experience and the situation itself influence the information requirement. Furthermore, some negative views on automated quality assessment seem to be very pessimistic, perhaps partly due to the perceived risk of being replaced by machines.

Our findings turned out to be interesting for other application fields as well. While gathering or analysing information and implementing information systems to encourage the task, there is always one question that is hard to answer: How can we realise information systems, which enable the automatic selection of relevant data and, simultaneously, grant end-users the option to adapt this automation, thus allowing tailorable quality assessment pursuant to their requirements?

In terms of big data, some restrictions are apparent: Although social media provides high-volume, high-velocity and a high-variety (McAfee & Brynjolfsson, 2012) of social data (Dijcks, 2012), the access is limited allowing client applications such as Social Media API and Social-QAS to merely gather small portions of data (Reuter & Scholl, 2014). Even with continuously gathering new data and filling the database, the volume and velocity of data processing in client applications like those will be small compared to the daily data creation in social media (Kaisler et al., 2013). Therefore, in high-volume scenarios, valuable information according to the user-selected quality criteria may be missed. In future work, it is important to examine how the end-user can be better integrated into the analysis process by applying machine learning to ensure the adaptability and alignment of the analysis of social media in the dynamic context of end-users.

Our work still has some limitations. Not all the criteria that are relevant for quality assessment are included within Social-QAS. Furthermore, according to the context, the number of criteria might overburden the cognitive skills of end-users. It is therefore important to define standards and to allow end-users to adapt them, whereby different tailoring power might then require different skills, according to MacLean et al. (1990); thus, local developers may be required (Gantt & Nardi, 1992).

The work presented above inspired us to develop the Social Media Observatory (SMO) (Kaufhold et al., 2022)—a user interface which allows for social media messages to be monitored, analysed, and classified (Kaufhold et al., 2020a). Creating social media datasets, creating machine learning classifiers, disseminating messages, as well as managing users, are all facilitated by the SMO. Originally, the SMO was created as interface for the SMA (Reuter et al., 2016c). The current version's main features are now included in Figure 5.4: Displayed on the dashboard are characteristics of the loaded dataset (e.g., language, media, number of results, post frequency, and sentiment), as well as visualizing posts on a map and in social feeds. Besides basic settings, e.g., to refresh the dashboard, it further supports visual interactive filtering. An additional feature to the SMO includes an annotation tool to create datasets for machine learning classifiers. This feature ensures that classifiers for credibility and relevance assessment can be designed and used to filter out unreliable and irrelevant information from the dashboard view. Furthermore, the interface comprises a feedback mechanism. This allows emergency services to correct any of the algorithm's misclassifications and thus improve the accuracy of classifiers.

Figure 5.4 Social Media Observatory (SMO) dashboard with interactive charts, feed and list view

5.6   Summary and Next Steps

Although emergency services mentioned sharing information with the public (85%) as the most important use of social media in emergencies, gaining situational awareness (71%) also received high approval (Section 3.3.2.1). This chapter therefore explored situation assessment and, based on an empirical study, found that (1) the fact that citizen-generated content may be flawed requires information assessment, and that automation might support this, however "it is a member of the emergency team who has to take responsibility for actions taken and who also has to decide if the information is used or not". Based on this, this chapter presents (2) a technical concept for a tailorable social media gathering and quality assessment service for social media as well as an (3) evaluation, which shows that "users accept […] automatism as they have the possibility to control the assessment and are able to comprehend why something was assessed in a particular way".

Nevertheless, this only presents the perspective of emergencies services. After examining the collection and analysis of social big data from a technological perspective, the next step is to use the concepts developed in this chapter in the scenario of self-organisation of digital volunteers (Chapter 6).

Self-Organisation of Digital Volunteers across Social Media

6

Recent disasters have shown an increase in the significance of social media for both affected citizens and volunteers alike in the coordination of information and organisation of relief activities, often independently of and in addition to the official emergency response. Existing research mainly focuses on the ways in which individual platforms are used by volunteers in response to disasters. This chapter examines the use of social media during the European Floods of 2013 and proposes a novel cross-social-media application for volunteers.

First, the results of an empirical study are presented. Public reporting during the event indicated, and our analysis confirms that Twitter, Facebook (FB), Google Maps and other services were frequently used by affected citizens and volunteers to coordinate help activities among themselves. We conducted a qualitative analysis of selected emergent volunteer communities in Germany on FB and Twitter among others, and subsequently conducted interviews with FB group founders and activists. Our aim was to analyse the use of social media during this particular event, especially with regard to the activities of digital volunteers. Our study illustrates the relevance of social media for German citizens in cases of disaster, focusing especially on the role of the moderator. Our particular focus was the embedding of social media in the organisational work conducted by said volunteers, emphasising both the patterns of social media use and resulting challenges. We show that different social media platforms were used in different ways: Twitter was primarily used for status updates while FB-pages were mostly intended to provide an overview of a broad range of information. FB-groups also coordinated a multitude of activities.

Supplementary Information The online version contains supplementary material available at https://doi.org/10.1007/978-3-658-39720-3_6.

© The Author(s), under exclusive license to Springer Fachmedien Wiesbaden GmbH, part of Springer Nature 2022
C. Reuter, *A European Perspective on Crisis Informatics*,
https://doi.org/10.1007/978-3-658-39720-3_6

Second, the results of our design case study (Wulf et al., 2011) are presented, which aims to examine how real and virtual relief activities might be supported by specific tools. These activities are initiated and coordinated through the use of social media. Challenges were identified based on this study and an attempt was made to address these challenges by means of XHELP, our cross-social-media application for volunteers in emergencies, particularly for moderators of emerging groups. We finally evaluated XHELP with 20 users.

*This chapter has been published as two articles: "**The Self-Organisation of Digital Volunteers across Social Media: The Case of the 2013 European Floods in Germany**" by Marc-André Kaufhold and Christian Reuter in the Journal of Homeland Security and Emergency Management (JHSEM) (Kaufhold & Reuter, 2016) [Paper H] as well as "**XHELP: Cross-Platform Social-Media Application for Volunteer Moderators**" by Christian Reuter, Thomas Ludwig, Marc-André Kaufhold and Volkmar Pipek in the Proceedings of the Conference on Human Factors in Computing Systems (CHI) (Reuter et al., 2015b) [Paper I]. Almost this entire chapter has been published as Paper I, however the empirical study in Section 6.2 has been published as part of Paper H.*

6.1   Related Work

6.1.1   Real and Digital Volunteers in Emergencies

Basically, organised volunteering during disasters is not a novel phenomenon: Nearly 40 years ago, these "emergent groups" were characterised as "private citizens who work together in pursuit of collective goals relevant to actual or potential disasters but whose organisation has not yet become institutionalized" (Stallings & Quarantelli, 1985). According to Quarantelli (1984), the essential conditions for their emergence are (a) a legitimising social environment, (b) a perceived threat, (c) a supporting social climate, (d) a network of social relationships, and (e) the availability of specific (immaterial) resources. Based on the analysis of self-organisation and community management during disasters (Comfort, 1994) recommends to develop a "search, exchange and maintenance of information", to "engage responsible organisations in a regular process of communication" and to "invest in information technology and infrastructure that will allow community organisations—to operate as a complex system". The broad acceptance of social media has, however, widened the possibility for crisis communication from authorities to citizens as well as the coordination of voluntary activities (Reuter et al., 2012). Reuter et al. (2013) distinguish between activities in the "real" and the "virtual" world. A distinction becomes apparent between real "emergent groups" (Stallings & Quarantelli, 1985), which usually act in the form of neighbourly help and on-site work, and virtual "digital volunteers" (Starbird & Palen, 2011), who originate from the Internet and work online. Accordingly, one of the main challenges is to bring these communities together.

6.1.2   Volunteers and Social Media

The emergence of digital volunteers and "voluntweeters" (Starbird & Palen, 2011) (digital volunteers in the Twitter sphere) and their use of social media has been studied in the context of various disasters: Users organise and disseminate crisis-related information (Heverin & Zach, 2010), seek information about peoples' status (Qu et al., 2011), express solidarity (Starbird & Palen, 2012) or coordinate both material and immaterial resources (Perng et al., 2012). Starbird and Palen (2011) suggested that personal relationships with people affected and the pure desire to help were the initial reasons for using Twitter during disasters. The prospect of *identifying, amplifying* and *redirecting information* was examined in multiple studies, which highlight the role of retweeting, and outline the phenomena of information *broadcasting* or information processing through filtering (Starbird & Palen, 2012). Another important aspect is the *verification* of information as there are obvious issues with regard to the perceived credibility of social media content in comparison with other media. Information with no clear source, for instance, can be implicated in the spread of rumour (Oh et al., 2013). Even so, activities of *structuring and synthesising* become apparent (Vieweg et al., 2010). The studies cited analysed how Twitter can contribute to the production of an overall, coherent picture which enables an appropriate response to the developing situation (Reilly et al., 2007), and indicate that tweets including situational updates or geolocations are more likely to be retweeted than others. Volunteer role classifications include "helper", "reporter", "retweeter", "repeater" and "reader" (Reuter et al., 2013) as well as "information broker", gathering and reporting information (Vieweg et al., 2008). Kaufhold and Reuter (2014) suggest "moderators", who establish supportive platforms for real and virtual activities, mediate offers of and requests for assistance, mobilise resources and integrate information of various sources.

6.1.3   Volunteers—Potentials and Obstacles

Digital volunteerism, then, might have both positive and negative consequences. Many studies highlight the "chaotic" or disorganised work of volunteers (Kaewk-itipong et al., 2012; Valecha et al., 2013), whose activities are indisputably valuable, but which also often lead to confusion. Activities in danger-zones have the potential to increase not only the complexity of tasks but also uncertainty and the pressure on emergency services, especially if the volunteers themselves are endangered (Perng et al., 2013). Valecha et al. (2013) suggest that "whenever there is greater uncertainty reduction needed, there will be a larger amount of collaboration on the platform", while uncertainty can be generated and ampli-fied by redundant information and mistakes due to the chaotic "disorganised" work of volunteers. Accordingly, Kaewkitipong et al. (2012) describe the actions taken by the emergency services to correct the mistakes caused by the "emerg-ing risks of the chaotic use of social media". Another suggested remedy lies with so-called "community scouts" (Reuter et al., 2012). In one case, a group of "trusted volunteers" was respectively formed to monitor social media and transfer "semi-official" reports to officials (St. Denis et al., 2012).

Different social media platforms entail different forms of communication (Hughes et al., 2014). Nevertheless, most studies focus on the use of Twitter, per-haps due to the ease of data access or the frequency of use (Reuter et al., 2012). However, in many European countries such as Germany—where our study per-taining to the European floods was conducted—56% of all Internet users actively use FB, whereas the active usage of Twitter is significantly lower at just 6% (BITKOM, 2013). Yet, Birkbak (2012) claims to have published one of the first comparative case studies of public FB groups in emergencies, showing that more research is needed. The use of more "closed" social media creates new design requirements, e.g. to make them more listenable. Thus, "data showed that replies by emergency managers to questions from the public were often buried within response threads to individual messages" (Hughes et al., 2014). They suggest that "to make online media streams more "listenable" for on-the-ground emergency managers, new [...] tools are needed that allow emergency managers to better track, respond to, and document public information".

Research efforts have been largely geared to identify as design requirements. Reuter et al. (2013) propose (a) the integration of ICT for volunteers into exist-ing networks, (b) the fostering of voluntary groups coming into existence, (c) connection between virtual and real activities, and (d) interfaces with official cri-sis management. Furthermore, based on interviews with emergency services and digital volunteers, Cobb et al. (2014) suggest (a) the coordination and integration of voluntary activities, (b) the connection between different tools and tasks as well as (c) the option to share their own activities in order to generate learning effects for spontaneous and often less experienced volunteers. They argue to query multiple social networks with filter options.

6.1.4 Existing Approaches and Tools

A number of public, scientific or commercial applications have been developed for coping with social media (Pohl, 2013). While they are being directly or indirectly developed for crisis management, they often contain limitations, as will be explained in the following. They either have (a) syntactical requirements, (b) do not support cross-media communication, or (c) are not integrated in networks users are familiar with (Table 6.1).

Table 6.1 Several Existing Approaches and Tools

Tool and Reference	a	b	c
Brandwatch (Brandwatch, 2014)			✗
Geofeedia (Geofeedia Inc, 2014)			✗
Hands2Help (Hofmann et al., 2014)	✗	✗	✗
HierarchicalTopics (Dou et al., 2013)			✗
Hootsuite (Hootsuite Media Inc, 2014)			✗
SensePlace2 (Robinson et al., 2013)		✗	✗
Sproutsocial (Sprout Social, 2014)			✗
Tweak the Tweet (Starbird & Stamberger, 2010)	✗	✗	
TweetDeck (Twitter, 2014)		✗	✗
Twitcident (Terpstra et al., 2012)		✗	✗
TwitInfo (Marcus et al., 2011)		✗	✗
UberMetrics (uberMetrics Technologies GmbH, 2014)			✗
Ushahidi (Okolloh, 2009)		✗	✗
Visual Backchannel (Dörk et al., 2010)		✗	✗

TweetDeck (Twitter, 2014) is a publicly available tool for real-time tracking, organising and engagement. It enables Tweet publication, management and search (based on quantitative criteria). Multiple approaches aim to provide visualisation which supplements the common activity- or list-based view of social media. For instance, *Visual Backchannel* (Dörk et al., 2010) offers a multi-faceted visual overview enriching queried tweets with a temporal topic stream, a spiral of involved people and an image cloud. *TwitInfo* (Marcus et al., 2011) additionally presents a message frequency graph and evaluates the overall positive and negative sentiment of the analysed set of tweets in a pie chart. *HierarchicalTopics* (Dou et al., 2013) is an approach for visually exploring large text collections; however, the system is not customised for citizens. Other platforms concentrate on the map-based visualisation of data: *Ushahidi* (Okolloh, 2009), for example, is a platform for the collection and visualisation of information and interactive mapping. Supporting multiple data streams, e.g., text messages via smartphone app, e-mail, Twitter, and web forms, it allows the dissemination of reports which can be displayed via list or geo-reference in a map view. Similar to *SensePlace2* (Robinson et al., 2013), Ushahidi enables the chronological filtering of messages. The downside of Ushahidi is, however, that it requires the deployment of a separate platform, while SensePlace2 is not publicly available. Although a closed system, *Hands2Help* (Hofmann et al., 2014) is a mobile app concept which intends to coordinate volunteers in terms of supply and demand of help, enabling ad hoc registration and allowing efficient allocation and monitoring. An exceptional solution is the *Tweak the Tweet* (Starbird & Stamberger, 2010) micro syntax for Twitter, allowing for the automatic classification of information by means of specific hashtags and tweet structure. So far, it is the only approach which is integrated in an existing network, but has syntactical requirements and is limited to Twitter.

Furthermore, there are plenty of commercial platforms providing cross-media functionalities: Hootsuite, Sproutsocial, *Brandwatch* (Brandwatch, 2014), Twitcident and *UberMetrics* (uberMetrics Technologies GmbH, 2014) each support the monitoring, filtering and analysis of various social media utilising a dashboard feature. However, these dashboard reports and visualisations focus on categories such as business performance, competitor benchmarking and brand analytics. Using dashboards for volunteer activities therefore requires the identification of relevant information categories. For example, *Geofeedia* (Geofeedia Inc, 2014) focuses on the monitoring of specific and configurable geographic locations. In addition to the presented functionalities, *Hootsuite* (Hootsuite Media Inc, 2014) and *Sproutsocial* (Sprout Social, 2014) both provide message publication and scheduling for public engagement as well as a team collaboration module which, for instance, allows the setup of permissions and roles, additional to the assignment and management of tasks. Moreover, *Twitcident* (Terpstra et al., 2012), which addresses emergency services, contributes the functionalities of event and incident detection. In conclusion, these approaches provide the features of dashboards, geographic monitoring, bidirectional message publication and task management. All these functions could be useful in supporting volunteer activities, but as commercial B2B products they are not available to a broad audience and do not address all requirements for volunteer moderators.

To summarise, almost all approaches (Table 6.1) have limitations with regard to volunteer moderators in disasters: Most of them either demand syntactical requirements from the user (Starbird & Stamberger, 2010); do not provide cross-platform structures, e.g. focus solely on Twitter (Dörk et al., 2010; Marcus et al., 2011; Okolloh, 2009; Robinson et al., 2013; Terpstra et al., 2012; Twitter, 2014), or require the use of a new platform and therefore fail to integrate ICT for volunteers into existing networks.

6.1.5 State of Play

Despite the outlined design requirements mentioned above, there is little existing research which focuses on the development of technical artifacts to support the rich coordination activities of digital volunteers—especially on how to support the "community scouts" (Reuter et al., 2012) or "trusted volunteers" (St. Denis et al., 2012) who appear in the form of very active "moderators" (Kaufhold & Reuter, 2014) during crises. Thus, our design case study seeks to enhance the state of the art by providing a cross-social-media case study based on the 2013 European floods in order to derive challenges, which in turn inform the design, development and evaluation of a technical artefact to support the current practices of volunteers in disasters and "to make online media streams more 'listenable'" (Hughes et al., 2014).

Our research questions are as follows: *How were different types of social media used during the European floods? How was social media used to organise volunteers?* And: *What are the challenges for collaboration support?*

6.2 Empirical Study

6.2.1 Methodology

Our empirical study aims to examine the use of social media for the coordination of volunteer relief activities. For this, we initially analysed six FB-communities, evaluated tweets and conducted seven semi-structured interviews (Table 6.2). We also make occasional use of further sources. Our work is thus based on the case study approach described by e.g. Stake (1995) and Yin (2014), which allows for the detailed exploration of a phenomenon within some bounded context (see also Creswell, 2013). The approach by Yin, in particular, allows for comparative work across multiple cases and distinguishes exploratory and explanatory case studies. Our work on the 2013 floods clearly explores data across what we can reasonably describe as a bounded context (the floods), but which nevertheless compares across three individual cases.

The FB analysis explored messages in three groups and from three pages from three federal states in order to analyse processes regarding interaction, structuring and task sharing. Starting on June 6th, FB-group and page activities were down-loaded and updated regularly as complete HTML documents to extend and refine our analysis. The last update was performed on October 31st. Additionally, news articles in the context of the floods were archived as PDF files and more than 50 screenshots were saved in order to document the use of Google Maps in the affected areas.

In addition, from June 6th to June 27th 2013 nearly 80,000 tweets containing the term or hashtag "Hochwasser" (English: flood) were archived using the tool "Tweet Archivist Desktop". We used the term "Hochwasser" because it was listed among the top trends in Twitter and was mentioned in several media. Our Twitter analysis consisted of two steps: First, we explored the whole dataset to extract quantitative features (e.g., overall number and temporal distribution of tweets, retweets, media, embedded URLs; tweets and retweets per user; other hashtags used along with "Hochwasser") and conceive the structure and topics of the information space. Subsequently, we focused on a reduced dataset of 1,602 tweets (containing relevant keywords like "urgent", "need", "offer" or "help") to examine how and in what ways relief activities were shaped in and by Twitter.

In the next step of our empirical study, we recruited moderators and helpers of the FB-communities in question via e-mail and private FB-messages, conduct-ing both local and phone interviews to gain insights into their work practices, ways of mobilising resources (Perng et al., 2012) and self-organisation processes (Starbird & Palen, 2011) as well as identifying the potential ways to support them. The interviews were designed to specifically address our interests. Initially, the interviewees were asked whether they belonged to an organisation of civil protection or had competencies regarding professional crisis response. Follow-ing this, we focused on the tasks and activities of the respondents, whereby we were particularly interested in the relationship between online or virtual activity and mobilisation 'on the ground'. The third part concentrated on task-sharing processes, during which potential cooperation with emergency services

Table 6.2 The Three Cases of Our Empirical Study

Case	A	B	C
State	Saxony-Anhalt	Lower Saxony	Bavaria
FB-Pages	Hochwassernews Magdeburg (Flood News Magdeburg)	Hochwasser Niedersachsen (Flood Lower Saxony)	Passau räumt auf (Passau cleans up)
FB-Groups	Hochwasser Magdeburg—HilfsGESUCHE (Flood Magdeburg—Requests for help)	Hochwasser Niedersachsen—BIETE/SUCHE[1] (Flood Lower Saxony—Offer/Search)	Mamas Helfen (Moms help)
Twitter	Search term: flood ("Hochwasser")		
Interviews	A (moderator) D (helper; employed at police)	B (moderator) E (helper; employed at water management) G (helper; employed at fire service)	C (moderator) F (moderator)

[1] The group was renamed to "Hochwasser—die Helfer-Gruppe (Flood—the Helper-Group)" on July 20, 2015.

was discussed. Finally, the interviews posed questions at an ICT level by evaluating FB functions and discussing technical support potential. Interviews were audio-recorded and transcribed for further analysis.

In our subsequent analysis we employed "open" coding (Strauss & Corbin, 1998) i.e. gathering data into approximate categories to reflect the issues raised by respondents based on repeated readings of the data and its organisation into "similar" statements. These categories reflect the structure of the following results section. While the analysis was conducted in German, the quotes selected for this chapter were translated to English by the authors.

6.2.2   The Study Case: European Floods 2013 in Germany

The European floods in June 2013 were an event in which volunteer activity played a major role. 35 federal states in seven European countries had to declare a state of disaster in multiple districts, including 55 districts in Germany including the federal states of Bavaria, Lower Saxony and Saxony-Anhalt. Figure 6.1 shows how severely the regions were affected. This disaster caused the deaths of eight people in Germany and cost the states an estimated 6.7 billion Euros. The German armed forces (19,000 soldiers) and fire services (75,000 firefighters) participated in the relief efforts, along with the German Red Cross and other relief organisations who provided medical and other care. Besides the large number of professional forces and voluntary organisations who were involved, many volunteers and affected people participated by building up flood barriers, filling and piling up sandbags, donating work material and goods for victims, distributing food and providing emergency shelters.

The use of social media in this case has been acknowledged and even utilised by the traditional media. Volunteer activities were planned and coordinated, emotional support was given and eyewitness reports were shared using these media. Aside from Twitter, FB was the most-used application. 157 pages and groups relating to the keyword "Hochwasser" (English: flood) were created and more than 600,000 people were members of such groups or liked the pages. For 47% of these communities the focus was on local geographical locations such as counties, towns or districts. 34% dealt with forwarding and exchanging information and 27% were considered as relief platforms (Karsten, 2013).

In the following sections, we describe three cases and six related FB-communities that we examined within our study. We chose three different areas to establish a modest degree of generalizability across federal borders. We selected FB-pages that indicated above-average activity and reach (in terms of FB-likes) to

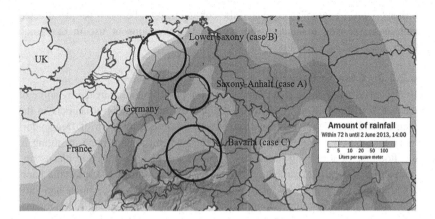

Figure 6.1   Amount of Rainfall and Cases during the Floods

act as a broadcasting medium (Sutton, 2010), and FB-groups representing local (self-help) communities that also showed a brisk degree of activity and more specifically dealt with the mediation of help supply and demand (Reuter et al., 2013).

6.2.2.1   Case A: Saxony-Anhalt

In *Saxony-Anhalt*, the floods had a significant impact on the town of Magdeburg where about 23,000 people had to be evacuated east of the Elbe River. Also, a transformer station was threatened, meaning that a potential ingress of water would have endangered the electricity supply of 30,000 households for several months. The team of the FB-page "Flood News Magdeburg", for instance, aimed to browse through, evaluate, select and share relevant information about the developing situation. Additionally, the FB-group "Flood Magdeburg—Requests for help" tried to provide a holistic situational overview with links to further groups or pages and information on hotlines and "donation camps".

6.2.2.2   Case B: Lower Saxony

The case of *Lower Saxony* shows communities seeking to support help activities distributed throughout the whole federal state. The description on the FB-page "Flood Lower Saxony" defines its goal as collecting and exchanging information about the flood, e.g., water levels, photos documenting the damage, evacuations and situational trends regarding Lower Saxony. The FB-group "Flood Lower

Saxony—Offer/Search" coordinated the communication between people affected and those offering assistance and presented conventions of use in the group description and as a fixed post.

6.2.2.3 Case C: Bavaria

In *Passau (Bavaria)*, the water supply was temporarily contaminated by some of the heaviest floods ever to affect the Danube River. Teaching at schools in the vicinity and the region was disrupted, while in the nearby town of Deggendorf more than 6,000 citizens had to be evacuated when the dam burst, resulting in the flooding of low-lying areas. The team of the FB-page "Passau cleans up" established a local and structured organisation consisting of headquarters, coordinator, and scout units to support the overall coordination of relief activities in Passau. The FB-group "Moms help" originating with a group of (pregnant) women, supported relief activities and took an active role in the response and advanced recovery phase.

6.2.3   Results I: Different Types of Social Media and ICT during the Floods

Focusing mainly on the use of FB and Twitter during the floods, the following sections present the analysis of the use and reception of specific functions of FB-groups and pages, as well as the integration of social media with other ICT.

6.2.3.1   Use Differences among different Services

Although Twitter was used extensively in flood situations, especially for distributing information and situational updates, our results show that it generally tended to take the form of a broadcast medium for shaping cross-platform structures and extending coverage (Reuter et al., 2015b): The coordination of relief activities was rarely observed in the Twitter sphere alone, but took place within a complex ecology of both online and offline facilities. This could, to some extent, be a corollary of low Twitter penetration in Germany, but it is consistent with Hughes et al. (Hughes et al., 2014) who showed differences in use across media platforms. Accordingly, Twitter seems to be used for real-time notification, and FB for community engagement (St. Denis et al., 2014). In our case, local and subject-specific groups emerged on FB, who cooperated extensively with other groups/pages. In addition, the interviewees mentioned their awareness of certain functionalities in social networking which induced them to stick to platforms they were familiar with (in this case FB) during the floods (A, 17:18; B, 50:36; C, 40:26).

6.2.3.2 Facebook Group and Page Functionalities

6.2.3.2.1 Group Discussion and Group Description

On entering a group or page in FB, the *group discussion,* or the *page* chronicle (see Section 6.2.3.2) are the most prominently visible features. While the chronicle lists items sorted exclusively by the date of their creation, in a group discussion, the date of the item comments also influence the position of the item. Exceptions are 'fixed postings' which are always at the top of the list and which were used in all cases either to (a) introduce the purpose of the group, (b) present the group's conventions and use of its functions, (c) give a general overview of the emergency and existing infrastructure, or (d) prioritise important or recent information. In the cases A and B, the fixed posting more or less consisted of the *group description*, including policy statements, probably because the fixed posting is more accessible and central on the user's screen. To reflect the group's purpose, statements like these were disseminated:

- "Help offers are collected here, so that voluntarily helpers have a contact point" (Flood Magdeburg—Requests for help, case A).
- "Although we are no longer under water, there are still plenty of help requests, so we needed to find something new [...]. We need YOU as a family mentor" (Moms help, Case C).
- "If ever there is another disaster in future, we would like to offer this platform to mediate help" (Flood Lower Saxony—Offer/Search, case B).

While in case A, the statement reflects the general purpose of the group, case C indicates that the focus of activity was shifted during the course of emergency and case B even strives to be a platform for future disasters. In terms of conventions, case A attempts to lay out a protocol, suggesting that a posting such as a help request should contain at least an address and the goods or services (lifts, sleeping places, etc.) needed, and that users should only publish help requests in a clearly stated fashion. In case B, interested people are told that help requests are organised on the discussion wall and files have been created with information on provisions, shelters, furniture, or materials to enable subject-specific communication via comments (see Section 6.2.3.2.2). Contrary to case A, they explicitly ask posters not to "post addresses, phone numbers or contact points without consultation". Two distinct approaches to issues of privacy could clearly be distinguished and are examined further below. Both groups mention that they will delete inappropriate (case A) or successfully processed (case B) postings. Furthermore, the mediation process of family mentoring is described in detail in case C.

"Flood Magdeburg—Requests for help" in particular tried to give an overview of the emergency by providing (a) a list of other FB-groups and pages that have a more global (e.g. Saxony-Anhalt), regional (e.g. Magdeburg, Elbe-Havel) or topical (e.g. help offers, emergency shelters) focus and (b) a list of official donation hotlines and donation camps.

6.2.3.2.2 Group Files and Documents
Group files (resp. documents) were used as descriptive sources and to enable topic-related communication (Figure 6.2 and Figure 6.3).

Figure 6.2   "Moms Help" Group Discussion

Interviewee B quotes her previous knowledge and the availability of group functions (files, documents and photos) as crucial factors in the use of FB during the floods, to structure efforts:

Figure 6.3   "Moms Help" List of Files

> *"If you create a group you can get people, who you promote to admin, so that you can divide labour. Then I can create folders in a group to sort certain things like help offers and requests in this case, which we managed with files, or that you can use photo albums to classify certain categories. You could structure this, which was crucial for me" (B, 50:26).*

While in most cases the administrators managed the document's title and content, other members used the comment section of the document for communication. For instance, "Moms help" started to mediate "family mentors" in mid-October with the help of FB-documents, whereby one document enabled potential family mentors to show their willingness and the second provided a sorted list of those already registered, ordered by postcode. Other files consisted of lists of one's own or foreign group administrators, blocked users, group supporters or general information. In another document, members were instructed to publish their help offers, and the document itself gave an example of how to structure these. Also, the files were tagged by the abbreviations "done for now" and "current" or by an exclamation mark to express the status or the urgency (Figure 6.3). Using the file function to organise help offers was described as a critical task:

> *"We originally tried to do this by using files but within three days we had reached our limitations. Answers were inserted into files as comment, but once there are 200 comments; nobody reads 250 comments to find out: 'Ah, the gumboots were up there'"* (C, 50:12).

6.2.3.2.3 Page Chronicle and Page Info Section

In contrast, the *page chronicle* is generally managed by the page team members, so that regular users can only comment on page postings and a specific comment section, kept apart from the chronicle itself. Page teams often used the *page info section* to clarify their objectives. The team of "Flood News Magdeburg" regularly published status updates regarding the severity of the situation, volunteer and material requirements and general information about recommended equipment as well as posts with empathetic intent, such as thanking volunteers for their efforts. They describe their task to browse through existing information, to evaluate it, to select information considered to be relevant, and to share it on its page. It can thus be thought of as generating collective intelligence (Hollan et al., 2000). In addition, the activities of structuring and synthesising information can be observed on the wall summarising information on several areas affected by the floods:

> *Update: 01:50*
> *+ + + approx. 30–40 fresh and well rested volunteers are required at Zollstraße to relieve tired helpers + + +*
> *+ + + The Wissenschaftshafen is debatable as contact point according to our information; please inform us about the current situation via PM. + + +*
> *+ + + Fresh helpers are also required in Pechau + + +*
> *If you have been up and about for a long time, please go to bed and rally your strength for the upcoming days.*

Discussions often emerged in the comment section of these messages, where potential helpers initially expressed their need for information and elements of a verification process became visible: There was a higher probability that information would be assumed to be correct if it was confirmed by the page moderator (Table 6.3, left). In contrast, the statements made by other users were sometimes questioned with greater intensity, indicating a certain degree of self-regulation through the crowd's mistrust of unconfirmed information (Table 6.3, right).

Table 6.3 Two Examples of Information Verification

[02:00] Eric: Where exactly in Pechau and Zollhaus??	[02:36] Janine: In Westerhuesen I think they are also looking (for helpers)!!!!
[02:00] Basti: I'm driving to Zollstrasse. Where do I have to register???	[02:40] Christian: #Janine Krause sure? Where exactly?
[02:02] Thomas: It will be explained at the sports field in Pechau. Leave the car there	[03:18] Markus: New contact point. Virchowstraße.
[02:02] Flood News Magdeburg: In Pechau, register at the sports field! At Zollstraße, you will see it directly on arrival.	[03:20] Jana: How certain?
	[03:20] Simon: Is that certain, Markus????
[02:03] Mirko: In Pechau you will be met at the sports field and at Zollstraße everything is lit up.	[03:40] Markus: Certain, but they are still constructing on-site. It makes little sense to come here yet.

Figure 6.4 Photo with Emotional and Cohesive Appeal. (Sources: "Flood Lower Saxony—Offer/Search")

The *photo function* was also utilised by several groups and pages. For instance, in "Flood Lower Saxony—Offer/Search" (Figure 6.4 and Figure 6.5) various photos are to be seen which document damage and other effects of the crisis, and the (process of) help activities such as 'piling sandbags' or relief and evacuation efforts. Comments on flood-related photos on the one hand usually contained emotional messages expressing solidarity, sympathy and identification with the helpers. Interviewee F states that they published those photos intentionally:

"We always uploaded pictures of people [...] and I think this was very good for the emotional processing (of the floods) that this mutual photo exchange took place here. And in a way, it was good for motivation too, of course." (F, 24:00).

On the other hand, coordination efforts occasionally took place and new help offers were disseminated in the comment section of the photos, indicating that the emotional appeal of photos can also serve the purpose of mobilising additional helpers and resources (White et al., 2014).

Figure 6.5   Photo with Emotional and Cohesive Appeal. (Source: "Flood Lower Saxony")

6.2.3.2.4 Problems with Private Messages: 'Oh I didn't see it'

Besides public page and group functions, *private messages* were also used in certain situations. To filter and verify information as well as support a clear overview, interviewee B adjusted the group policy in such a way that comments were not published on the wall until an administrator had confirmed them. Therefore, interviewees also used private messages to contact helpers and affected people:

"At busy times, especially in the initial phase [...], suddenly there were 17 private messages from people who wanted something from the group. Then I could simply open a new tab for each person and work through it and also re-sort the information in files" (B, 50:26).

However, this procedure has the disadvantage that messages to contacts who are not part of one's friend list are automatically moved into the folder "other" and the user is not notified:

> *"Many people aren't aware of the folder 'other' and FB gives no notification of other messages. And 2–3 weeks later the answer came back: 'Oh I didn't see it.' For emergency situations, it would be great if you could answer more directly" (A, 33:10).*

6.2.3.3 Twitter—Retweets and Situational Updates

Representing 17.93% of the entire Twitter dataset, the account @_BB_RADIO_H2O has regularly and automatically published information on water levels based on data provided by the Federal Waterways Administration. As these tweets contain situational updates and geo-referenced information, they contribute to overall situational awareness. Tweets generated by other accounts comprise links to webcams, which give the users an idea of what the situation is like on the ground. With 13.86%, the account @Hochwasser2013 mainly published retweets. Under the accounts @FeuerwehrRT and @THW the fire service and the THW (federal agency for technical relief) retweeted tweets automatically, including the hashtags #hochwasser and #feuerwehr (fire department) and #thw. A great number of captured accounts were mainly limited to disseminating retweets, which constitute 46.45% of the dataset. The news channel "MDR Sachsen-Anhalt" showed a high level of activity with 1,071 tweets (1.34%) on the account @MDR_SAN. On June 3rd, 4:03 AM, MDR offered to retweet important messages: "@MDRaktuell: #Flood: Where are #Volunteers needed? Please tweet, we retweet". Alongside MDR, many other accounts based on traditional media, especially TV and radio stations, print media and their associated websites also produced some of the highest numbers of (re)tweets.

To further analyse tweets related to civic relief activities, we reduced the data set by excluding official accounts dealing with politics, media and companies. When reflecting the remaining data, it became apparent that help activities in particular can be identified by recurring expressions such as "urgent", "needed", "offer", or "help". Filtering the data set according to these expressions alone resulted in a set of 1,602 tweets. Overall, only a small amount actually dealt with relief activities. The majority belonged to situational updates (e.g. water levels). Among the communities examined, only "Flood Lower Saxony" used the account *@hochwasserniede* to distribute information on Twitter, but each tweet contained a URL referencing their activities on FB. Furthermore, none of the interviewees had a personal Twitter account or considered creating one during the floods.

6.2.3.4 ICT used alongside Facebook and Twitter

6.2.3.4.1 Geo Mapping with Google Maps

Social media relief activities were supplemented by a vast range of external tools. The team of the FB-page, "Flood News Magdeburg", for instance, created a *Google map* (similar work was done in other cities). On this map, flooded areas, shelters, sandbag filling stations, threatened dikes, a need for relief forces or transport facilities were illustrated with the help of various markers, polygons and attached information windows (Figure 6.6). In addition, the description of the map was used to introduce its purpose or additional resources. In the comment section, numerous comments were made by helpers who appreciated such maps and wanted to support the up-to-dateness of the map with situational updates (Table 6.4, left). These comments reveal the potential of crisis maps to visualise geo-referenced information, but clearly show the challenges that lie in ensuring information is both clear and up-to-date (Table 6.4, right).

Table 6.4 Positive Reception and Obstacles of Google Maps

Marko: The map is really brilliant. Keep it up-to-date, we will gladly continue to work with it. Eriu: Really helpful application for the coordination of flood relief activities. Anon: Many thanks for this great map. Using it yesterday, I found a suitable place of action and after work was done there, I found the next place.	Jschlademann: GREAT MAP!!! THANKS! Please update: The physiotherapy practice on Ernst-König-Strasse doesn't require help anymore. The annotation can be deleted. MANY THANKS!! Philipp: Why isn't the street at the surface mine listed as blocked at the map? It has been completely flooded for several days now. Joshwa: Please update, some entries are older than 8 hours and make the map unclear and useless for potential helpers:/

Furthermore, interviewee B indicated problems adapting to Google Maps as she tried to *"create a map where volunteers sign in […], but did not understand how to set a marker"* (B, 56:59).

Figure 6.6   Google Maps in the City of Halle

6.2.3.4.2 Organised Support: Live Blog and Google Docs

The public broadcasting company "MDR" organised a moderated *live-blog*: besides selected tweets and FB-posts, manual posts by users (and their own recommendations e.g. accounts for donations or seek/offer-platforms) were made available (Figure 6.7, left). Furthermore, MDR used *Google docs* to share a public spreadsheet regarding flood-related information and guidance. In order to obtain and list volunteers' addresses and phone numbers, the team around interviewee F created a Google form: *"And then we created a Google form and distributed it via campus blog and student council Facebook pages. We got more than 1000 entries overnight [...]"* (F, 01:53).

6.2.3.4.3 Custom Web Tools

Custom web tools were developed in addition to the ones mentioned above, to further structure the process of capturing and matching help requests and offers. In the area around Dresden, tweets were automatically generated by the account @FluDDHilfe whenever a user had created a help request or offer on the *fluddhilfe.de* website (Figure 6.7, right). By cross-referencing in this way, the developer established a bidirectional connection between both platforms. Interviewee F also mentions the use of the *flut.stomt.de* website, a similar tool to collect help requests and offers in different regions, highlighting coordinative features: *"And it was really nice that you could enter how many helpers were required and*

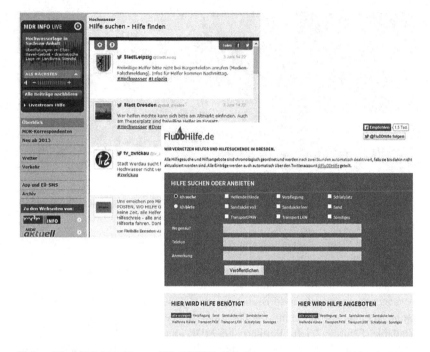

Figure 6.7   MDR Live Blog and FluDDHilfe Website

click "*I will go there*" and then the tool's counter (of required helpers) went down"
(F, 35:43).

In addition to these publicly accessible artifacts, interviewee C used a local *Excel* spreadsheet to organise demands from people and collection points, while interviewee B, along with other administrators, used *Dropbox* to make certain information and documents available to a limited audience of users.

6.2.4   Results II: (Self-)Organisation with Social Media

Social media was used to advance communication, to supplement existing channels and to support overall organisational efforts to overcome the consequences of the floods. Data concerning information processing activities and the qualitative characteristics of social media information in this context will be presented in the following sections.

6.2.4.1 Organisation and Task Sharing in Volunteer Communities

In all the cases we examined, there were elements of task sharing within the internal team of moderators. The team of the Lower Saxony case split tasks as follows:

> *"She went to Schönhausen and Breitenhagen and gained her own impressions. At the time, I was still reacting at a distance. She then called me [...]: 'This and that is needed. Could you please check if anybody has that?" (B, 15:52).*

Interviewee B followed up by checking existing FB-documents or asking for offers. In terms of other virtual communities, a *private coordination* process was established in a way that addresses and other personal data were treated confidentially for the purpose of data privacy: *"That means there is a private group of moderators where there are some admins who made a reliable impression"* (B, 43:50). Interviewee E also states that many resources were organised privately (E, 06:17) and that too few affected citizens articulated their demands over FB for efficient provision, possibly due to lack of internet or relevant facilities and/or skills within the disaster situation (E, 27:40). According to interviewee G, trucks of resources were transferred to the disaster zone, where the respective resources were not needed at all:

> *"After the floods, the few deployments from the various help organisations that I saw were catastrophic. When people returned to the locality for two or three days, I cannot pull up with countless trucks containing furniture, if no houses have been cleared out yet" (G, 06:07).*

Interviewee E reported a similar incident of someone *"sending 120 beds to Breitenhagen"*, although the *"people of Breitenhagen did not want any old hotel beds"* (E, 35:56). Besides the inefficient allocation of resources, problems with transportation allocation arose because the coordinators were subject to a degree of information overload (far too many messages) (E, 34:06).

In Passau, interviewee C describes a cross-platform division of work where volunteers provided collection points, published them in newspapers and later on were supplied with material donations. Afterwards, the moderator team arranged distribution and transport to the affected population. Within FB, and in contrast to the Lower Saxony case, a *public coordination* process was established in Passau: *"We cooperated with Flood Help Bavaria, Passau [...] and all the others who really were active there. We posted the help offers and requests everywhere"* (C, 20:00). Nevertheless, the cross-platform dissemination of posts had the drawback of potential information inconsistencies, because status updates were not always announced on every platform:

> *"The problem was that we had eight help requests in eight groups [...]. There were conversations like 'I already got help, everything is done'—'Really? The request is still open over here'—'Oh sorry, I forgot to update it'. The response between the groups or help activities did not work"* (C, 55:56).

In addition to that, the relief efforts in Passau were supplemented by the student initiative 'Passau cleans up'. After using Google forms to collect volunteers' addresses and phone numbers, a coordination network was built up:

> *"At the beginning, we set up a mailing list. We built up a local coordination network, meaning we had [...] two headquarters. Then there were (seven) coordination points with coordinators, whereby each coordinator had 3–5 scouts who walked through the streets along with fire service and THW personnel, coordinating how many volunteers and what kind of equipment was needed. This was communicated back to the coordinators, who then forwarded the information to the headquarters. From the headquarters, we sent the volunteers and their equipment to the relevant location"* (F, 04:28).

In order to reach a broader audience (further to their *campus blog*), i.e., for sharing the Google forms, clarifying conflicting or inaccurate information, and reducing fearmongering, the students created a FB-page for the communication of information (F, 05:11). The page was also used to gather help offers and requests via private messages and public page posts (F, 10:11).

6.2.4.2 Roles of Digital Volunteers: The Moderator

Several social media roles (see Section 6.2.4.2) could be observed in our case studies which were connected both to the core activity of helping as well as to the gathering, amplification and moderation of information. The interviews clearly focused on the role of moderators, but also provided us with insight into their cooperation with other types of users.

In the beginning, the role of the *moderators*, represented by interviewees A, B, C and F, often initially encompassed simple activities, but then evolved into a more comprehensive role of founding and organising communities of affected citizens and volunteers. Interviewee C started her voluntary work by collecting information about activities in the neighbourhood, but also went on to organise not only appeals for donations but also to manage collection points (C, 04:48). Likewise, interviewee B describes in detail how she mediated messages containing offers by volunteers to people affected by the floods and how she organised transports:

> *"Messages about hygiene articles and disinfectants were managed privately in the background. People just said. 'I have such-and-such. Where should I send the packet?' And then I sent them a PDF with the address" (B, 09:49).*

Interviewee A started her activities on "Flood News Magdeburg" by identifying demands for help and mediating volunteers, which led to the foundation of "Flood Magdeburg—Requests for help":

> *"There were plenty of requests: 'Where can I help?' If you registered there and visited the page 10 minutes later, you wouldn't be able to find your own posting anymore. New postings were published every few seconds and you couldn't find anything" (A, 03:45).*

She thus describes her task as *"providing a clear view of (relevant) information and sorting out (spam)"* (A, 29:09). However, her aim was also to reduce time-consuming exposure for others by *"clicking all the pages and getting the messages"* (A, 28:37) and further by *"updating information, answering requests, and maintaining contact with on-site volunteers to get current information"* (A, 05:20). Furthermore, according to interviewee F, the team of "Passau cleans up" paid great attention to the style of their message to create acceptance on the part of both citizens and moderators:

> *"We paid great attention to our style of writing. We tried to formulate it in a way that made it clear help was mutual and not condescending. And of course, you've got to try to express yourself in a way that is not too complex because there are people out there who kept on saying 'Well it's not just students you know but the town population, too' because it was only students who were mentioned in the press. So, you see we were a bit afraid that if we conveyed things in a complex way, we would lose volunteers; that they would pack it in because they thought we were arrogant" (F, 28:39).*

Summarising the moderators' core activities, they entailed the mediation of volunteer activity and matched citizens' demands with offers of help by utilising and integrating social media functions and ICT which contributed to the process of structuring the rich information supply.

Another prominent role is the *helper* who performs real, virtual or even combined activities to support affected people. On-site helpers often commented on page postings to supplement or update published information, and used information offered by postings or Google maps to find new places requiring help or to ascertain which (material) resources were sought. Interviewee E, for instance, was involved in the filling of sandbags, clean-up activities (E, 03:32) and the collection of donations for affected citizens (E, 14:14). She also provided psychological assistance from home, something she was not prepared for initially (E, 2:49).

Our research also identified the role of the *amplifier*, or *retweeter*, in the context of Twitter. The automatic retweet services and the manual retweet offers described in Section 6.2.3.3 contributed to the amplification of specific information. Although FB does not provide direct functionality such as retweets, some FB-page teams described their task as to identify, evaluate, select, and publish—and therefore amplify—relevant information. A common activity of "Flood News Magdeburg" was to disseminate structured and synthesised postings to provide a situational overview. Additionally, FB provides mechanisms for adjusting the relative weight of information, due to its more segmented structure and rights management: For instance, interviewee B adjusted "Flood Lower Saxony—Offer/Search" in such a way that messages were only published if a moderator approved them, thus preventing the spread of inappropriate and irrelevant information. Furthermore, successfully processed requests were deleted afterwards.

Page teams typically not only performed the role of the amplifier but also that of the *reporter*, acting as a news channel that integrated external resources such as traditional media articles, water level services and links to further specific or regional communities. Indeed, on-site helpers, members of moderator teams (see Section 6.2.3.3) and affected citizens acted as eyewitnesses to this role, confirming the observation that citizens adopted multiple roles simultaneously (Reuter et al., 2013).

6.2.4.3 Cooperation with Official Emergency Management

In relation to official emergency management, regional differences regarding the depth of cooperation with volunteers could be observed. While interviewee A was only in touch with the fire service and THW during food distribution, B maintained contact with local emergency service organisations via telephone, so that they could *"ask incident control how many people they still needed"* (B, 20:56).

However, it was not usually possible to establish communication with the emergency services via FB (B, 38:45). Equally, in Passau communication was realised not through FB, but through direct contact to officials:

> *"Indeed, within one and a half weeks we had been invited to the 'round table', to the big crisis meeting which everyone important was attending. That's where it was all coordinated, who should work together with whom" (C, 22:20).*

As the administration of "Moms help" did not constitute an official emergency management organisation, they joined the charitable organisation "Caritas" to give their work a status (C, 22:20). The initiative "Passau cleans up" ensured contact with official emergency forces in their internal organisation in a rather different way:

> *"Scouts walked through the streets talking to the official forces, asking how many volunteers they needed, and then passed the information 'We need 50 people with shovels and boots' on by word of mouth to the coordinators. They called us (the headquarters), where one member managed a spreadsheet in front of the office, equipped the volunteers and sent them to the coordinators. The scouts picked the volunteers up from there and took them along" (F, 37:20).*

This respondent, though acknowledging that she did not know how to support this process using social media, strongly supported the idea that state institutions like the municipality, fire services or THW should be educated in dealing with social media. The author of "Info Page Flood Bavaria 2013" pointed out that although he gathered information from blogs and established media, he relied above all on messages of users, because such messages provided information up to two hours in advance of other sources. According to interviewee D, some coordination difficulties arose due to reliance on official information, whereby too many volunteers sometimes went to the contact points mentioned, while there were too few helpers at other places (D, 02:34). Because of this suboptimal volunteer coordination, up-to-date information about required numbers of helpers was published on FB, which meant that indecisive helpers no longer went to these locations. In this case, the incident commander could not comprehend why fewer people were arriving, because he was not aware of the current situation on FB (E, 14:14). Such circumstances indicate that the emergency services' inclusion of social media information would improve the optimal allocation of both information and (material) resources.

6.2.5   Results III: Discussion of Challenges and Patterns

Our examination of social media use revealed some recurring patterns, extending those detected in our preliminary study (Kaufhold & Reuter, 2014; Reuter et al., 2015b). Table 6.5 summarises the identified challenges regarding the use of ICT and, in particular, social media during the European floods of 2013, and identifies the most common actions that were undertaken intended to overcome these challenges. However, while some challenges could be addressed to a fairly satisfactory degree, most have a considerable room for improvement.

Table 6.5 Identified Challenges and Actions

#	Challenge identified in our study	Actions and Implications
1	Clarity and Representation of Relevant Content	Display the community's goals or purpose Display conventions of interaction Apply a structure and channelling of information
2	Feedback and Updates in Interaction Relationships	Ensure the timely arrival of information Update outdated information
3	Organisational Identification and Resilience	Use of photos for emotional processing, solidarity and motivation 'Exploit' style of message writing to maximise acceptance Design proper collaboration between involved stakeholders
4	Integration of Technologies and Interaction Types	Model organisational embedment of ICT Support different tasks with suitable ICT Consider public and private ways of interaction
5	Moderation and Autonomous Work	Use ICT to relieve moderating tasks Foster self-regulation of participants Consideration of different levels of skills regarding ICT
6	Maintenance of Quality of Information	Amplification of relevant information Provision of current information Provision of geo-visualised information Provision of 'appealing' information

These challenges will be further described and elaborated in the following.

6.2.5.1 Clarity and Representation of Relevant Content

The description of the FB-group, a fixed posting, and/or the page's info section were used to display the overall goals of the community and to provide conventions on how to behave or use existing infrastructure. This seems to be a crucial aspect for optimising the process of communication. There also seems to be a fundamental requirement to structure information flow, e.g., use of the file function to create specific documents dealing with certain topics. The annotations within the document titles furthermore indicate the need to display a status representing developments on this topic. These efforts seem to aim towards making relevant help requests more available and listenable (Hughes et al., 2014) to the users, to maintain a clear overview within the interaction platform and to support the interaction between roles, such as moderators, helpers and people in need.

6.2.5.2 Feedback and Updates in Interaction Relationships

According to our interviewees, a considerable amount of communication took place via private messages for the purposes of privacy as well. Birkbak (2012) already reported on the benefits of an architecture like FB including both public and private spaces. However, there is a high risk that timely feedback will not be received since messages received from people not in one's friend list are filtered into the folder "other". One major challenge is therefore to ensure the timely arrival of information. Moreover, our study showed that cross-platform collaboration requires proper information-update procedures to counter information inconsistencies and redundant resource allocation.

6.2.5.3 Organisational Identification and Resilience

To motivate affected citizens and volunteers, to generate identification with the helper's efforts and to provide emotional support, it was common practice to upload photos showing the impact of the flood and related relief activities to counter it. As a consequence, comments usually contained emotional messages expressing solidarity, sympathy and identification with the helpers, showing the potential of social media to influence a community's resilience in a positive way. Furthermore, the style of message writing seems fundamental to gain a broad acceptance among different cultural or social groups. However, the challenge of how to ensure proper collaboration among authorities, professional response and volunteer communities has to be examined in a more comprehensive and profound manner.

6.2.5.4 Integration of Technologies and Interaction Types

Regarding the organisational integration of social media, different *degrees of relevance* were observed. While "Passau cleans up" used social media for the most part to supplement the spread of information and gather some basic information, their central resource was the local organisation with headquarters, coordinators and scouts. "Flood Lower Saxony—Offer/Search" used FB as their core platform for coordinating relief activities and information flow. In all cases, Twitter was primarily used to distribute information but not to coordinate. Also, different *degrees of privacy* were implemented ranging from "Flood Magdeburg—Requests for help", where people were encouraged to publicly exchange their address and contact data, to "Flood Lower Saxony—Offer/Search", where sensitive data was instead exchanged by private messages and managed with the support of external tools which were only visible to the creator or to a limited audience of invited people. In relation to tools, different *degrees of technological integration* were studied. In order to master a multitude of different tasks, "Passau cleans up" used blogs, Google docs and external web tools. "Flood News Magdeburg" integrated a Google map into their efforts and "Flood Lower Saxony" disseminated tweets alongside their core FB activities. Tools such as Google Maps and OpenStreetMap could also tighten the connection between real and virtual volunteer activities (Reuter et al., 2013) and support disaster response through voluntary community mapping (Soden & Palen, 2014).

6.2.5.5 Moderation and Autonomous Work

Moderators progressed from simple activities to more complex ones (Starbird & Palen, 2011). It also became apparent that the moderation of a community entails considerable effort and is a very time-consuming process; ICT could reduce the quantity of moderation activities by fostering the self-regulation of participants. However, the interviews indicated that there were problems regarding the adaption to new technology in emergency situations, which prevented a richer integration of technology in some communities.

6.2.5.6 Maintain Quality of Information

From the perspective of information quality, several information processing activities as well as supporting functions and tools were identified. Consistent with previously conducted studies (Starbird, 2013; Vieweg et al., 2010), we found that page teams and moderators sought to identify, select and amplify relevant information, and provided structured and synthesised posts of information. While geo-visualised information was a perceived aspect of improving the quality of information (Ludwig et al., 2015a), the immediacy of information was seen as a central benefit of social media in supporting the overall coordination of relief activities. In addition, the style of message writing was also seen as an aspect of quality, insofar as it influenced acceptance among the various citizens and volunteers. For instance, emotionally supportive photos in conjunction with messages written in an appropriate style seem important to promote a positive climate among participants.

6.2.6 Interim Summary

This section examined the actions of virtual communities in disasters by analysing the contents of social media posts and conducting semi-structured interviews with FB-group and page founders, focusing on the use of social media and ICT in disasters with regards to organisational and information-specific characteristics. The case study of the 2013 European floods bolsters evidence for the relevance of social media during disasters for German citizens, but also shows perceived deficiencies of current emergency management practices in relation to the use of social media.

In order to answer our first research question *"How were different types of social media used during the European floods?"* (Section 6.2.3), we found that Twitter was used as a platform for status updates, the information space of which was largely constructed through automatic retweet services. While FB-pages were mostly intended to provide an overview and to filter the vast information supply, FB-groups also coordinated a multitude of virtual and real relief activities. This confirms the findings of Hughes et al. (Hughes et al., 2014). Other tools, such as Google Maps, Live Blog and Google Docs and custom web tools have also been used for specific purposes often related to FB and Twitter. However, among the examined communities the overall importance of social media varied, and different levels of privacy and technological integration were applied.

To approach our second research question *"How was social media used to organise volunteers?"* (Section 6.2.4), we conclude that in addition to affected citizens and (digital) volunteers, some particularly dedicated volunteers adopted the role of moderators to mediate the supply and demand of help through social media and other ICT. Moderators exploited the given functionality of social media and tools they were familiar with to structure the processes of exchanging information, promoting cohesion and organising volunteers. In contrast, considering organisational barriers of using social media (Reuter et al., 2016b) the cooperation with official emergency management rather relied on local communication, meetings and telephone calls.

To address the third research question *"What are the challenges for collaboration support?"* (Section 6.2.5) we outlined six challenges including (#1) clarity and representation of relevant content, (#2) feedback and updates in interaction relationships, (#3) organisational identification and resilience, (#4) integration of technologies and interaction types, (#5) moderation and autonomous work, and (#6) maintaining quality of information.

Compared to related work, our approach provides several contributions: (A) While there are many studies about social media and digital volunteers in the US, fewer studies investigated events in Europe. The point to be emphasised here is that comparative work which might draw out geographical organisational and mobilisation differences ought to be valuable. (B) Looking at the 2013 European floods case, existing work focuses "only" on Twitter (Fuchs et al., 2013; Reuter & Schröter, 2015), concentrates on one particular city (Mildner, 2013; Wittmann et al., 2015) or is rather design oriented (Backfried et al., 2015; Reuter et al., 2015b; Sackmann et al., 2014), and does not describe the overall case. In contrast, our study covered different media "beyond Twitter", examining the event in three locations across Germany and made use of both social media and interview data. (C) We also particularly focused on the moderator as an important role on social media emergency response, something that we think has been a little underestimated until now.

Although Twitter was extensively used in flood situations for distributing information and situational updates, our results show that it tended to mainly take the form of a broadcast medium for shaping cross-platform structures and extending coverage. The coordination of relief activities was rarely observed in the Twitter sphere alone, but took place within a complex ecology of both online and offline facilities. This could, to some extent, be a corollary of low Twitter penetration in Germany, but it is consistent with Hughes et al. (Hughes et al., 2014) showing differences of use across media platforms. Accordingly, Twitter is used for real-time notification, and FB for community engagement (St. Denis et al., 2014). In our case, local and subject-specific groups emerged on FB, which cooperated extensively with other groups/pages. These observations lead to our design challenges:

First, *clarity and representation of relevant content*: The issue of "collective activity", so that all participants, officials and volunteers can access accurate and up-to-date information, can be supported by the identification or the assessment of information through search and filter functions. The interviews indicate that information tends to be sorted thematically with the aid of files. Additional functions for organising information with search and filter options especially with geographical references are desirable. The purpose of such functions would be to render relevant help requests more available and listenable (Hughes et al., 2014) to the users, to maintain a clear overview within the interaction platform and to support the interaction between moderators, helpers and people in need. These people are currently organised in different groups and use a variety of pages—and sometimes several pages—to articulate their demands.

Second, *moderation and autonomous work*: Interviews show that the moderator's role (an extension of the Reuter et al. (2013) role model) is to mediate demands, requests and offers for help; to mobilise volunteers as well as material and immaterial resources and to integrate information from media, official authorities and other organisations. This is evidently a serious role and entails considerable overhead. It is noticeable that private rooms are sometimes used for coordination, especially when privacy is of importance or sensitive data needs to be available on a limited basis. It is obvious that moderating a group is a very time-consuming process. ICT could reduce the amount of moderation activities by fostering the self-regulation of the participants.

Third, *feedback and updates in interaction relationships*: Incoming messages from people not appearing on one's friends list are not flagged and are filtered into the residual FB folder "other". This process impedes the giving of timely feedback. Regarding Google Maps, the requirements for up-to-datedness of geo-referenced objects could, in addition, be supported by notifications or time-based filtering.

Fourth, *integration of technologies and interaction types*: It is apparent that in a complex ecology, different tools are used for different purposes. Twitter is particularly used for distributing situational updates. Interviewees saw the benefit of an embedded FB application as long as it is quickly accessible and fills feature gaps. Using maps such as Google Maps could also tighten the connection between real and virtual volunteer activities. When integrating these services, additional accounts should be avoided because not every user has accounts on networks such as Twitter or Google +. It should be remembered that not everyone is equally "savvy"; imposing an unnecessary learning effort during a crisis situation is not to be recommended.

6.3 XHELP: Cross-Social-Media Application for Volunteers

We developed the platform XHELP in order to support these requirements and with the overall aim of supporting the role of group moderator through functionality for assessing and distributing information. We are aware that such functionalities might also be of interest to other target groups. However, based on our research, volunteer moderators are our main target group so far. A cross-platform search and posting function should simplify the current practices and reduce organisational efforts. Since most of the relief activities we saw were organised via FB groups and pages, XHELP has been implemented as an embedded FB application. The advantages of such an approach are that an additional registration process is not necessary and potential entry barriers will be reduced. To evaluate the potential synergy effects of integrating several social networks, the functions of the web application will not just relate to FB, but will also integrate Twitter. Besides using XHELP inside FB, the user can also assess XHELP as an ordinary web version.

6.3.1   Cross-Social-Media Search and Filter Function

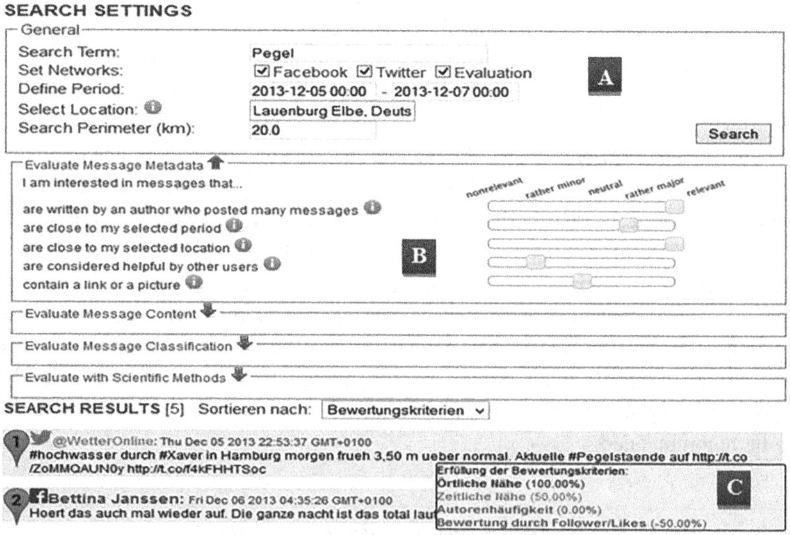

SEARCH SETTINGS
General
Search Term: Pegel
Set Networks: ☑ Facebook ☑ Twitter ☑ Evaluation   A
Define Period: 2013-12-05 00:00   - 2013-12-07 00:00
Select Location: ⓘ   Lauenburg Elbe, Deuts
Search Perimeter (km):   20.0   Search

Evaluate Message Metadata
I am interested in messages that...   nonrelevant rather minor neutral rather major relevant

are written by an author who posted many messages ⓘ
are close to my selected period ⓘ
are close to my selected location ⓘ   B
are considered helpful by other users ⓘ
contain a link or a picture ⓘ

Evaluate Message Content
Evaluate Message Classification
Evaluate with Scientific Methods

SEARCH RESULTS [5] Sortieren nach: Bewertungskriterien ⌄

1 @WetterOnline: Thu Dec 05 2013 22:53:37 GMT+0100
   #hochwasser durch #Xaver in Hamburg morgen frueh 3,50 m ueber normal. Aktuelle #Pegelstaende auf http://t.co
   /ZoMMQAUN0y http://t.co/f4kFHHTSoc
                                                        Erfülung der Bewertungskriterien:
                                                        Örtliche Nähe (100.00%)
2 Bettina Janssen: Fri Dec 06 2013 04:35:26 GMT+0100 Zeitliche Nähe (50.00%)   C
   Hoert das auch mal wieder auf. Die ganze nacht ist das total lauf Autorenhäufigkeit (0.00%)
                                                        Bewertung durch Follower/Likes (-50.00%)

Figure 6.8   Search Settings and Results

To support the relief activities of volunteers and group moderators in particular, a function for searching and filtering information is needed, as we have seen.

Figure 6.9
Geo-Localisation

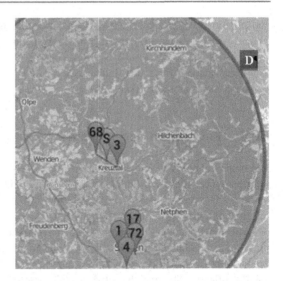

Groups and pages are often regionally based and therefore require filtering by location, while time-based filtering enables a further selection of the information supply. As moderators in particular search their groups for information in order to coordinate offers of and demands for help, it is essential to include data from groups and pages of the specific user in the search. The search function obtains the data from a social media API developed for this purpose. The API provides relevant messages from FB and Twitter in the OpenSocial format (http://openso cial.org/) and offers parameters for the time- and location-based filtering of posts. Using tokens, we can also access data from the user's restricted FB groups, if s/he has agreed and installed the XHELP FB app. In order to further support the aspects required for filtering and assessing information by users, the social media API is combined with a *quality assessment service* (Reuter et al., 2014). This tool enables the weighting of 12 different assessment criteria (time, space, reputation, metadata, sentiment analysis, fear factor, happiness factor among others) for search requests in addition to the filter options mentioned above. This means that the order of the search results can be controlled (Figure 6.8).

In the *general* section, users can type in search strings, choose the media to be searched and specify both a search period and a location, including a search radius (**A**). It is also possible to relevant FB groups or pages. The subsequent collapsible field-sets offer optional assessment criteria to impact the order of search results. Alternatively, the search results can be sorted by time, local proximity,

and platform (**B**). If a user defines more than one criterion, the degrees of ful-
filment will be shown in percentage and colour during a mouse-over (**C**). Next
to the list of the search results is a map (Figure 6.9) visualising the set location
as a green marker, the search radius as a blue circle and the search results with
geo-coordinates as red markers (**D**).

6.3.2 Publication and Management of Relevant Messages

The empirical study revealed that groups are closely linked to regional areas, but
information requirements cannot always be met within the confines of the area in
question. The posting function (Figure 6.10) of the application aims to support
information retrieval by moderators and volunteers by providing the opportunity
of publishing messages on multiple channels simultaneously. Here, Twitter is
provided as a publication channel in our evaluation without the need of a Twitter
account. In a real-world setting, this would not be feasible or would at least be
legally difficult. Clicking the label "Create new posting" (Figure 6.10) on the
left navigation bar shows the view of a message publication. The user types the
message into a text box before selecting the channels for publication (**E**).

Closely tied to the posting function is a dashboard view that summarises
created posts along with relevant metadata. Since postings are published cross-
platform, the user has to be supported in the management of these postings and
related comments by providing an overview. The dashboard is intended to give
the user an overview of his/her activities and to enable direct interaction with the
responding authors without visiting each channel individually.

The dashboard contains the overview "My Postings" (Figure 6.11). Alongside
the postings published within XHELP, it contains the user's postings or commented postings that were created beyond the application on the source platform
to give an entire overview of the user's activities. Once a post is commented on,
it will be attached chronologically with a reference to its source platform (**F**).
For the sake of clarity, the dashboard displays a maximum of five comments per
posting; and with an arrow symbol in the top right-hand corner of a posting,
the user can collapse or expand the comments on a posting. Users can respond
to each comment and delete their own. The top right-hand corner of a posting
contains symbols for deleting and finalising the correspondent posting (**G**). With
the "finalise posting" function, the user has a dialog-based opportunity to write a
concluding posting informing all related groups, pages, and media. The empirical
study showed that users published their requests in multiple groups but neglected
to inform each group individually whether requests had been settled. In order not

CREATE NEW POSTING

Internal Title ⓘ

Message (0 Zeichen)

E

Select Groups, Pages and Platforms of Publication:
☐ Publish Message on Twitter ⓘ
Groups:
☐ Hochwasser Opfer 2013 (alles wird verschenkt)
☐ Privates Helfer- und Hilfenetzwerk für Alle
☐ Hochwasser Magdeburg - HilfsGESUCHE
☐ HochwasserNiedersachsen - BIETE / SUCHE !!!
Pages:
☐ Mamas helfen Info Portal
☐ Hochwasser Niedersachsen

Publish Posting

Figure 6.10 Create new Posting

to waste resources on matters already dealt with and to prevent *dead postings*, XHELP supports the user in finalising and/or deleting successfully completed requests or postings and informing the participants of interaction. The postings will not be displayed in "My Postings" anymore, but are still accessible in the left navigation bar.

In summary, XHELP blends together multiple aspects of existing (commercial) approaches within the scope of volunteer activities: It provides dashboard features (Brandwatch, 2014; Twitter, 2014; uberMetrics Technologies GmbH, 2014), bidirectional and cross-media communication (Sprout Social, 2014), and with "finalise posting" a basic task management function (Hootsuite Media Inc, 2014). Moreover, the information search is enriched by map-based visualisation (Geofeedia Inc, 2014; Okolloh, 2009). Additionally, XHELP has no syntactical requirements and is embedded into an established context of use.

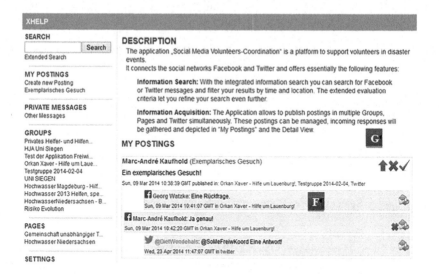

Figure 6.11   Dashboard with "My Postings"

6.3.3   Evaluation with Volunteers and Citizens

To assess the concept and the potential value of the web-application XHELP, an evaluation of the search for as well as filtering and assessment of information functions and of cross-channel functionality (FB, Twitter) was conducted. The philosophy behind the evaluation process was derived from the notion of "situated evaluation" (Twidale et al., 1994) in which qualitative methods are used in order to draw conclusions about real-world use of a technology using domain experts. The aim here is not to measure the relationship between evaluation goals and outcomes but to derive subjective views from experts about how useful and relevant the technology might be in use. XHELP was therefore evaluated with 20 users (E01-E20) whereof six participated on a first version of the prototype and were not involved in the follow-up. Of the remaining 14, four participants had been initiators and moderators of FB pages during European floods (three of them had already been interviewed during the empirical case study). Their experience as active volunteers generated some valuable feedback.

The evaluation was based on a scenario-based walkthrough coupled with subsequent semi-structured interviews. The scenario was designed to introduce the participants to the character of a disaster and the role of the volunteer (only if he/she was not already an experienced volunteer). It was based on hurricane Xaver which caused heavy damages on the coast of Germany in December 2013. The participants were given a general description of their role with regard to dealing with the information demands of affected citizens with the help of XHELP. The participants were then given the opportunity to explore the application, on the basis that they would be given a concrete task to tackle afterwards. The first step of the task required them to search for and filter specific information pertaining to water levels. For this purpose, the search function was extended with an evaluation mode. Search results were premised on preselected data records to ensure the comparability of the participants' results. The second step instructed them to ask for additional information about the condition of the dikes using the publication function, whereupon our team created some responses from both platforms to enable the use of the response and finalise functions. Following the think-aloud protocol (Nielsen, 1993), participants were asked to express their thoughts while completing the task.

The semi-structured interviews which followed were intended to encourage reflection on the evaluation process, on ease of use and on the overall usefulness of the application. The questions were specifically oriented towards overall impressions, the advantages and disadvantages of XHELP, coverage of information demands, possible overload, and problems of cross-platform information acquisition. The interviews were analysed and categorised systematically. We employed "open" coding i.e. gathering data into approximate categories to reflect the issues raised by respondents based on repeated readings of the data and its organisation into "similar" statements. We clustered positive and negative aspects of the (a) search and (b) dashboard functionality, as well as the (c) usability and (d) potentials of functional enhancement. Taking into account the quantity and originality of aspects as well as the participants' domain expertise, we created a rating for each cluster. The most noteworthy contributions will be presented subsequently and thereafter shaped into design requirements.

6.3.3.1   Results I: Cross-Platform Search and Assessment

Ten interviewees regarded the search refinement and sorting of results as being valuable, especially when dealing with large amounts of data. In contrast, some negative views were expressed. Eight interviewees deemed the selection of criteria to be too extensive, resulting in complex searches which might hamper quick results. Additionally, E20 suggested that some means of assessing the emotional content of messages was needed, since it bore some consequences for perceived accuracy:

> *"If someone is upset about something that isn't correct at all and then spreads wrong information and next other people follow it, it has to be counteracted rapidly" (E20).*

Two participants argued that an automatic information assessment might result in over-reliance on the application and could potentially result in the loss of relevant search results. E20 doubted that an information search with search terms was useful for identifying offers of, and demands for donated items:

> *"But then, if I search for donations, they don't show up, but rather I have to enter 'dusk mask'. But I cannot always search through all search terms. If it is somehow possible to reasonably filter offers of donation computer-linguistically that would be certainly handy" (E20).*

More positively, nine interviewees deemed search functions based on chronological and regional proximity to be important. The visualisation of a search radius, the ability to identify their own location and the possibility to see search results on a map were all seen as enriching information value. Broadly, this is because these functions enabled better judgment about information relevance in relation to rationality, priority and reliability (E17). A search for general, repeated and crisis-specific verbs or syntaxes that *"are easily and always tracked in the background for a certain disaster"* (E20), would therefore be a useful addition.

6.3.3.2   Results II: Cross-Platform Dissemination of Posts

Altogether, we saw benefits in terms of the reduction of the overhead. Publishing posts in multiple groups, pages and platforms simultaneously was seen to be much easier. Through the centralised presentation, an overview could also be obtained:

> *"I really like it. It saves a lot of work, because before, you had to visit every single page and that wasted too much time: You do not have enough people that can help"* (E19).

Seven interviewees thought that the application speeded up their information searches over different information sources and the broader bandwidth of platforms. During the selection of dissemination channels, six participants selected Twitter to increase the audience of readers. Three people indicated explicitly that they value the opportunity to publish postings in Twitter without having to create an own account:

> "You essentially built a bridge [...]. This is awesome, because many distribute their information through Twitter and have the opportunity to use Twitter without even owning an account or looking for followers or whatever" (E18).

Further, four participants expressed a positive attitude towards finalising a posting, or at least the opportunity to publish summary messages, on all channels simultaneously. This circumstance and the resulting reduction of effort are emphasised by E18:

> "What I really liked was the function to finish a posting, or to extend or change the demands; you did not need to search in twenty groups 'Where is the post?' to edit or comment it, but rather it was done immediately" (E18).

6.3.3.3 Results III: Reliability of Gathered Information

During the evaluation, eight participants expressed concerns about the reliability of information, which they gathered with the search or dissemination functionality, and identified different ways in which they went about validating information. For example, two interviewees searched for the public profile of the message author to gain an impression of this person:

> "Then I would try to evaluate the information based on the history of the person, which means if a person published quite a few postings in the past that were meaningful and correct, then I would be more likely to believe in the correctness of information" (E12).

Three interviewees wanted to check the reliability by confirmation from other users and two sought direct contact with the author. The consultation of other sources is linked to some other concerns, as stated by E16:

> "Someone might ascribe too much weight to information on these networks which has not been validated officially. Because I remember that there were several false reports [...]. That could raise panic or something" (E16).

E16 suggests (similarly to E8) that false reports are a serious problem. Beyond that, she considers local information to be more reliable than remote information.

6.3.3.4   Results IV: Potential of Functional Enhancement

A number of comments were made about improving XHELP's functionality. Five participants requested the possibility of self-selecting groups, pages and networks, ensuring that only relevant crisis information is managed within the application:

> "An incredible amount of people [...] have hundreds of groups. To select the relevant groups again and again from post to post [...] is too time-consuming. Maybe you can select [...] groups to be associated with the app" (E18).

Further, three interviewees see potential in the integration of additional social networks, e.g. Google +. Another person mentions the integration of news webpages within the search functionality (E15). To increase XHELP's breadth of usage, E18 wishes "that if the application is released, it will be released on smartphones [...], because many people are on the road and do the whole [response work] not at PC or laptop, but on a smartphone" (E18).

Furthermore, E18 suggests improved contact support among the users of the application to connect people with similar objectives. Thus, new relations between volunteers or communities can emerge:

> "Maybe it would be interesting to see other users of the app [or] who are searching for the same thing and using the app and who have the same interests as me" (E11).

If task completion is to be achieved cooperatively, E20 asked for a joint view within the application:

> "It would be very important for the organisers of the same group [...] to have the same overview, because otherwise you do things twice or three times [...], so you simply need the same information" (E20).

Overall, five participants asked for the ability to evaluate obtained information. Three of them explicitly mentioned the ability to sort comments or select a "best answer":

> "It would be nice [...] if you had the option to actually mark the question answered or to highlight the respondent who answered the question. So that anybody searching for the answer does not have to go through all the comments initially" (E12).

Concerning the search function, two interviewees requested the ability to manually evaluate search results along with the automatic assessment and to be able to put selected results into a favourite view (E08). Similarly, E20 proposes a function to exclude unreliable sources and to purposefully search for messages of certain, reliable or official authors. Authorities themselves are seen to be reliable information sources. Thus, E15 wishes *"that the corresponding official establishments such as police, fire service etc. write appropriate messages, in the knowledge that people can access them in any case through this application"* (E15). E19 complains that otherwise official information is disclosed *"much too late and not comprehensively"* (E19) to self-organised helpers.

6.4   Design Requirements

The evaluation reveals four design requirements as being essential to enhance the value of an application that provides a cross-social-media support for volunteers during emergencies:

First, *overview and avoiding barriers of usage*: The basic principle of a FB application that enables interaction patterns, and the display of content from social media already in use is demonstrably beneficial, according to our respondents. The evaluation, however, showed that there is need for an information management tool which allows some kind of overview and transcends existing barriers. Extended configurations imply further possibilities for improving the information overview, especially in terms of providing a common overview that moderators and teams can rely on.

Second, *user-defined information management*: A custom information management is required because of the varying preconditions, assessments and working procedures of the participants. Options were requested for selecting relevant application channels to include or exclude information from groups or sites that they saw as relevant or irrelevant to their demands. Furthermore, the scenario showed that users wanted a component to manage favourites, e.g. storing valuable search results or relevant answers obtained using the cross-platform posting function.

Third, *support for self-assessment* and *information verification*: The participants wanted support for information assessment according to specific qualitative criteria to enable them to search purposefully through the vast flood of data on social media. At the same time, they expressed a desire to self-evaluate posts or comments and to highlight relevant comments. Such a function could be used to improve the filtering and classification of upcoming search queries (Cobb et al., 2014). As the data is investigated, the process can be assisted by giving easy access to a message creator's public profile, supporting the establishment of contacts and enriched information about the poster. Since official crisis response information is considered to be more trustworthy, the integration of that data into the process of information assessment or into the application is desirable.

Fourth, *amplify potential for cross-platform networking*: Interviewees see advantages in cross-platform information processing because faster responses are possible, and the general view of the integrated platforms reduces management effort. The functionality of finalising postings is perceived as assistance to formulating cross-platform status updates and to completing help activities.

6.5   Summary

This chapter examines the work of volunteer communities in disasters focusing on the empirical analysis of social media activities as well as interviews with moderators of volunteer groups in FB and the evaluation of the novel web-application XHELP. This is intended to support volunteers during crisis events.

The case study of the European floods in 2013 emphasises the relevance of social media in Germany for the first time. Twitter has been used broadly as a platform for status updates, while FB pages gave a situational overview and FB groups coordinated a multitude of virtual and real help activities. This confirms the findings of Hughes et al. (2014). Among affected citizens and volunteers, some particularly motivated people adapted the role of "moderators" to mediate offers of and demands for help with the use of the technical functions of the social networks. This extends the role model of Reuter et al. (2013). Our examination shows the main challenges, which are (1) clarity and representation of relevant content; (2) moderation and autonomous work; (3) feedback and updates in interaction relationships; and (4) integration of technologies and interaction types for the design of social media for volunteers in crises.

Evaluating our web-application XHELP, we showed that a cross-platform search, especially with time and location filtering options, contributes to the channelling of the information flow. Furthermore, cross-platform posting provides an overview and reduces overhead with its centralised management. The embedding of Twitter is seen as an opportunity to increase the range of search and distribution activities. The interviewees mentioned the reduction of search criteria, the possibility of self-assessment and the filtering of information to gain an overview of the relevant activities as potential sources for improvement. The main results of the evaluation can be summarised as (1) avoiding barriers of usage with supportive tools; (2) user-defined application configuration and information management;

(3) support for self-assessment and information verification; and (4) amplifying the potentials of cross-platform networking.

Compared to related work, our approach provides several contributions: Addressing the "chaotic" use of social media (Kaewkitipong et al., 2012; Valecha et al., 2013), we implemented functionalities to render social media "more listen-able" as suggested by Hughes et al. (2014) (which is also interesting for crowd monitoring), e.g., by showing related discussions on various social media and by using a cross-social-media function to finalise postings. In order to support current working practices, Cobb et al. (2014) suggest querying multiple social networks with filters. We have implemented such a function. Our app enables its users to disseminate messages (including backchannel (Dörk et al., 2010)) to various social networks. We consider that our approach enhances the state of the art by presenting empirical data, a concept and its implementation which e.g., amplifies the potential of cross-platform networking. Other tools, such as Ushahidi, automate the collection of incident reports and facilitate the mapping of report locations (McClendon & Robinson, 2012), but are developed as external platforms which have to be deployed manually. Our app is integrated into FB and supports established interaction types (Reuter et al., 2013) while still having a cross-platform focus without the burden of syntactical requirements (Starbird & Palen, 2011). The potential integration of additional social media platforms promises to further enhance the cross-platform concept in future. XHELP will then be able to support volunteer's emergent collaboration (Reuter, 2014b) not only across time and space, but also across platform, group and page.

Discussion and Conclusion

7

In 2001, the first case of social media being used for disaster relief was recorded. Since then, social media and its usage for public safety and security—before, during, and after crises, emergencies, or disasters—has been developing continuously and becoming more and more pervasive. As a reaction to this, many studies in the field of crisis informatics have been published, investigating the way in which social media was used and perceived in crisis events of any type and size.

This thesis aimed to answer the following main research question from a European perspective: **What are citizens' and authorities' attitudes towards social media for public safety and security?** The essential findings of my contribution to the topic are summarised in this section.

7.1 The State of the Art in Crisis Informatics

Being familiar with the most recent scientific research and the state of the art in the field is an essential foundation to conduct relevant research. Therefore chapter 2 summarises studies that focus on the use of social media during many of the most significant emergency events that have happened worldwide since 2001. It is shown that while former studies primarily investigated crisis events in the USA, the number of studies focusing on other countries has been increasing. The wide range of different studies investigating different countries also involves the comparative and systematic analysis of various emergency contexts. The social media platform Twitter plays an important role in the crisis informatics literature as it supports the collection of data and is highly accessible.

Different *types of research* can be found in the crisis informatics literature. Firstly, many researchers use empirical methods such as data collection

© The Author(s), under exclusive license to Springer Fachmedien Wiesbaden GmbH, part of Springer Nature 2022
C. Reuter, *A European Perspective on Crisis Informatics*, https://doi.org/10.1007/978-3-658-39720-3_7

or interviews to investigate the influence of social media on behaviour in crisis management. Secondly, the handling of data, i.e., collecting, processing and interpreting large amounts of social data, is a further focus of research. To support an effective usage of social media in times of crisis, some researchers concentrate on deriving suitable testing systems and showing design implications. Thirdly, interdisciplinary and cross-field research is carried out, enabling researchers to approach more complex problems and research questions take a more comprehensive perspective.

Considering authorities and citizen as two important groups, four different *use patterns* are derived. Firstly, the communication between citizens (C2C), that involves emergent and (digital) volunteer groups who constitute a framework for self-coordination and help. Secondly, the communication from authorities to citizens (A2C), comprising all measures of crisis communication. Thirdly, the communication from citizens to authorities (C2A), in which not only the analysis of big data or social media but also concepts of crowdsourcing and crowd tasking play an important and role. And finally, the communication among authorities (A2A) that makes use of inter-organisational social networks.

After summarising the current state of social media use in emergencies, this thesis investigates different stakeholders' perceptions of the use of social media in emergencies in Europe. It aims to not focus just on Twitter, and to research more than one particular crisis, while including both perspectives of emergency services and citizens by utilising representative surveys across Europe. Chapter 3 therefore researches emergency services' and Chapter 4 citizens' perceptions of social media in emergencies.

7.2   Attitudes of Emergency Services' Staff

Chapter 3 focuses on authorities' perspective, aiming to answer the question RQ1: **What is the attitude of the staff of emergency services across Europe towards the organisational usage of social media?**

It shows that social media is mostly used by organisations to share information, particularly recommendations concerning the prevention of accidents and emergencies with citizens (A2C). Whilst not even half of the respondents reported to use social media at least occasionally to receive messages from the public (C2A), even fewer, only 5%, indicated that their organisations often use social media in this context. However, an important finding of the survey is that several organisations actually use social media before, during, or after an emergency. It is shown, particularly by the qualitative answers, that social media is often used to share tips with the public both before and during an emergency. While suggestions before an emergency concentrate on preventive information, during an emergency they include safety advice. Furthermore, during an emergency, social media helps with the dissemination of warnings and information concerning the current situation and status of an emergency. At the same time, organisations monitor social media activity. After emergencies, organisations use social media to make multimedia supported reports available to the public and to coordinate clean-up activities. In the future, most of the emergency services are likely to share information—such as recommendations concerning both the prevention of accidents and the right behaviour during emergencies—with the public more often via social media and, in general, to use social media more frequently. However, this is not applicable to all organisations to the same extent.

Not only skilled staff, i.e. trained personnel with required knowledge and professional communication capabilities, but also an open attitude to the usage of social media information is essential for an efficient and widespread social media use by emergency services. Furthermore, an organisation must meet the technical requirements such as a reliable internet infrastructure and a software supporting users coordinating their activities in multiple social networks. To promote social media usage, it can be useful to show examples of good practice and to create a positive attitude inside the organisation. However, legal concerns such as data protection and internal aspects such as compliance issues, mistrust, and difficulties of dealing with the complexity of social media information have led to usage barriers. By collecting data in 2014 and 2017 across Europe, with a total of 1,169 answers, empirical evidence to enhance an effective use of social media for emergency services is provided. The analysis shows that personal experience has an effect on how organisational usage of social media is perceived and how emergency service staff view the future use of social media. Furthermore, it shows that the use has increased.

7.3 Citizens' Perception towards Social Media in Emergencies

Having studied authorities' perspective, chapter 4 considers the perception of citizens, aiming to address the question RQ2: **How do citizens across Europe, especially in the Netherlands, Germany, Italy, and the United Kingdom, use social media during emergencies?**

The chapter shows that during emergency situations, social media is already being used by many citizens in Europe who want to both gain and distribute information. Considering the representative survey: While one third (29%) of the surveyed citizens indicated that they had used social media for sharing information, almost 40% of them (39%) used social media to inform themselves. This confirms an earlier finding: "Social media supports citizens in their search for reliable information to reduce their uncertainty about the situation far beyond the regular but late information provided by authorities" (Jurgens & Helsloot, 2017). Weather conditions or warnings (47%), feelings or emotions (40%) and road or traffic conditions (35%) were the most frequently shared topics. Also, the survey reveals that citizens expect their usage to increase in the future with view to emergency purposes.

Another essential finding of the survey is that the frequency of social media usage in private and emergency contexts varies from country to country and from citizen to citizen. It can be shown that men and people older than 50 are less likely to make use of social media to share and look for information than women and younger people. This finding could be due to the fact that 29% of respondents who are 50 years of age or older do not have a smartphone without which social media cannot be used away from home. This group of people runs the risk of being excluded from important information that emergency services or other citizens share via social media before, during, or after an emergency, as social media use in general is increasing—however, they should then use other channels. In this context, an important challenge to address is that the most vulnerable people in an emergency, e.g., older or disabled citizens, will not necessarily benefit from the dissemination of social media use among emergency services. Finally, the first citizen study shows that emergency functions of social media such as Twitter Alerts and Facebook Safety Checks were relatively unknown among the citizens interviewed, more than half of them (56%) had never heard of at least one of them. More precisely, 60% did not know about Twitter Alerts and for 68% Facebook Safety Checks was an unknown function.

Further, the chapter focuses on the impact of risk cultures in social media use in emergencies. Usage of social media during emergencies and respective perceptions vary across countries. This work applies the theory of risk cultures to the social media use in order to find out if it can also be applied to this area. The study shows differences of current use of social media in emergencies, expectations towards authorities monitoring social media, intensity of perceiving barriers regarding the use as well as variances concerning the (likelihood of future) use of mobile apps. While German and British participants' frequency of use of social media is medium and low, respectively, Italian and Dutch respondents use them relatively frequently. At the same time, our findings stress that across the four European countries, participants assessed similar advantages, such as dissemination of information, and barriers, such as false rumours, with respect to use social media during emergencies. Equal distribution across nations, age, and gender showed significant relationships with social media usage which, among other findings, suggests being helpful for effective implementation of management structures using new technologies. With regard to citizens' expectations towards monitoring by authorities and attitudes towards the use of mobile emergency apps, our findings are consistent with prior research on risk cultures (Cornia et al., 2016; Dressel & Pfeil, 2017).

The fact that most citizens (69%) expect emergency services to monitor their social media platforms more regularly and that almost half of them (41%) expect a response within an hour leads to the following conclusion: Not only citizens' social media use in emergencies is increasing, but also their expectation of emergency services using social media to communicate with citizens. Using social media, emergency services can consider information shared by citizens. Fifty-six percent of citizens are convinced that only few emergency services make use of data on social media as they are concerned with other things than responding to requests for help or information during an emergency. This is reflected by the fact that emergency services rather use social media to share information with the public, than to monitor activities and use the respective data during an emergency. Furthermore, many respondents indicated that factors encouraging them to share information via social media depended on a clearer purpose for sharing information, especially if they knew that emergency services would actually use the information shared. Thus, from the citizens' view, emergency services do not behave in the way that citizens expect them to.

7.4 Situational Assessment of Emergency Services

In order to ease the use of social media for emergency services, e.g. to monitor activities, appropriate applications are needed. Therefore, Chapter 5 focuses on tailorable situation assessment with social media, answering the question RQ3: **How can situational assessment of emergency services be supported by social media?**

Based on an empirical pre-study and analysis of the technical properties of social media, the chapter presents key challenges, like multi-platform support, data formats or meta data, and implements the prototype Social-QAS to show how crisis management actors can use an adjustable quality assessment to better assess the situation using citizen-generated information from social media. The service incorporates identified quality criteria for information from social media. Furthermore, an important characteristic is the individual adjustability enabling the user to adapt the quality criteria to the respective context.

This adjustability not only includes tailoring options regarding the quality assessment criteria but also regarding the source platform selection. In general, the options enable a greater flexibility—addressing the different needs, e.g. related to risk cultures or individual preferences. This is very important because situation assessment is very subjective depending on personal skills and experience, and because information needs to differ depending on the context. Overall, Social-QAS and its successor, the Social Media Observatory, imply a number of benefits in comparison to other applications. Next to emergency services receiving information, flexible assessment and free accessibility support the work of unbound volunteers. To sum up, it is useful to be flexible by tailoring options for source platform selection and quality assessment criteria since situation assessment revealed itself to be very subjective. Consequently, personal feelings, experiences and the situation itself influence the information requirement.

7.5   Self-Organisation of Digital Volunteers with Social Media

Chapter 6 focuses on the use of social media by citizen themselves, aiming to answer the question RQ4: **How can self-organisation of digital volunteers be supported by social media?**

Our study during the European floods in 2013 confirms that different social media platforms were used for different purposes: Firstly, Twitter was used to give regular status and situation updates, whereby automatic retweet services played an important role in structuring the information space. Secondly, Facebook pages and groups were used with different intentions. On the one hand, Facebook pages enabled gaining an overview of the situation and supported handling large amounts of information via a filter function. On the other hand, Facebook groups built a framework for the coordination of virtual and real relief activities. Some questioned the possibility of involving volunteers, however, our study showed that many rather easy tasks, where coordination is the main effort, exist. Or as described: "The role of ordinary citizens might be questioned if disaster response was a complex task, but this is often not the case. It was not difficult to see who needs help and help them by driving them to hospital. It was not difficult to stand at a door and ask people to go to another entrance. It was not difficult for a fishing boat to search the ocean for aircraft or human debris" (Scanlon et al., 2014). Still, the coordination of these activities is sometimes challenging.

Finally, some other tools such as Google Maps, Live Blog, Google Docs or custom web tools were used, often in combination with Twitter or Facebook. Nevertheless, it is important to differentiate between the examined communities, as both the overall importance of social media and the applied levels of privacy and technological integration varied. Moderators act as intermediaries between supply and demand of help in social media and other ICTs by structuring the process of exchanging information, promoting cooperation, and organising voluntary services. This important role is not only taken by affected citizens and (digital) volunteers, but also by organised volunteers, like volunteer fire brigades. However, arrangements with official emergency management were made via local communication, meetings, and telephone.

The chapter also addresses the challenges for volunteers. These include, clarity and representation of relevant content, feedback and updates in interaction relationships, organisational identification and resilience, integration of technologies and interaction types, moderation and autonomous work, and maintaining quality of information. The FB application XHELP was implemented to meet these requirements as most relief activities are organised in FB groups and pages. It not only has a cross-platform search function but also a posting function to reduce high organisational efforts and facilitate procedures. Its users can benefit from reduced entry barriers and time savings as an additional registration process is no longer necessary.

Further advantages became apparent when evaluating XHELP. Because of time and location filtering options that are part of the cross-platform search, the information flow is channelled. Regarding the cross-platform posting function, benefits especially result from the provided overview and reduced overhead through centralised management. Finally, the integration of Twitter increases the benefit of the whole application by enabling a wider range of search and distribution activities. However, there is still room for improvement. Some of the participants wish for less search criteria and a possibility to gain an overview of relevant activities through self-assessment and filtering of information. To sum up, the main connecting points are: (1) avoiding barriers of usage with supportive tools; (2) user-defined application configuration and information management; (3) support for self-assessment and information verification; and (4) amplifying the potentials of cross-platform networking.

7.6   Policy Recommendations and Limitations

Based on the findings of the aforementioned studies with citizens and authorities, their attitudes and experiences and possibilities for situation assessment or volunteer support, some policy recommendations can be derived:

1. **Multiple perspectives:** Research on social media in emergencies and resulting concepts or policies *should consider multiple, e.g. authorities' and citizens', perspectives.* Addressing these views is especially important from a public administration and political science standpoint and is in accordance with sociotechnical theory (Pasmore, 1988) as the most important theory of public administration and IT (Reddick, 2012, p. 4) on the impact of technology on social and organisational change. Accordingly, the governing process is not just based on legal authority (wherefore authorities would be the only necessary actor), but depends on all stakeholders' participation (including citizens) and their attitudes towards social media and their actual (private) use of social media, which this thesis found to be the "driving force in shaping the opinion on organisational use" (Section 3.3.3). If all perspectives are included, crisis informatics is probably more successful, as it possibly addresses more requirements.

2. **Benefits and costs:** It is also vital to *evaluate benefits and costs or risks for all stakeholders.* Benefits include foreseeable effects as reasons for technology implementation, but also more difficult to predict opportunity-based and emergent changes (Orlikowski & Hofman, 1997); costs and risks also include effects that were neither foreseeable nor wanted. While this work found that emergency service personnel in Europe have the opinion that providing preventive and situational communication via social media are the most important use cases (and probably the most valuable or time efficient, belonging to A2C) (Section 3.3.2.2), we found that citizens also have high expectations towards authorities with regard to other use cases, such as monitoring social media or the expectation of receiving answers to messages in social media from emergency services within one hour (both C2A) (Section 4.2.2.4). The latter can both be seen as an emergent effect, which was not necessarily planned by emergency services. However, as governments are increasingly able to use ICT, they face a growing demand for open government (de Vries, 2016), and social media is one possibility for this. Further risks are false rumours, unreliable information, or data privacy issues. As a takeaway, the value of use cases

differs based on the perspective and needs of the respective user group. Evaluating possible effects beforehand, but also during and after the implementation is recommended.

3. **Resource constraints:** Another important factor is that emergencies mostly imply time and resource constraints. Social media policies should therefore only focus *on cases where the positive effects outweigh the negative.* Or, as mentioned in the introduction: "big crisis data should not be considered as a magic bullet which can save lives just because they are available" (Boersma & Fonio, 2017). Emergency services should therefore evaluate which use cases and expectations they really can address also *during* an emergency and which not, in order to not create more complexity, chaos or information overload (Kaufhold, 2021). Based on the assessment of the situation, strategies with different levels of involvement and resource intensity could be implemented, including information dissemination and crisis communication (lower), monitoring social media (medium) or active two-way communication and coordination (higher efforts).

4. **Use patterns:** It is also important to be very aware that both functionalities and usage differ among social media platforms (Section 6.2.3). The knowledge about *different use patterns for different social media services* (some are suitable for publishing information, others for group work) should be applied. Using social media without any also rudimentary form of two-way communication is probably not expected by citizens, and will therefore not be fully accepted by them (Section 4.2.2.4). Policymakers should also consider existing social media and their use, as citizens are most likely to use the communication channels, they use in everyday life also during emergencies. Both policies and tools for emergency services or volunteers should therefore avoid barriers of usage (Section 6.2.5.4), ensuring existing users and data can be included.

5. **Target groups:** Social media policies for emergency services *should especially focus on persons that are already using social media.* Not many people will start using social media during an emergency. Our structural equation modelling found that the private usage of social media is a driving force in shaping emergency service staffs' opinion on organisational use (Section 3.3.3). Crisis managers are likely to use the same technology they are familiar with on a day-to-day basis also during crises (Groenendaal & Helsloot, 2021). Additionally, emergency services' staff mentioned staff skills and organisational culture as most important factors, compared to software, equipment, or funding (Section 3.3.2.3).

6. **Cultural differences:** Policies for social media *should be aware of different risk cultures* (Cornia et al., 2016) in order to implement appropriate communication strategies (Section 4.3.1). State-oriented (Germany), individualistic (the Netherlands) or fatalistic (the United Kingdom, formerly Italy) risk cultures differ regarding trust in authorities or who is responsible for managing crisis situations (authorities or citizens themselves) and therefore different services may be effective. The adaption of best practices to other countries might therefore not necessarily be successful without adjustments, also within a country demographic or regional differences may also be important to consider. International learning effects, e.g. between state-oriented and individual-oriented risk cultures, could be promising to strengthen European resilience. However, being aware of differences and therefore being flexible is a core recommendation.

7. **Automation:** The implementation of technical applications to ease the processing of social media should also consider that automation can help, however that emergency services need *reasons, and not just recommendations, to implement decisions* (Section 5.4.4). The fact that citizen-generated content may be flawed requires information assessment, which can be supported by automation, however "it is a member of the emergency team who has to take responsibility for actions taken and who also has to decide if the information is used or not". As long as the situation is dynamic and actors are diverse, tailorability of applications is necessary to address all needs—and applications should always justify why some conclusions are derived based on existing data.

Of course, the work presented in this thesis has many limitations. Although individual limitations of the different parts of the studies have already been mentioned in the respective sections (3.2.3.2, 3.3.4.3, 4.2.3, 4.3.4.3, 5.5, 6.4), there are some limitations on the level of the thesis as a whole:

- The study is based on empirical work and mostly on *surveys* with emergency services and citizens, which is why only those people who participate in surveys are covered in this thesis. In some parts of this work, real activities on social media have been studied, however, perceptions are largely based on self-reporting. Studies observing real behaviour in social media are therefore always needed as a complement.
- Furthermore, most studies worked with *online surveys*, therefore only people willing and able to work online were considered. Therefore, participants are more tech-savvy than the average, and some numbers mentioned in this work

may actually be lower. Nevertheless, it should be emphasised that social media is not an all-encompassing solution for the entire communication in crisis situations, but only a piece of the puzzle that can effectively complement it for certain target groups, such as people who use social media actively. For some people and during a certain type of emergency, warning and information via radio or television is best, for others crisis apps or social media complement crisis communication. Accordingly, this preselection might even be helpful, even though online surveys were conducted here.

- Although the study especially regarding citizens is based on large representative samples in the Netherlands, Germany, the United Kingdom and Italy, *not all European countries* are considered and also within the countries studied large differences were found. Europe is therefore no homogeneous unit with regard to crisis informatics. Nevertheless, some aspects mentioned in these countries could be interpreted with regard to certain risk cultures, wherefore they might be transferrable to other countries that have a similar risk culture.

Crisis informatics is a very important field of study and nowadays increasingly so from a European perspective, as long as the number of large-scale emergencies affecting Europe increases. This thesis aims to provide a necessary complement to the successful implementation of social media in emergencies with a European view (a view of selected European countries) from the perspective of public administration and political science.

References

Acar, Adam; & Muraki, Yuya. (2011). Twitter for crisis communication: lessons learned from Japan's tsunami disaster. *International Journal of Web Based Communities*, vol. 7, no. 3, pp. 392–402. https://doi.org/10.1504/IJWBC.2011.041206

Agichtein, Eugene; Castillo, Carlos; Donato, Debora; Gionis, Aristides; & Mishne, Gilad. (2008). Finding High-Quality Content in Social Media. In *Proceedings of the International Conference on Web Search and Data Mining* (pp. 183–193). https://doi.org/10.1145/1341531.1341557

Aichholzer, Julian. (2017). *Einführung in lineare Strukturgleichungsmodelle mit Stata* (1st ed.). Wiesbaden: Springer VS. https://doi.org/10.1007/978-3-658-16670-0

Akhgar, Babak; Fortune, Dave; Hayes, Richard E.; Guerra, Barbara; & Manso, Marco. (2013). Social media in crisis events: Open networks and collaboration supporting disaster response and recovery. In *2013 IEEE International Conference on Technologies for Homeland Security (HST)* (pp. 760–765). IEEE. https://doi.org/10.1109/THS.2013.6699099

Al-Saggaf, Yeslam; & Simmons, Peter. (2015). Social media in Saudi Arabia: Exploring its use during two natural disasters. *Technological Forecasting and Social Change*, vol. 95, pp. 3–15. https://doi.org/10.1016/j.techfore.2014.08.013

Alam, Firoj; Imran, Muhammad; & Ofli, Ferda. (2017). Image4Act: Online Social Media Image Processing for Disaster Response. In *Proceedings of the 2017 IEEE/ACM International Conference on Advances in Social Networks Analysis and Mining 2017* (pp. 601–604). New York, USA: Association for Computing Machinery. https://doi.org/10.1145/3110025.3110164

Alam, Firoj; Joty, Shafiq; & Imran, Muhammad. (2018a). Domain Adaptation with Adversarial Training and Graph Embeddings. In *Proceedings of the 56th Annual Meeting of the Association for Computational Linguistics (Volume 1: Long Papers)* (pp. 1077–1087). Melbourne, Australia: Association for Computational Linguistics. https://doi.org/10.18653/v1/P18-1099

Alam, Firoj; Ofli, Ferda; & Imran, Muhammad. (2018b). Processing Social Media Images by Combining Human and Machine Computing during Crises. *International Journal of Human-Computer Interaction*, vol. 34, no. 4, pp. 311–327. https://doi.org/10.1080/10447318.2018.1427831

© The Editor(s) (if applicable) and The Author(s), under exclusive license to Springer Fachmedien Wiesbaden GmbH, part of Springer Nature 2022
C. Reuter, *A European Perspective on Crisis Informatics*,
https://doi.org/10.1007/978-3-658-39720-3

Alam, Firoj; Ofli, Ferda; & Imran, Muhammad. (2020). Descriptive and visual summaries of disaster events using artificial intelligence techniques: case studies of Hurricanes Harvey, Irma, and Maria. *Behaviour & Information Technology (BIT)*, vol. 39, no. 3, pp. 288–318. https://doi.org/10.1080/0144929X.2019.1610908

Albris, Kristoffer. (2017). The switchboard mechanism: How social media connected citizens during the 2013 floods in Dresden. *Journal of Contingencies and Crisis Management (JCCM)*, pp. 1–8. https://doi.org/10.1111/1468-5973.12201

Alexander, David E. (2013). Social Media in Disaster Risk Reduction and Crisis Management. *Science and Engineering Ethics*, vol. 20, no. 3, pp. 717–733. https://doi.org/10.1007/s11948-013-9502-z

Allen, Christopher. (2004). Tracing the Evolution of Social Software. Retrieved from http://www.lifewithalacrity.com/2004/10/tracing_the_evo.html

Alpaslan, Özerdem; & Gianni, Rufini. (2012). L'Aquila's reconstruction challenges: has Italy learned from its previous earthquake disasters? *Disasters*, vol. 37, no. 1, pp. 119–143. https://doi.org/10.1111/j.1467-7717.2012.01296.x

American Red Cross. (2012a). More Americans Using Mobile Apps in Emergencies. Retrieved April 14, 2018, from https://www.prnewswire.com/news-releases/more-americ ans-using-mobile-apps-in-emergencies-168144726.html

American Red Cross. (2012b). Social Media in Disasters and Emergencies: Online Survey of 1,017 Respondents and Telephone Survey of 1,018 Respondents. Retrieved from https://slideplayer.com/slide/1448104/

An, Jisun; Kwak, Haewoon; Mejova, Yelena; Oger, Sonia Alonso Saenz De; & Fortes, Braulio Gomez. (2016). Are you Charlie or Ahmed? Cultural pluralism in Charlie Hebdo response on Twitter. In *International AAAI Conference on Web and Social Media* (pp. 1–10). Retrieved from https://ojs.aaai.org/index.php/ICWSM/article/view/14709/14558

Anderson, Kenneth M.; & Schram, Aaron. (2011). Design and implementation of a data analytics infrastructure in support of crisis informatics research: NIER track. *2011 33rd International Conference on Software Engineering (ICSE)*, pp. 844–847. https://doi.org/10.1145/1985793.1985920

Andrews, Cynthia; Fichet, Elodie; Ding, Yuwei; Spiro, Emma S.; & Starbird, Kate. (2016). Keeping Up with the Tweet-dashians: The Impact of "Official" Accounts on Online Rumoring. In *Proceedings of the Conference on Computer-Supported Cooperative Work & Social Computing (CSCW)* (pp. 452–465). New York, USA: ACM Press. https://doi.org/10.1145/2818048.2819986

Ardito, Carmelo; Costabile, M. Francesca; Desolda, Giuseppe; Lanzilotti, Rosa; Matera, Maristella; & Picozzi, Matteo. (2014). Visual composition of data sources by end users. In *Proceedings of the International Working Conference on Advanced Visual Interfaces* (pp. 257–260). New York, USA: ACM Press. https://doi.org/10.1145/2598153.2598201

Arif, Ahmer; Robinson, John J.; Stanek, Stephanie A.; Fichet, Elodie S.; Townsend, Paul; Worku, Zena; & Starbird, Kate. (2017). A Closer Look at the Self-Correcting Crowd: Examining Corrections in Online Rumors. In *Proceedings of the Conference on Computer-Supported Cooperative Work & Social Computing (CSCW)* (pp. 155–168). New York, USA: ACM. https://doi.org/10.1145/2998181.2998294

Arif, Ahmer; Shanahan, Kelley; Chou, Fangju; Dosouto, Yoanna; Starbird, Kate; & Spiro, Emma S. (2016). How Information Snowballs: Exploring the Role of Exposure in Online

Rumor Propagation. In *Proceedings of the Conference on Computer-Supported Cooperative Work & Social Computing (CSCW)* (pp. 466–467). New York, USA: ACM Press. https://doi.org/10.1145/2818048.2819964

Backfried, Gerhard; Schmidt, Christian; & Quirchmayr, Gerald. (2015). Cross-Media Linking in Times of Disaster. In *Proceedings of the International Conference on Information Systems for Crisis Response and Management (ISCRAM)*. Kristiansand, Norway.

Baird, Malcolm E. (2010). *The Phases of Emergency Management*. Retrieved from https://www.memphis.edu/ifti/pdfs/cait_phases_of_emergency_mngt.pdf

Bassett, C. (2015). Plenty as a response to austerity? Big Data expertise, cultures and communities. *European Journal of Cultural Studies*, vol. 18, no. 4–5, pp. 548–563. https://doi.org/10.1177/1367549415577394

Batrinca, Bogdan; & Treleaven, Philip C. (2014). Social media analytics: a survey of techniques, tools and platforms. *AI & Society*, vol. 30, no. 1, pp. 89–116. https://doi.org/10.1007/s00146-014-0549-4

Behnke, Nathalie; & Eckhard, Steffen. (2022). A systemic perspective on crisis management and resilience in Germany. *Dms – Der Moderne Staat – Zeitschrift Für Public Policy, Recht Und Management*, vol. 15, no. 1, pp. 3–19. https://doi.org/10.3224/dms.v15i1.11

Bello-Orgaz, Gema; Jung, Jason J.; & Camacho, David. (2016). Social big data: Recent achievements and new challenges. *Information Fusion*, vol. 28, pp. 45–59. https://doi.org/10.1016/j.inffus.2015.08.005

Benessia, Alice; & De Marchi, Bruna. (2017). When the earth shakes … and science with it. The management and communication of uncertainty in the L'Aquila earthquake. *Futures*, vol. 91, pp. 35–45. https://doi.org/10.1016/j.futures.2016.11.011

Benz, Arthur; Broschek, Jörg; & Lederer, Markus. (2021). *A Research Agenda for Multilevel Governance*. Edward Elgar Publishing.

Berger, Peter L.; & Luckmann, Thomas. (1967). *The social construction of reality : a treatise in the sociology of knowledge* (1st ed.). New York: Doubleday.

Bica, Melissa; Palen, Leysia; & Bopp, Chris. (2017). Visual Representations of Disaster. In *Proceedings of the Conference on Computer-Supported Cooperative Work & Social Computing (CSCW)* (pp. 1262–1276). https://doi.org/10.1145/2998181.2998212

Birkbak, Andreas. (2012). Crystallizations in the Blizzard: Contrasting Informal Emergency Collaboration In Facebook Groups. In *Proceedings of the Nordic Conference on Human-Computer Interaction (NordiCHI)* (pp. 428–437). Copenhagen, Denmark: ACM. https://doi.org/10.1145/2399016.2399082

BITKOM. (2013). *Soziale Netzwerke 2013 – Eine repräsentative Untersuchung zur Nutzung sozialer Netzwerke im Internet*. Berlin, Germany. Retrieved from https://www.bitkom.org/sites/default/files/file/import/BITKOM-Publikation-Soziale-Netzwerke.pdf

Boersma, Kees; & Fonio, Chiara. (2017). *Big data, surveillance and crisis management*. Routledge. https://doi.org/10.4324/9781315638423

Boin, Arjen; Comfort, Louise K.; & Demchak, Chris C. (2010). The Rise of Resilience. In *Designing Resilience* (pp. 1–12). Pittsburgh University Press.

Bontempo, R. N.; Bottom, W. P.; & Weber, E. U. (1997). Cross-Cultural Differences in Risk Perception: A Model-Based Approach. *Risk Analysis*, vol. 17, no. 4, pp. 479–488. https://doi.org/10.1111/j.1539-6924.1997.tb00888.x

Borges, Clemente Rafael; & Macías, José Antonio. (2010). Feasible database querying using a visual end-user approach. In *Proceedings of the ACM SIGCHI symposium on Engineering interactive computing systems* (pp. 187–192). New York, New York, USA: ACM Press. https://doi.org/10.1145/1822018.1822047

Brandwatch. (2014). Brandwatch Analytics: A social media monitoring platform for businesses who care what customers say. Retrieved from http://www.brandwatch.com/bra ndwatch-analytics

Bruns, Axel; & Burgess, Jean. (2012). Local and Global Responses to Disaster: #eqnz and the Christchurch Earthquake. In *Proceedings of the Disaster and Emergency Management Conference* (pp. 86–103). Brisbane, QLD: AST Management Pty Ltd.

Brynielsson, Joel; Johansson, Fredrik; Jonsson, Carl; & Westling, Anders. (2014). Emotion classification of social media posts for estimating people's reactions to communicated alert messages during crises. *Security Informatics*, vol. 3, no. 7. https://doi.org/10.1186/s13388-014-0007-3

Bukar, Umar Ali; Jabar, Marzanah A.; Sidi, Fatimah; Nor, Rnh Binti; Abdullah, Salfarina; & Ishak, Iskandar. (2022). How social media crisis response and social interaction is helping people recover from Covid-19: an empirical investigation. *Journal of Computational Social Science*, vol. 5, no. 1, pp. 781–809. https://doi.org/10.1007/s42001-021-00151-7

Bukar, Umar Ali; Jabar, Marzanah A.; Sidi, Fatimah; Nor, Rozi Nor Haizan Binti; Abdullah, Salfarina; & Othman, Mohamed. (2020). Crisis Informatics in the Context of Social Media Crisis Communication: Theoretical Models, Taxonomy, and Open Issues. *IEEE Access*, vol. 8, pp. 185842–185869. https://doi.org/10.1109/ACCESS.2020.3030184

Burnap, Pete; Williams, Matthew L.; Sloan, Luke; Rana, Omer; Housley, William; Edwards, Adam; … Voss, Alex. (2014). Tweeting the terror: modelling the social media reaction to the Woolwich terrorist attack. *Social Network Analysis and Mining*, vol. 4, no. 1, pp. 1–14. https://doi.org/10.1007/s13278-014-0206-4

Cameron, Mark A.; Power, Robert; Robinson, Bella; & Yin, Jie. (2012). Emergency Situation Awareness from Twitter for Crisis Management. In *Proceedings of the 21st international conference companion on World Wide Web* (pp. 695–698). New York, USA: ACM Press. https://doi.org/10.1145/2187980.2188183

Canadian Red Cross. (2012). *Social Media during Emergencies*. Retrieved from https://www. redcross.ca/crc/documents/Social-Media-in-Emergencies-Survey-Oct-2012-English.pdf

Cappiello, Cinzia; Daniel, Florian; Matera, Maristella; Picozzi, Matteo; & Weiss, Michael. (2011). Enabling End User Development through Mashups: Requirements , Abstractions and Innovation Toolkits. In *Proceedings of the International Symposium on End-User Development (IS-EUD)* (pp. 9–24). https://doi.org/10.1007/978-3-642-21530-8_3

Caragea, Cornelia; Mcneese, Nathan; Jaiswal, Anuj; Traylor, Greg; Kim, Hyun-woo; Mitra, Prasenjit; … Yen, John. (2011). Classifying Text Messages for the Haiti Earthquake. In *Proceedings of the International Conference on Information Systems for Crisis Response and Management (ISCRAM)* (pp. 1–10). Lisbon, Portugal.

Castillo, Carlos. (2016). *Big Crisis Data – Social Media in Disasters and Time-Critical Situations*. New York, USA: Cambridge University Press.

Castillo, Carlos; Mendoza, Marcelo; & Poblete, Barbara. (2011). Information credibility on twitter. In *Proceedings of the 20th international conference on World wide web* (pp. 675–684). New York, USA: ACM Press. https://doi.org/10.1145/1963405.1963500

Chang, Chia-Chin; Hung, Shiu-Wan; Cheng, Min-Jhih; & Wu, Ching-Yi. (2015). Exploring the intention to continue using social networking sites: The case of Facebook. *Technological Forecasting and Social Change*, vol. 95, pp. 48–56. https://doi.org/10.1016/j.tec hfore.2014.03.012

Chaturvedi, Ankur; Simha, Anoop; & Wang, Zhen. (2015). ICT infrastructure and social media tools usage in disaster/crisis management. In *Regional Conference of the International Telecommunications Society (ITS)*. Los Angeles, USA.

Chauhan, Apoorva; & Hughes, Amanda Lee. (2016). Online Media as a Means to Affect Public Trust in Emergency Responders. In *Proceedings of the International Conference on Information Systems for Crisis Response and Management (ISCRAM)*. Retrieved from http://idl.iscram.org/files/apoorvachauhan/2016/1390_Apoo rvaChauhan+AmandaLeeHughes2016.pdf

Chauhan, Apoorva; & Hughes, Amanda Lee. (2017). Providing Online Crisis Information: An Analysis of Official Sources during the 2014 Carlton Complex Wildfire. In *Proceedings of the 35th International Conference on Human Factors in Computing Systems (CHI 2017)* (pp. 3151–3162). https://doi.org/10.1145/3025453.3025627

Chen, Bingyang; Wang, Xiao; Zhang, Weishan; Chen, Tao; Sun, Chenyu; Wang, Zhenqi; & Wang, Fei-Yue. (2022). Public Opinion Dynamics in Cyberspace on Russia–Ukraine War: A Case Analysis With Chinese Weibo. *IEEE Transactions on Computational Social Systems*, vol. 9, no. 3, pp. 948–958. https://doi.org/10.1109/tcss.2022.3169332

Chen, Qiang; Min, Chen; Zhang, Wei; Ma, Xiaoyue; & Evans, Richard. (2021). Factors driving citizen engagement with government TikTok accounts during the COVID-19 pandemic: Model development and analysis. *Journal of Medical Internet Research*, vol. 23, no. 2, pp. e21463. https://doi.org/10.2196/21463

Chowdhury, Soudip Roy; Imran, Muhammad; Asghar, Muhammad Rizwan; Amer-Yahia, Sihem; & Castillo, Carlos. (2013). Tweet4act: Using Incident-Specific Profiles for Classifying Crisis-Related Messages. In T. Comes, F. Fiedrich, S. Fortier, J. Geldermann, & L. Yang (Eds.), *International Conference on Information Systems for Crisis Response and Management (ISCRAM)* (pp. 834–839). Baden-Baden, Germany.

Church, Karen; & Oliver, Nuria. (2011). Understanding Mobile Web and Mobile Search Use in Today's Dynamic Mobile Landscape. In *Proceedings of the 13th International Conference on Human Computer Interaction with Mobile Devices and Services* (pp. 67–76). Stockholm: ACM.

Cinelli, Matteo; Quattrociocchi, Walter; Galeazzi, Alessandro; Valensise, Carlo Michele; Brugnoli, Emanuele; Schmidt, Ana Lucia; … Scala, Antonio. (2020). The COVID-19 Social Media Infodemic. *Scientific Reports*, vol. 10, pp. 1–18. https://doi.org/10.1038/s41 598-020-73510-5

Cobb, Camille; McCarthy, T.; Perkins, Annuska; & Bharadwaj, Ankitha. (2014). Designing for the Deluge: Understanding & Supporting the Distributed, Collaborative Work of Crisis Volunteers. In *Proceedings of the Conference on Computer Supported Cooperative Work & Social Computing (CSCW)* (pp. 888–899). Baltimore, USA: ACM. https://doi. org/10.1145/2531602.2531712

Coche, Julien; Rodriguez, Guillermo Romera; Montarnal, Aurelie; Tapia, Andrea; & Benaben, Frederick. (2021). Social media processing in crisis response: an attempt to shift from data to information exploitation. In *HICSS 2021–54th Hawaii International Conference on System Sciences* (pp. 2285–2294).

Comfort, Louise K. (1994). Self-Organization in Complex Systems. *Journal of Public Admin-istration Research and Theory*, vol. 4, no. 3, pp. 393–410.

Comfort, Louise K. (2007). Crisis Management in Hindsight: Cognition, Communication, Coordination, and Control. *Public Administration Review*, vol. 67, no. s1, pp. 189–197. https://doi.org/10.1111/j.1540-6210.2007.00827.x

Constantinides, Panos. (2013). The failure of foresight in crisis management: A secondary analysis of the Mari disaster. *Technological Forecasting and Social Change*, vol. 80, no. 9, pp. 1657–1673. https://doi.org/10.1016/j.techfore.2012.10.017

Coombs, W. Timothy. (2009). Conceptualizing Crisis Communication. In R. L. Heath & D. O'Hair (Eds.), *Handbook of Risk and Crisis Communication* (pp. 99–118). New York, USA: Routledge.

Coppola, Damon P. (2006). *Introduction to International Disaster Management*. Burlington, USA: Elsevier Science & Technology.

Cornia, Alessio; Dressel, Kerstin; & Pfeil, Patricia. (2016). Risk cultures and dominant approaches towards disasters in seven European countries. *Journal of Risk Research*, vol. 19, no. 3, pp. 288–304. https://doi.org/10.1080/13669877.2014.961520

Costabile, Maria Francesca; Member, Senior; Fogli, Daniela; Mussio, Piero; & Piccinno, Antonio. (2007). Visual Interactive Systems for End-User Development : A Model-Based Design Methodology, vol. 37, no. 6, pp. 1029–1046.

Coutaz, Joelle; & Crowley, James L. (2016). A First-Person Experience with End-User Development for Smart Homes. *IEEE Pervasive Computing*, vol. 15, no. 2, pp. 26–39. https://doi.org/10.1109/MPRV.2016.24

Creswell, John W. (2013). *Research design: Qualitative, quantitative, and mixed methods approaches*. New York, NY: SAGE Publications.

Criado, J. Ignacio; Guevara-Gómez, Ariana; & Villodre, Julián. (2020). Using Collaborative Technologies and Social Media to Engage Citizens and Governments during the COVID-19 Crisis. The Case of Spain. *Digital Government: Research and Practice*, vol. 1, no. 4. https://doi.org/10.1145/3416089

Cronbach, Lee J. (1951). Coefficient alpha and the internal structure of tests. *Psychometrika*, vol. 16, no. 3, pp. 297–334.

de Albuquerque, João Porto; Herfort, Benjamin; Brenning, Alexander; & Zipf, Alexander. (2015). A geographic approach for combining social media and authoritative data towards identifying useful information for disaster management. *International Journal of Geo-graphical Information Science*, vol. 29, no. 4, pp. 667–689. https://doi.org/10.1080/136 58816.2014.996567

de Vries, Michiel S. (2016). *Understanding Public Administration*. Red Globe Press.

de Vries, Michiel S.; & Sobis, Iwona. (2018). Trust in the Local Administration: A Compar-ative Study between Capitals and Non-Capital Cities in Europe. *The NISPAcee Journal of Public Administration and Policy*, vol. XI, no. 1, pp. 209–228.

Denef, Sebastian; Bayerl, Petra Saskia; & Kaptein, Nico. (2013). Social Media and the Police—Tweeting Practices of British Police Forces during the August 2011 Riots. In *Proceedings of the Conference on Human Factors in Computing Systems (CHI)* (pp. 3471–3480). Paris, France: ACM Press. https://doi.org/10.1145/2470654.2466477

Dijcks, Jean-Pierre. (2012). Oracle: Big data for the enterprise. *Oracle White Paper*, , no. June, pp. 16. Retrieved from https://www.oracle.com/technetwork/database/bi-datawareh ousing/wp-big-data-with-oracle-521209.pdf

Doerner, Christian; Draxler, Sebastian; Pipek, Volkmar; & Wulf, Volker. (2009). End Users at the Bazaar: Designing Next-Generation Enterprise-Resource-Planning Systems. *IEEE Software*, vol. 26, no. 5, pp. 45–51. https://doi.org/10.1109/MS.2009.127

Doll, William J.; & Torkzadeh, Gholamreza. (1988). The Measurement of End-User Computing Satisfaction. *MIS Quarterly*, vol. 12, no. 2, pp. 259. https://doi.org/10.2307/248851

Dörk, Marian; Gruen, Daniel; Williamson, Carey; & Carpendale, Sheelagh. (2010). A Visual backchannel for large-scale events. *IEEE Transactions on Visualization and Computer Graphics*, vol. 16, pp. 1129–1138. https://doi.org/10.1109/TVCG.2010.129

Dou, Wenwen; Yu, Li; Wang, Xiaoyu; Ma, Zhiqiang; & Ribarsky, William. (2013). HierarchicalTopics: Visually exploring large text collections using topic hierarchies. *IEEE Transactions on Visualization and Computer Graphics*, vol. 19, no. 12, pp. 2002–2011. https://doi.org/10.1109/TVCG.2013.162

Douglas, Mary; & Wildavsky, Aaron. (1983). *Risk and Culture: An Essay on the Selection of Technological and Environmental Dangers*. Berkeley: University of California Press.

Dressel, Kerstin. (2015). Risk culture and crisis communication. *International Journal of Risk Assessment and Management*, vol. 18, no. 2, pp. 115–124. https://doi.org/10.1504/IJRAM.2015.069020

Dressel, Kerstin; & Pfeil, Patricia. (2017). Socio-cultural factors of risk and crisis communication: Crisis communication or what civil protection agencies should be aware of when communicating with the public in crisis situations. In M. Klafft (Ed.), *Risk and Crisis Communication for Disaster Prevention and Management* (pp. 64–76). epubli.

Economics, Trading. (2019). European Union GDP Per Capita. Retrieved from https://tradingeconomics.com/european-union/gdp-per-capita.

Eisenstein, Jacob. (2013). What to do about bad language on the internet. In *Proceedings of the Conference of the North American Chapter of the Association for Computational Linguistics: Human Language Technologies (NAACL)* (pp. 359–369). Atlanta, USA.

Eismann, Kathrin; Posegga, Oliver; & Fischbach, Kai. (2016). Collective Behaviour, Social Media, and Disasters: a Systematic Literature Review. In *Twenty-Fourth European Conference on Information Systems (ECIS)* (pp. 1–20). Atlanta, USA: AISeL.

Endsley, Mica R. (1995). Toward a Theory of Situation Awareness in Dynamic Systems. *Human Factors: The Journal of the Human Factors and Ergonomics Society*, vol. 37, pp. 32–64.

Endsley, Tristan; Wu, Yu; Eep, James; Reep, James; Eep, James; & Reep, James. (2014). The Source of the Story: Evaluating the Credibility of Crisis Information Sources. In S. R. Hiltz, M. S. Pfaff, L. Plotnick, & P. C. Shih (Eds.), *Proceedings of the International Conference on Information Systems for Crisis Response and Management (ISCRAM)* (pp. 158–162). University Park: ISCRAM.

Eriksson, Mats. (2018). Lessons for Crisis Communication on Social Media: A Systematic Review of What Research Tells the Practice. *International Journal of Strategic Communication*, vol. 12, no. 5, pp. 526–551. https://doi.org/10.1080/1553118X.2018.1510405

Fathi, Ramian; Thom, Dennis; Koch, Steffen; Ertl, Thomas; & Fiedrich, Frank. (2020). VOST: A case study in voluntary digital participation for collaborative emergency management. *Information Processing & Management*, vol. 57, no. 4, pp. 102174. https://doi.org/10.1016/J.IPM.2019.102174

Federal Emergency Management Agency. (2018). *Robert T. Stafford Disaster Relief and Emergency Assistance Act, as amended, and Related Authorities as of August 2016*. Retrieved from https://www.fema.gov/media-library/assets/documents/15271

Feldman, David; Contreras, Santina; Karlin, Beth; Basolo, Victoria; Matthew, Richard; Sanders, Brett; ... Luke, Adam. (2016). Communicating flood risk: Looking back and forward at traditional and social media outlets. *International Journal of Disaster Risk Reduction*, vol. 15, pp. 43–51. https://doi.org/10.1016/j.ijdrr.2015.12.004

Ferguson, Julie; Schmidt, Arjen; & Boersma, Kees. (2018). Citizens in crisis and disaster management: Understanding barriers and opportunities for inclusion. *Journal of Contingencies and Crisis Management (JCCM)*, vol. 26, no. 3, pp. 326–328. https://doi.org/10.1111/1468-5973.12236

Fichet, Elodie; Robinson, John; & Starbird, Kate. (2015). Eyes on the Ground: Emerging Practices in Periscope Use during Crisis Events. In *Proceedings of the Information Systems for Crisis Response and Management (ISCRAM)*. Ager, Norway.

Field, Andy. (2009). *Discovering Statistics Using SPSS* (3rd ed.). London, United Kingdom: Sage.

Fischer, Diana; Posegga, Oliver; & Fischbach, Kai. (2016). Communication Barriers in Crisis Management: A Literature Review. In *Twenty-Fourth European Conference on Information Systems (ECIS)* (pp. 1–18). Atlanta, GA, GA: AISeL.

Fischer, Gerhard; & Scharff, E. (2000). Meta-Design – Design for Designers. In D. Boyarski & W. Kellogg (Eds.), *Proceedings of the International Conference on Designing Interactive Systems* (pp. 396–405). New York, USA: ACM.

Flizikowski, Adam; Hołubowicz, Witold; Stachowicz, Anna; Hokkanen, Laura; & Delavallade, Thomas. (2014). Social Media in Crisis Management – the iSAR + Project Survey. In S. R. Hiltz, M. S. Pfaff, L. Plotnick, & P. C. Shih (Eds.), *Proceedings of the International Conference on Information Systems for Crisis Response and Management (ISCRAM)* (pp. 707–711). Brussels, Belgium: ISCRAM.

Fortunati, Leopoldina; & Taipale, Sakari. (2014). The advanced use of mobile phones in five European countries. *The British Journal of Sociology*, vol. 65, no. 2, pp. 317–337. https://doi.org/10.1111/1468-4446.12075

Friberg, Therese; Prödel, Stephan; & Koch, Rainer. (2010). Analysis of information quality criteria in crisis situation as a characteristic of complex situations. In *Proceedings of the 15th International Conference on Information Quality*. Little Rock, USA.

Fuchs, Georg; Andrienko, Natalia; Andrienko, Gennady; Bothe, Sebastian; & Stange, Henrik. (2013). Tracing the German Centennial Flood in the Stream of Tweets: First Lessons Learned. In *SIGSPATIAL International Workshop on Crowdsourced and Volunteered Geographic Information* (pp. 2–10). Orlando, USA.

Fung, Isaac Chun-Hai; Tse, Zion Tsz Ho; Cheung, Chi-Ngai; Miu, Adriana S.; & Fu, King-Wa. (2014). Ebola and the social media. *The Lancet*, vol. 384, no. 9961, pp. 2207. https://doi.org/10.1016/S0140-6736(14)62418-1

Gabel, Sabrina; Aldehoff, Larissa; & Reuter, Christian. (2019). Discussing Conflict in Social Media – The Use of Twitter in the Jammu and Kashmir Conflict. *Perspectives on Terrorism*. https://doi.org/10.1177/1750635220970997

Ganis, Matthew; & Kohirkar, Avinash. (2012). Ensuring the Accuracy of Your Social Media Analysis. *Cutter IT Journal*, vol. 25, no. 10, pp. 13–18.

Gantt, M.; & Nardi, Ba. (1992). Gardeners and gurus: patterns of cooperation among CAD users. In *Conference on Human Factors in Computing Systems – Proceedings* (pp. 107–117). https://doi.org/10.1145/142750.142767

Gao, Huiji; Barbier, Geoffrey; & Goolsby, Rebecca. (2011). Harnessing the Crowdsourcing Power of Social Media for Disaster Relief. *IEEE Intelligent Systems*, vol. 26, no. 3, pp. 10–14. https://doi.org/10.1109/MIS.2011.52

Gaspar, Rui; Gorjão, Sara; Seibt, Beate; Lima, Luisa; Barnett, Julie; Moss, Adrian; & Wills, Josephine. (2014). Tweeting during food crises: A psychosocial analysis of threat coping expressions in Spain, during the 2011 European EHEC outbreak. *International Journal of Human-Computer Studies*, vol. 72, no. 2, pp. 239–254. https://doi.org/10.1016/j.ijhcs.2013.10.001

Geofeedia Inc. (2014). Geofeedia: There's more to social discovery than keywords and hashtags. Retrieved from https://web.archive.org/web/20140612012652/http://geofeedia.com/how-it-works

Gierlach, Elaine; Belsher, Bradley E.; & Beutler, Larry E. (2010). Cross-Cultural Differences in Risk Perceptions of Disasters. *Risk Analysis*, vol. 30, no. 10, pp. 1539–1549. https://doi.org/10.1111/j.1539-6924.2010.01451.x

Giles, Jim. (2005). Internet encyclopaedias go head to head. *Nature*, vol. 438, no. December, pp. 900–901. https://doi.org/10.1038/438900a

Goolsby, Rebecca. (2010). Social media as crisis platform. *ACM Transactions on Intelligent Systems and Technology*, vol. 1, no. 1, pp. 1–11. https://doi.org/10.1145/1858948.1858955

Gorp, Annemijn F. Van. (2014). Integration of Volunteer and Technical Communities into the Humanitarian Aid Sector: Barriers to Collaboration. In *Proceedings of the International Conference on Information Systems for Crisis Response and Management (ISCRAM)* (pp. 620–629).

Grace, Rob. (2021). Overcoming barriers to social media use through multisensor integration in emergency management systems. *International Journal of Disaster Risk Reduction*, vol. 66, pp. 102636. https://doi.org/10.1016/j.ijdrr.2021.102636

Grammel, Lars. (2009). Supporting end users in analyzing multiple data sources. In *2009 IEEE Symposium on Visual Languages and Human-Centric Computing (VL/HCC)* (pp. 246–247). IEEE. https://doi.org/10.1109/VLHCC.2009.5295248

Groenendaal, Jelle; & Helsloot, Ira. (2021). Why technology not always adds value to crisis managers during crisis: The case of the Dutch nation-wide crisis management system LCMS. In *Proceedings of the Information Systems for Crisis Response and Management (ISCRAM)* (pp. 1–10). Blacksburg, USA. Retrieved from http://idl.iscram.org/files/jellegroenendaal/2021/2386_JelleGroenendaal+IraHelsloot2021.pdf

Gui, Xinning; Kou, Yubo; Pine, Kathleen H.; & Chen, Yunan. (2017). Managing Uncertainty: Using Social Media for Risk Assessment during a Public Health Crisis. In *Proceedings of the Conference on Human Factors in Computing Systems (CHI)* (pp. 4520–4533). New York, NY, USA: Association for Computing Machinery. https://doi.org/10.1145/3025453.3025891

Haddow, George; Bullock, Jane; & Coppola, Damon. (2007). *Introduction to Emergency Management* (3rd ed.). Burlington: Butterworth-Heinemann.

Haesler, Steffen; Schmid, Stefka; Vierneisel, Annemike Sophia; & Reuter, Christian. (2021). Stronger Together: How Neighborhood Groups Build up a Virtual Network during the

COVID-19 Pandemic. *Proceedings of the ACM: Human Computer Interaction (PACM): Computer-Supported Cooperative Work and Social Computing*, vol. 5, no. CSCW2. https://doi.org/10.1145/3476045

Hagar, Christine. (2007). The information needs of farmers and use of ICTs. In B. Nerlich & M. Doring (Eds.), *From Mayhem to Meaning: Assessing the social a nd cultural impact of the 2001 foot and mouth outbreak in the UK*. Manchester, United Kingdom: Manchester University Press.

Harrald, John R.; Egan, Dennis M.; & Jefferson, Theresa. (2002). Web Enabled Disaster and Crisis Response : What Have We Learned from the September 11 th. In *Proceedings of the Bled eConference* (pp. 69–83). Retrieved from https://domino.fov.uni-mb.si/proceedings.nsf/proceedings/d3a6817c6cc6c4b5c1256e9f003bb2bd/$file/harrald.pdf

Haunschild, Jasmin; & Reuter, Christian. (2021). Perceptions of Police Technology Use and Attitudes Towards the Police – A Representative Survey of the German Population. In *Workshop-Proceedings Mensch und Computer*. Bonn: Gesellschaft für Informatik e. V. https://doi.org/10.18420/muc2021-mci-ws08-255

Heer, Jeffrey; & Boyd, D. (2005). Vizster: visualizing online social networks. In *IEEE Symposium on Information Visualization (INFOVIS)* (pp. 32–39). IEEE. https://doi.org/10.1109/INFVIS.2005.1532126

Helsloot, Ira; & Groenendaal, Jelle. (2013). Twitter: An Underutilized Potential during Sudden Crises? *Journal of Contingencies and Crisis Management (JCCM)*, vol. 21, no. 3, pp. 178–183. https://doi.org/10.1111/1468-5973.12023

Helsloot, Ira; & Ruitenberg, Arnout. (2004). Citizen Response to Disasters : a Survey of Literature and Some Practical Implications. *Journal of Contingencies and Crisis Management (JCCM)*, vol. 12, no. 3, pp. 98–111. https://doi.org/10.1111/j.0966-0879.2004.00440.x

Helsloot, Ira; Vries, David de; Groenendaal, Jelle; Scholtens, Astrid; in 't Veld, Michiel; Melick, Gaby van; ... Blaha, Manfred. (2015). Deliverable D6.1. & D6.2. Guidelines for the use of new media in crisis situations. https://doi.org/10.5281/ZENODO.16235

Henderson, Austin; & Kyng, Morten. (1991). There's no place like home: Continuing Design in Use. In J. Greenbaum & M. Kyng (Eds.), *Design at work cooperative design of computer systems* (pp. 219–240). Lawrence Erlbaum Associates.

Hess, Jan; Reuter, Christian; Pipek, Volkmar; & Wulf, Volker. (2012). Supporting End-User Articulations in Evolving Business Processes: A Case Study to explore Intuitive Notations and Interaction Designs. *International Journal of Cooperative Information Systems (IJCIS)*, vol. 21, no. 4, pp. 263–296. https://doi.org/10.1142/S0218843012500049

Heverin, Thomas; & Zach, Lisl. (2010). Microblogging for Crisis Communication: Examination of Twitter Use in Response to a 2009 Violent Crisis in the Seattle-Tacoma, Washington Area. In *Proceedings of the Information Systems for Crisis Response and Management (ISCRAM)* (pp. 1–5). Brussels, Belgium, USA: ISCRAM.

Hewitt, Kenneth. (2012). Culture, hazard and disaster. In B. Wisner, J. C. Gaillard, & I. Kelman (Eds.), *The Routledge Handbook of Hazards and Disaster Risk Reduction* (pp. 85–96). London; New York: Routledge.

Hickey, Gary; & Kipping, Cheryl. (1996). A multi-stage approach to the coding of data from open-ended questions. *Nurse Researcher*, vol. 4, no. 1, pp. 81–91. https://doi.org/10.7748/nr.4.1.81.s9

Hiltz, S. Roxanne; Hughes, Amanda Lee; Imran, Muhammad; Plotnick, Linda; Power, Robert; & Turoff, Murray. (2020). Exploring the usefulness and feasibility of software requirements for social media use in emergency management. *International Journal of Disaster Risk Reduction*, vol. 42, pp. 101367. https://doi.org/10.1016/j.ijdrr.2019.101367

Hiltz, Starr Roxanne; Diaz, Paloma; & Mark, Gloria. (2011). Introduction: Social Media and Collaborative Systems for Crisis Management. *ACM Transactions on Computer-Human Interaction (TOCHI)*, vol. 18, no. 4, pp. 1–6.

Hiltz, Starr Roxanne; Kushma, Jane; & Plotnick, L. (2014). Use of Social Media by US Public Sector Emergency Managers: Barriers and Wish Lists. In S. R. Hiltz, M. S. Pfaff, L. Plotnick, & P. C. Shih (Eds.), *Proceedings of the International Conference on Information Systems for Crisis Response and Management (ISCRAM)* (pp. 600–609). Brussels, Belgium: ISCRAM. https://doi.org/10.13140/2.1.3122.4005

Hiltz, Starr Roxanne; & Plotnick, Linda. (2013). Dealing with Information Overload When Using Social Media for Emergency Management: Emerging Solutions. In *Proceedings of the International Conference on Information Systems for Crisis Response and Management (ISCRAM)* (pp. 823–827). Baden-Baden, Germany.

Hofmann, Marlen; Betke, Hans; & Sackmann, Stefan. (2014). Hands2Help – Ein App-basiertes Konzept zur Koordination Freiwilliger Helfer/ Hands2Help – An App-based Concept for Coordination of Disaster Response Volunteers. *I-Com – Zeitschrift Für Interaktive Und Kooperative Medien*, vol. 13, no. 1, pp. 29–36.

Hollan, James; Hutchins, Edwin; & Kirsh, David. (2000). Distributed cognition: Toward a New Foundation for Human-Computer Interaction Research. *ACM Transactions on Computer-Human Interaction (TOCHI)*, vol. 7, no. 2, pp. 174–196. https://doi.org/10.1145/353485.353487

Hootsuite Media Inc. (2014). Hootsuite: Everything you need in one place. Retrieved from https://hootsuite.com/

Huang, Cheng-Min; Chan, Edward; & Hyder, Adnan a. (2010). Web 2.0 and internet social networking: a new tool for disaster management?--lessons from Taiwan. *BMC Medical Informatics and Decision Making*, vol. 10, pp. 57. https://doi.org/10.1186/1472-6947-10-57

Hughes, Amanda Lee. (2014). Participatory Design for the Social Media Needs of Emergency Public Information Officers. In *Proceedings of the International Conference on Information Systems for Crisis Response and Management (ISCRAM)*. University Park, PA, USA. Retrieved from http://idl.iscram.org/files/hughes/2014/603_Hughes2014.pdf

Hughes, Amanda Lee; & Palen, Leysia. (2009). Twitter Adoption and Use in Mass Convergence and Emergency Events. In J. Landgren & S. Jul (Eds.), *Proceedings of the Information Systems for Crisis Response and Management (ISCRAM)* (Vol. 6, pp. 248–260). Gothenburg, Sweden. https://doi.org/10.1504/IJEM.2009.031564

Hughes, Amanda Lee; & Palen, Leysia. (2012). The Evolving Role of the Public Information Officer: An Examination of Social Media in Emergency Management. *Journal of Homeland Security and Emergency Management (JHSEM)*, vol. 9, no. 1, pp. Article 22. https://doi.org/10.1515/1547-7355.1976

Hughes, Amanda Lee; & Palen, Leysia. (2014). *Social Media in Emergency Management: Academic Perspective.* (J. E. Trainor & T. Subbio, Eds.), *Critical Issues in Disaster Science and Management: A Dialogue Between Scientists and Emergency Managers.* Washington, DC, USA: Federal Emergency Management Agency.

Hughes, Amanda Lee; Palen, Leysia; Sutton, Jeannette; Liu, Sophia B.; & Vieweg, S. (2008). "Site-Seeing" in Disaster: An Examination of On-Line Social Convergence. In *Proceedings of the International Conference on Information Systems for Crisis Response and Management (ISCRAM)*. Washington D.C., USA.

Hughes, Amanda Lee; & Shah, R. (2016). Designing an Application for Social Media Needs in Emergency Public Information Work. In *Proceedings of the International Conference on Supporting Group Work (CSCW)* (pp. 399–408). New York, USA: ACM Press. https://doi.org/10.1145/2957276.2957307

Hughes, Amanda Lee; St. Denis, Lise Ann; Palen, Leysia; & Anderson, Kenneth M. (2014). Online Public Communications by Police & Fire Services during the 2012 Hurricane Sandy. In *Proceedings of the Conference on Human Factors in Computing Systems (CHI)* (pp. 1505–1514). Toronto, Canada: ACM Press. https://doi.org/10.1145/2556288.2557227

Hughes, Amanda Lee; Starbird, Kate; Leavitt, Alex; Keegan, Brian; & Semaan, Bryan. (2016). Information Movement Across Social Media Platforms During Crisis Events. *CHI'16 Extended Abstracts.*, pp. 1–5. https://doi.org/10.1145/2851581.2856500

Hughes, Amanda Lee; & Tapia, Andrea H. (2015). Social Media in Crisis: When Professional Responders Meet Digital Volunteers. *Journal of Homeland Security and Emergency Management (JHSEM)*, vol. 12, no. 3, pp. 679–706. https://doi.org/10.1515/jhsem-2014-0080

IBM. (2014). Statistical Package for the Social Sciences. Retrieved October 18, 2017, from https://www14.software.ibm.com/

IFRC. (2015). *World Disaster Report 2015: Focus on local actors, the key to humanitarian effectiveness.* Genf: International Federation of Red Cross and Red Crescent Societies. https://doi.org/10.1017/CBO9781107415324.004

Imran, Muhammad; Castillo, C.; Lucas, J.; Meier, P.; & Vieweg, S. (2014). AIDR: Artificial Intelligence for Disaster Response. In *Proceedings of the Companion Publication of the 23rd International Conference on World Wide Web Companion* (pp. 159–162). Republic and Canton of Geneva, Switzerland: International World Wide Web Conferences Steering Committee. https://doi.org/10.1145/2567948.2577034

Imran, Muhammad; Castillo, Carlos; Diaz, Fernando; & Vieweg, Sarah. (2015). Processing Social Media Messages in Mass Emergency: A Survey. *ACM Computing Surveys*, vol. 47, no. 4, pp. 1–38. https://doi.org/10.1145/2771588

Imran, Muhammad; Castillo, Carlos; Diaz, Fernando; & Vieweg, Sarah. (2018). Processing Social Media Messages in Mass Emergency: Survey Summary. In *Companion Proceedings of the The Web Conference (WWW)* (pp. 507–511). Lyon, France. https://doi.org/10.1145/3184558.3186242

Imran, Muhammad; Meier, Patrick; & Boersma, Kees. (2017). The use of social media for crisis management. In *Big Data, Surveillance and Crisis Management* (p. 19). Routledge.

Imran, Muhammad; Ofli, Ferda; Caragea, Doina; & Torralba, Antonio. (2020). Using AI and Social Media Multimodal Content for Disaster Response and Management: Opportunities, Challenges, and Future Directions. *Information Processing and Management*, vol. 57, no. 5, pp. 1–9. https://doi.org/10.1016/j.ipm.2020.102261

index mundi. (2019). Age structure. Retrieved from https://www.indexmundi.com/world/age_structure.html

International Association of Chiefs of Police. (2010). 2010 Social Media Survey Results. Retrieved from https://www.slideshare.net/ssieg/2010-social-media-survey-results

International Association of Chiefs of Police. (2015). 2015 Social Media Survey Results. Retrieved from https://www.valorforblue.org/Documents/Clearinghouse/IACP_2015_Social_Media_Survey_Results.pdf

International Federation of Red Cross and Red Crescent Societies. (2020). *World Disaster Report 2020: Come Heat or High Water. Tackling the humanitarian impacts of climate crisis together*. Geneva. Retrieved from https://reliefweb.int/report/world/world-disasters-report-2020-come-heat-or-high-water-tackling-humanitarian-impacts

Internet World Stats. (2019). Internet Usage in the European Union. Retrieved from https://www.internetworldstats.com/stats9.htm

Jäckle, Sebastian; & Wagschal, Uwe. (2022). Trust in politics during the Covid-19 crisis. *Dms – Der Moderne Staat – Zeitschrift Für Public Policy, Recht Und Management*, vol. 15, no. 1, pp. 149–174. https://doi.org/10.3224/dms.v15i1.04

Jennex, Murray E. (2012). Social Media – Truly Viable For Crisis Response? In L. Rothkrantz, J. Ristvej, & Z. Franco (Eds.), *Proceedings of the Information Systems for Crisis Response and Management (ISCRAM)* (pp. 1–5). Vancouver, Canada.

Jiang, Hanchen; & Tang, Xiao. (2022). Effects of local government social media use on citizen compliance during a crisis: Evidence from the COVID-19 crisis in China. *Public Administrateion*. https://doi.org/10.1111/padm.12845

Johansson, Fredrik; Brynielsson, Joel; Quijano, Maribel Narganes; & Narganes Quijano, M. (2012). Estimating Citizen Alertness in Crises Using Social Media Monitoring and Analysis. *2012 European Intelligence and Security Informatics Conference*, pp. 189–196. https://doi.org/10.1109/EISIC.2012.23

Jurgens, Manon; & Helsloot, Ira. (2017). The effect of social media on the dynamics of (self) resilience during disasters: A literature review. *Journal of Contingencies and Crisis Management (JCCM)*, vol. 26, pp. 79–88. https://doi.org/10.1111/1468-5973.12212

Kaewkitipong, Laddawan; Chen, Charlie; & Ractham, Peter. (2012). Lessons Learned from the Use of Social Media in Combating a Crisis: A Case Study of 2011 Thailand Flooding Disaster. In *Proceedings of the Thirty Third International Conference on Information Systems (ICIS)* (pp. 1–17). Atlanta, GA: AISeL.

Kaisler, Stephen; Armour, Frank; Espinosa, J. Alberto; & Money, William. (2013). Big Data: Issues and Challenges Moving Forward. In *2013 46th Hawaii International Conference on System Sciences* (pp. 995–1004). IEEE. https://doi.org/10.1109/HICSS.2013.645

Kaplan, Andreas M.; & Haenlein, Michael. (2010). Users of the world, unite! The challenges and opportunities of Social Media. *Business Horizons*, vol. 53, no. 1, pp. 59–68. https://doi.org/10.1016/j.bushor.2009.09.003

Karsten, Andreas. (2013). Interoperabilität und Agilität: Sachstand und Herausforderung. In *Interorganisationale Zusammenarbeit im Krisenmanagement*. Siegen, Germany.

Kaufhold, Marc-André. (2021). *Information Refinement Technologies for Crisis Informatics: User Expectations and Design Principles for Social Media and Mobile Apps*. Wiesbaden, Germany: Springer Vieweg. https://doi.org/10.1007/978-3-658-33341-6

Kaufhold, Marc-André; Bayer, Markus; & Reuter, Christian. (2020a). Rapid relevance classification of social media posts in disasters and emergencies: A system and evaluation featuring active, incremental and online learning. *Information Processing and Management*, vol. 57, no. 1, pp. 102132. https://doi.org/10.1016/j.ipm.2019.102132

Kaufhold, Marc-André; Gizikis, Alexis; Reuter, Christian; Habdank, Matthias; & Grinko, Margarita. (2018a). Avoiding chaotic use of social media before, during, and after emergencies: Design and evaluation of citizens' guidelines. *Journal of Contingencies and Crisis Management (JCCM)*, pp. 1–16. https://doi.org/10.1111/1468-5973.12249

Kaufhold, Marc-André; Haunschild, Jasmin; & Reuter, Christian. (2020b). Warning the Public: A Survey on Attitudes, Expectations and Use of Mobile Crisis Apps in Germany. In *Proceedings of the 28th European Conference on Information Systems (ECIS), An Online AIS Conference* (pp. 15–17).

Kaufhold, Marc-André; Reuter, Christian; & Ludwig, Thomas. (2022). Big Data and Multi-Platform Social Media Services in Disaster Management. In *International Handbook of Disaster Research*. Springer.

Kaufhold, Marc-André; & Reuter, Christian. (2014). Vernetzte Selbsthilfe in Sozialen Medien am Beispiel des Hochwassers 2013 / Linked Self-Help in Social Media using the example of the Floods 2013 in Germany. *I-Com – Zeitschrift Für Interaktive Und Kooperative Medien*, vol. 13, no. 1, pp. 20–28. https://doi.org/10.1515/icom.2014.0004

Kaufhold, Marc-André; & Reuter, Christian. (2016). The Self-Organization of Digital Volunteers across Social Media: The Case of the 2013 European Floods in Germany. *Journal of Homeland Security and Emergency Management (JHSEM)*, vol. 13, no. 1, pp. 137–166. https://doi.org/10.1515/jhsem-2015-0063

Kaufhold, Marc-André; Rupp, Nicola; Reuter, Christian; Amelunxen, Christoph; & Cristaldi, Massimo. (2018b). 112.SOCIAL: Design and Evaluation of a Mobile Crisis App for Bidirectional Communication between Emergency Services and Citizen. In *Proceedings of the European Conference on Information Systems (ECIS)*. Portsmouth, UK: AIS. Retrieved from https://aisel.aisnet.org/ecis2018_rp/81/

Kaufhold, Marc-André; Rupp, Nicola; Reuter, Christian; & Habdank, Matthias. (2020c). Mitigating Information Overload in Social Media during Conflicts and Crises: Design and Evaluation of a Cross-Platform Alerting System. *Behaviour & Information Technology (BIT)*, vol. 39, no. 3, pp. 319–342. https://doi.org/10.1080/0144929X.2019.1620334

Kavanaugh, Andrea; Fox, Edward A.; Sheetz, Steven; Yang, Seungwon; Li, Lin Tzy; Whalen, Travis F.; … Fox, E. A. (2011a). Social Media Use by Government: From the Routine to the Critical. In *Proceedings of the International Digital Government Research Conference* (pp. 121–130). Maryland, USA.

Kavanaugh, Andrea; Yang, Seungwon; Li, Lin Tzy; Sheetz, Steven; & Fox, Edward A. (2011b). Microblogging in crisis situations: Mass protests in Iran, Tunisia, Egypt. In *Proceedings of the Conference on Human Factors in Computing Systems (CHI)* (pp. 1–7). Vancouver, Canada: ACM. Retrieved from http://www.princeton.edu/~jvertesi/Transnati onalHCI/Participants_files/Kavanaugh.pdf

Kemp, Simon. (2017). Digital in 2017: Global Overview. Retrieved from https://wearesocial.com/sg/blog/2017/01/digital-in-2017-global-overview/

Kemp, Simon. (2022). Digital 2022: April Global Statshot Report. Retrieved from https://datareportal.com/reports/digital-2022-april-global-statshot

Khan, Nawab Ali; Azhar, Mohd; Rahman, Mohd Nayyer; & Akhtar, Mohd Junaid. (2022). Scale Development and Validation for Usage of Social Networking Sites During Covid-19. *SSRN Electronic Journal*, vol. 70, pp. 102020. https://doi.org/10.2139/ssrn.3995265

Kievik, Milou; & Gutteling, Jan M. (2011). Yes, we can: motivate Dutch citizens to engage in self-protective behavior with regard to flood risks. *Natural Hazards*, vol. 59, no. 3, pp. 1475. https://doi.org/10.1007/s11069-011-9845-1

Kim, Jooho; Bae, Juhee; & Hastak, Makarand. (2018). Emergency information diffusion on online social media during storm Cindy in U.S. *International Journal of Information Management*, vol. 40, pp. 153–165. https://doi.org/10.1016/J.IJINFOMGT.2018.02.003

Kirchner, Jan; & Reuter, Christian. (2020). Countering Fake News: A Comparison of Possible Solutions Regarding User Acceptance and Effectiveness. *Proceedings of the ACM on Human-Computer Interaction*, vol. 4, no. CSCW2. https://doi.org/10.1145/3415211

Knoblauch, Hubert. (2010). *Wissenssoziologie* (2. Aufl.). Stuttgart: UVK-Verl.-Ges.

Koch, Michael. (2008). CSCW and Enterprise 2.0 – towards an integrated perspective. In *Proceedings of the Bled eConference* (pp. 416–427). Bled, Slovenia.

Kogan, Marina; Anderson, Jennings; Palen, Leysia; Anderson, Kenneth M.; & Soden, Robert. (2016). Finding the Way to OSM Mapping Practices: Bounding Large Crisis Datasets for Qualitative Investigation (pp. 2783–2795). https://doi.org/10.1145/2858036. 2858371

Kristensen, M.; Kyng, M.; & Palen, L. (2006). Participatory Design in Emergency Medical Service: Designing for Future Practice. In *Proceedings of the Conference on Human Factors in Computing Systems (CHI)* (pp. 161–170). New York, USA: ACM Press.

Kropczynski, Jess; Grace, Rob; Coche, Julien; Halse, Shane; Obeysekare, Eric; Montarnal, Aurélie; … Tapia, Andrea. (2018). Identifying actionable information on social media for emergency dispatch. In *Proceedings of the ISCRAM Asia Pacific*. Retrieved from https://hal.archives-ouvertes.fr/hal-01987793/

Kruskal, William H.; & Wallis, W. Allen. (1952). Use of ranks in one-criterion variance analysis. *Journal of the American Statistical Association*, vol. 47, no. 260, pp. 583–621.

Kuhn, Nicole S. (2022). American Indian and Alaska Native Youth's Experiences with COVID-19 Health Communication on TikTok. In *Interaction Design and Children* (pp. 679–682). New York, USA: Association for Computing Machinery. https://doi.org/10.1145/3501712.3538833

Kuttschreuter, Margôt; Rutsaert, Pieter; Hilverda, Femke; Regan, Áine; Barnett, Julie; & Verbeke, Wim. (2014). Seeking information about food-related risks: The contribution of social media. *Food Quality and Preference*, vol. 37, pp. 10–18. https://doi.org/10.1016/j.foodqual.2014.04.006

Lambert, Catherine E. (2020). Earthquake Country: A Qualitative Analysis of Risk Communication via Facebook. *Environmental Communication*, vol. 14, no. 6, pp. 744–757. https://doi.org/10.1080/17524032.2020.1719170

Latonero, Mark; & Shklovski, Irina. (2011). Emergency Management, Twitter, and Social Media Evangelism. *International Journal of Information Systems for Crisis Response and Management (IJISCRAM)*, vol. 3, no. 4, pp. 1–16. https://doi.org/10.4018/jiscrm.201 1100101

Leavitt, Alex; & Robinson, John J. (2017). The Role of Information Visibility in Network Gatekeeping: Information Aggregation on Reddit during Crisis Events. In *Proceedings of the ACM Conference on Computer-Supported-Cooperative Work and Social Computing (CSCW)* (pp. 1246–1261). New York, NY, USA: Association for Computing Machinery. https://doi.org/10.1145/2998181.2998299

Lee, Haein; Park, Hyejin; & Kim, Jinwoo. (2013). Why do people share their context information on Social Network Services? A qualitative study and an experimental study on users' behavior of balancing perceived benefit and risk. *International Journal of Human-Computer Studies*, vol. 71, no. 9, pp. 862–877. https://doi.org/10.1016/j.ijhcs.2013.01.005

Ley, Benedikt; Pipek, Volkmar; Reuter, Christian; & Wiedenhoefer, Torben. (2012). Supporting improvisation work in inter-organizational crisis management. In J. A. Konstan, E. H. Chi, & K. Höök (Eds.), *CHI '12. Proceedings of the 2012 ACM annual conference on Human Factors in Computing Systems, Austin, TX, 5–10 May 2012* (p. 1529). New York: ACM Press. https://doi.org/10.1145/2207676.2208617

Lieberman, Henry; Paterno, Fabio; & Wulf, Volker. (2006). *End-User Development*. Dordrecht, The Netherlands: Springer. https://doi.org/10.1007/1-4020-5386-X

Likert, R. (1932). A Technique for the Measurement of Attitudes. *Archives of Psychology*, vol. 140, pp. 1–55.

Lim, Seongtaek; Cha, Sang Yun; Park, Chala; Lee, Inseong; & Kim, Jinwoo. (2011). Idioculture in crowd computing: A focus on group interaction in an event-driven social media system. *International Journal of Human-Computer Studies*, vol. 69, no. 10, pp. 632–646. https://doi.org/10.1016/j.ijhcs.2011.02.001

Liu, Sophia B. (2014). Crisis Crowdsourcing Framework: Designing Strategic Configurations of Crowdsourcing for the Emergency Management Domain. *Computer Supported Cooperative Work (CSCW)*, vol. 23, no. 4–6, pp. 389–443. https://doi.org/10.1007/s10606-014-9204-3

Liu, Sophia B.; Palen, Leysia; & Sutton, Jeannette. (2008). In search of the bigger picture: The emergent role of on-line photo sharing in times of disaster. In *Proceedings of the International Conference on Information Systems for Crisis Response and Management (ISCRAM)*. Washington D.C., USA. Retrieved from http://idl.iscram.org/files/liu/2008/716_Liu_etal2008.pdf

Lo, Alex Y.; & Chan, Faith. (2017). Preparing for flooding in England and Wales: the role of risk perception and the social context in driving individual action. *Natural Hazards*, vol. 88, no. 1, pp. 367–387. https://doi.org/10.1007/s11069-017-2870-y

Ludwig, Thomas; Kotthaus, Christoph; Reuter, Christian; Dongen, Sören Van; & Pipek, Volkmar. (2017). Situated crowdsourcing during disasters: Managing the tasks of spontaneous volunteers through public displays. *International Journal on Human-Computer Studies (IJHCS)*, vol. 102, no. C, pp. 103–121. https://doi.org/10.1016/j.ijhcs.2016.09.008

Ludwig, Thomas; Reuter, Christian; & Pipek, Volkmar. (2013). What You See Is What I Need: Mobile Reporting Practices in Emergencies. In O. W. Bertelsen, L. Ciolfi, A. Grasso, & G. A. Papadopoulos (Eds.), *Proceedings of the European Conference on Computer Supported Cooperative Work (ECSCW)* (pp. 181–206). Paphos, Cyrus, United Kingdom: Springer. https://doi.org/10.1007/978-1-4471-5346-7_10

Ludwig, Thomas; Reuter, Christian; & Pipek, Volkmar. (2015a). Social Haystack: Dynamic Quality Assessment of Citizen-Generated Content during Emergencies. *ACM Transactions on Computer-Human Interaction (TOCHI)*, vol. 21, no. 4, pp. Article 17. https://doi.org/10.1145/2749461

Ludwig, Thomas; Reuter, Christian; Siebigteroth, Tim; & Pipek, Volkmar. (2015b). CrowdMonitor: Mobile Crowd Sensing for Assessing Physical and Digital Activities of Citizens during Emergencies. In B. Begole, K. Jinwoo, I. Kor, & W. Woontack (Eds.), *Proceedings of the Conference on Human Factors in Computing Systems (CHI)* (pp. 4083–4092). New York, USA, Korea: ACM Press. Retrieved from https://dl.acm.org/doi/https://doi.org/10.1145/2702123.2702265

Ludwig, Thomas; Siebigteroth, Tim; & Pipek, Volkmar. (2015c). CrowdMonitor: Monitoring Physical and Digital Activities of Citizens During Emergencies. In L. M. Aiello & D. McFarland (Eds.), *Social Informatics – SocInfo 2014 International Workshops, Barcelona, Spain, November 11, 2014, Revised Selected Papers* (pp. 421–428). Schweiz: Springer International Publishing. https://doi.org/10.1007/978-3-319-15168-7_51

MacLean, A.; Carter, K.; Lövstrand, L.; & Moran, L. (1990). User-Tailorable Systems: Pressing the Issues with Buttons. In *Proceedings of the Conference on Human Factors in Computing Systems (CHI)*. Seattle, USA.

Maguire, Brigit; & Hagan, Patrick. (2007). Disasters and communities: Understanding social resilience. *The Australian Journal of Emergency Management*, vol. 22, no. 2, pp. 16–20.

Marcus, Adam; Bernstein, MS; Badar, Osama; Karger, David R.; Madden, Samuel; & Miller, Robert C. (2011). Twitinfo: aggregating and visualizing microblogs for event exploration. In *Proceedings of the Conference on Human Factors in Computing Systems (CHI)* (pp. 227–236). Vancouver, Canada.

Mark, Gloria; & Semaan, Bryan. (2008). Resilience in collaboration: technology as a resource for new patterns of action. *Proceedings of the ACM 2008 Conference on Computer Supported Cooperative Work – CSCW '08*, pp. 137. https://doi.org/10.1145/1460563.1460585

Marris, Claire; Langford, Ian H.; & O'Riordan, Timothy. (1998). A Quantitative Test of the Cultural Theory of Risk Perceptions: Comparison with the Psychometric Paradigm. *Risk Analysis*, vol. 18, no. 5, pp. 635–647. https://doi.org/10.1111/j.1539-6924.1998.tb00376.x

Marx, Leo; & Smith, Merritt Roe. (1994). *Does Technology Drive History? The Dilemma of Technological Determinism*. MIT Press.

Massa, Daniele; & Spano, Lucio Davide. (2015). FaceMashup: Enabling End User Development on Social Networks Data BT. In P. Díaz, V. Pipek, C. Ardito, C. Jensen, I. Aedo, & A. Boden (Eds.), *5th International Symposium on End-User Development (IS-EUD)* (pp. 204–210). Cham, Germany: Springer International Publishing. https://doi.org/10.1007/978-3-319-18425-8_17

McAfee, Andrew; & Brynjolfsson, Erik. (2012). Big Data: The Management Revolution. *Harvard Business Review*, vol. 90, no. 10, pp. 61–67.

McClendon, Susannah; & Robinson, Anthony C. (2012). Leveraging Geospatially-Oriented Social Media Communications in Disaster Response. In *Proceedings of the International Conference on Information Systems for Crisis Response and Management (ISCRAM)*. Vancouver, Canada.

Medina, Rocio Zamora; & Diaz, Jose Carlos Losada. (2016). Social Media Use in Crisis Communication Management: An Opportunity for Local Communities? In M. Z. Sobaci (Ed.), *Social Media and Local Governments* (pp. 321–335). Cham, Germany: Springer International Publishing. https://doi.org/10.1007/978-3-319-17722-9_17

Mendonça, David. (2007). Decision support for improvisation in response to extreme events: Learning from the response to the 2001 World Trade Center attack. *Decision Support Systems*, vol. 43, no. 3, pp. 952–967. https://doi.org/10.1016/j.dss.2005.05.025

Mendoza, Marcelo; Poblete, Barbara; & Castillo, Carlos. (2010). Twitter Under Crisis: Can we trust what we RT? In *Proceedings of the First Workshop on Social Media Analytics (SOMA)* (pp. 71–79). New York, USA: ACM Press.

Mildner, Sven. (2013). Bürgerbeteiligung beim Hochwasserkampf – Chancen und Risiken einer kollaborativen Internetplattform zur Koordination der Gefahrenabwehr. In T. Köhler & N. Kahnwald (Eds.), *Online Communities: Enterprise Networks, Open Education and Global Communication: 16. Workshop GeNeMe '13 Gemeinschaften in Neuen Medien* (pp. 13–21). Dresden, Germany: TUDpress.

Mirbabaie, Milad; Bunker, Deborah; Stieglitz, Stefan; Marx, Julian; & Ehnis, Christian. (2020). Social media in times of crisis: Learning from Hurricane Harvey for the coronavirus disease 2019 pandemic response. *Journal of Information Technology*, vol. 35, no. 3, pp. 195–213. https://doi.org/10.1177/0268396220929258

Mirbabaie, Milad; & Marx, Julian. (2020). 'Breaking' news: uncovering sense-breaking patterns in social media crisis communication during the 2017 Manchester bombing. *Behaviour & Information Technology (BIT)*, vol. 39, no. 3, pp. 252–266. https://doi.org/10.1080/0144929X.2019.1611924

Mislove, Alan; Marcon, Massimiliano; Gummadi, Krishna P.; Druschel, Peter; & Bhattacharjee, Bobby. (2007). Measurement and Analysis of Online Social Networks. In *Proceedings of the 7th ACM SIGCOMM conference on Internet measurement* (pp. 29–42). https://doi.org/10.1145/1298306.1298311

Moi, Matthias; Friberg, Therese; Marterer, Robin; Reuter, Christian; Ludwig, Thomas; Markham, Deborah; … Muddiman, Andrew. (2015). Strategy for Processing and Analyzing Social Media Data Streams in Emergencies. In *Proceedings of the International Conference on Information and Communication Technologies for Disaster Management (ICT-DM)* (pp. 1–7). Red Hook, NY: IEEE. https://doi.org/10.1109/ICT-DM.2015.7402055

Morss, Rebecca E.; Demuth, Julie L.; Lazrus, Heather; Palen, Leysia; Barton, C. Michael; Davis, Christopher A.; … Watts, Joshua. (2017). Hazardous Weather Prediction and Communication in the Modern Information Environment. *Bulletin of the American Meteorological Society*, vol. 98, no. 12, pp. 2653–2674. https://doi.org/10.1175/BAMS-D-16-0058.1

Muralidharan, Sidharth; Dillistone, Kristie; & Shin, Jae-Hwa. (2011). The Gulf Coast oil spill: Extending the theory of image restoration discourse to the realm of social media and beyond petroleum. *Public Relations Review*, vol. 37, no. 3, pp. 226–232. https://doi.org/10.1016/j.pubrev.2011.04.006

Murphy, Tim; & Jennex, Murray E. (2006). Knowledge Management , Emergency Response , and Hurricane Katrina. *International Journal of Intelligent Control Systems*, vol. 11, no. 4, pp. 199–208.

Mysiak, J.; Testella, F.; Bonaiuto, M.; Carrus, G.; De Dominicis, S.; Ganucci Cancellieri, U.; … Grifoni, P. (2013). Flood risk management in Italy: challenges and opportunities for the implementation of the EU Floods Directive (2007/60/EC). *Natural Hazards and Earth System Sciences*, vol. 13, no. 11, pp. 2883–2890. https://doi.org/10.5194/nhess-13-2883-2013

Nagy, Ahmed; & Stamberger, Jeannie. (2012). Crowd Sentiment Detection during Disasters and Crises. In *Proceedings of the Information Systems for Crisis Response and Management (ISCRAM)* (pp. 1–9). Vancouver, Canada.

Nespeca, Vittorio; Comes, Tina; Meesters, Kenny; & Brazier, Frances. (2020). Towards coordinated self-organization: An actor-centered framework for the design of disaster management information systems. *International Journal of Disaster Risk Reduction*, vol. 51, pp. 101887.

Nielsen, Jakob. (1993). *Usability Engineering*. San Francisco, USA: Morgan Kaufmann.

Nilges, Joachim; Balduin, Norbert; & Dierich, Barbara. (2009). Information and Communication Platform for Crisis Management (IKK). In *Proceedings of the International Conference and Exhibition on Electricity Distribution (CIRED)* (pp. 1–3). Stevenage, UK, Czech Republic: IET.

Norris, Wendy. (2017). Digital Humanitarians. *Journalism Practice*, vol. 11, no. 2–3, pp. 213–228. https://doi.org/10.1080/17512786.2016.1228471

O'Reilly, Tim. (2005). What Is Web 2.0 – Design Patterns and Business Models for the Next Generation of Software. Retrieved from http://www.oreillynet.com/pub/a/oreilly/tim/news/2005/09/30/what-is-web-20.html

OECD. (2018a). Elderly population (indicator). https://doi.org/10.1787/8d805ea1-en

OECD. (2018b). Working age population (indicator). https://doi.org/10.1787/d339918b-en

OECD. (2018c). Young population (indicator). https://doi.org/10.1787/3d774f19-en

Oh, Onook; Agrawal, Manish; & Rao, Raghav. (2013). Community Intelligence and Social Media Services: A Rumor Theoretic Analysis of Tweets during Social Crises. *Management Information Systems Quarterly*, vol. 37, no. 2, pp. 407–426.

Okolloh, Ory. (2009). Ushahidi, or "testimony": Web 2.0 tools for crowdsourcing crisis information. *Participatory Learning and Action*, vol. 59, no. 1, pp. 65–70.

Olshannikova, Ekaterina; Olsson, Thomas; Huhtamäki, Jukka; & Kärkkäinen, Hannu. (2017). Conceptualizing Big Social Data. *Journal of Big Data*, vol. 4, no. 1. https://doi.org/10.1186/s40537-017-0063-x

Olteanu, Alexandra; Vieweg, Sarah; & Castillo, Carlos. (2015). What to Expect When the Unexpected Happens: Social Media Communications Across Crises. In *Proceedings of the ACM Conference on Computer-Supported-Cooperative Work and Social Computing (CSCW)* (pp. 994–1009). New York, NY: ACM. https://doi.org/10.1145/2675133.2675242

Onorati, Teresa; Díaz, Paloma; & Carrion, Belen. (2018). From social networks to emergency operation centers: A semantic visualization approach. *Future Generation Computer Systems*. https://doi.org/10.1016/j.future.2018.01.052

Organisation for Economic Co-operation and Development (OECD). (2007). Participative Web: User-Created Content. Retrieved from http://www.oecd.org/internet/ieconomy/38393115.pdf

Orlikowski, Wanda J.; & Hofman, J. Debra. (1997). An Improvisational Model for Change Management: The Case of Groupware Technologies. *Sloan Management Review*, vol. 38, no. 2.

Öztürk, Nazan; & Ayvaz, Serkan. (2018). Sentiment analysis on Twitter: A text mining approach to the Syrian refugee crisis. *Telematics and Informatics*, vol. 35, no. 1, pp. 136–147. https://doi.org/10.1016/J.TELE.2017.10.006

Palen, Leysia. (2008). Online Social Media in Crisis Events. *Educause Quarterly*, vol. 3, pp. 76–78.

Palen, Leysia; Anderson, Jennings; Bica, Melissa; Castillo, Carlos; Crowley, John; Pérez, Paloma Díaz; … Wilson, Tom. (2020). *Crisis Informatics: Human-Centered Research*

on Tech & Crises – A Guided Bibliography Developed by Crisis Informatics Researchers.
Retrieved from https://tinyurl.com/crisisinformatics

Palen, Leysia; & Anderson, Kenneth M. (2016). Crisis informatics: New data for extraordinary times. *Science*, vol. 353, no. 6296, pp. 224–225.

Palen, Leysia; & Liu, Sophia B. (2007). Citizen communications in crisis: anticipating a future of ICT-supported public participation. In *Proceedings of the Conference on Human Factors in Computing Systems (CHI)* (pp. 727–736). San Jose, USA: ACM Press. https://doi.org/10.1145/1240624.1240736

Palen, Leysia; Vieweg, Sarah; Liu, Sophia B.; & Hughes, Amanda Lee. (2009). Crisis in a Networked World: Features of Computer-Mediated Communication in the April 16, 2007, Virginia Tech Event. *Social Science Computer Review*, vol. 27, no. 4, pp. 467–480. https://doi.org/10.1177/0894439309332302

Palen, Leysia; Vieweg, Sarah; Sutton, Jeannette; Liu, Sophia B.; & Hughes, Amanda Lee. (2007). Crisis Informatics: Studying Crisis in a Networked World. In *Proceedings of the International Conference on E-Social Science*. Ann Arbor, USA. Retrieved from http://www.ncess.ac.uk/events/conference/2007/papers.htm

Parajuli, Rishi Ram. (2020). Citizen Disaster Science Education for effective disaster risk reduction in developing countries. *Geoenvironmental Disasters*, vol. 7, no. 1, pp. 12. https://doi.org/10.1186/s40677-020-00150-2

Pasmore, William A. (1988). *Designing Effective Organizations: The Sociotechnical Systems Perspective*. John Wiley & Sons.

Paulus, David; Fathi, Ramian; Fiedrich, Frank; de Walle, Bartel Van; & Comes, Tina. (2022). On the Interplay of Data and Cognitive Bias in Crisis Information Management. *Information Systems Frontiers*. https://doi.org/10.1007/s10796-022-10241-0

Perng, Sung-Yueh; Büscher, Monika; Wood, Lisa; Halvorsrud, Ragnhild; Stiso, Michael; Ramirez, Leonardo; & Al-Akkad, Amro. (2012). Peripheral response: Microblogging during the 22/7/2011 Norway attacks. In *Proceedings of the International Conference on Information Systems for Crisis Response and Management (ISCRAM)* (pp. 1–11). Vancouver, Canada.

Perng, Sung-Yueh; Büscher, Monika; Wood, Lisa; Halvorsrud, Ragnhild; Stiso, Michael; Ramirez, Leonardo; & Al-Akkad, Amro. (2013). Peripheral Response: Microblogging During the 22/7/2011 Norway Attacks. *International Journal of Information Systems for Crisis Response and Management (IJISCRAM)*, vol. 5, no. 1.

Perry, Ronald W.; Lindell, Michael K.; & Tierney, Kathleen J. (Eds.). (2001). *Facing the unexpected: disaster preparedness and response in the United States*. Washington, DC: Joseph Henry Press.

Pipek, Volkmar. (2005). *From tailoring to appropriation support: Negotiating groupware usage (PhD-Thesis)*. (Faculty of Science – Department of Information Processing Science – University of Oulu, Ed.). Oulu, Finland: Oulu University Press.

Pipek, Volkmar; Liu, Sophia B.; & Kerne, Andruid. (2014). Special Issue: Crisis Informatics and Collaboration. *Computer Supported Cooperative Work (CSCW) – The Journal of Collaborative Computing and Work Practices*, vol. 23, no. 4–6.

Pipek, Volkmar; Reuter, Christian; Ley, Benedikt; Ludwig, Thomas; & Wiedenhoefer, Torben. (2013). Sicherheitsarena – Ein Ansatz zur Verbesserung des Krisenmanagements durch Kooperation und Vernetzung. *Crisis Prevention – Fachmagazin Für*

Innere Sicherheit, Bevölkerungsschutz Und Katastrophenhilfe, vol. 3, no. 1, pp. 58–59. Retrieved from http://www.wineme.uni-siegen.de/paper/2013/crisisprevention2013_sicherheitsarena.pdf

Pipek, Volkmar; & Wulf, Volker. (2009). Infrastructuring: Toward an Integrated Perspective on the Design and Use of Information Technology. *Journal of the Association for Information Systems (JAIS)*, vol. 10, no. 5, pp. 447–473.

Plotnick, Linda; & Hiltz, Starr Roxanne. (2016). Barriers to Use of Social Media by Emergency Managers. *Journal of Homeland Security and Emergency Management*, vol. 13, no. 2, pp. 247–277. https://doi.org/10.1515/jhsem-2015-0068

Plotnick, Linda; Hiltz, Starr Roxanne; Kushma, Jane; & Tapia, Andrea. (2015). Red Tape : Attitudes and Issues Related to Use of Social Media by U . S . County- Level Emergency Managers. In *Proceedings of the Information Systems for Crisis Response and Management (ISCRAM)*. Kristiansand, Norway: ISCRAM. Retrieved from http://idl.iscram.org/files/lindaplotnick/2015/1225_LindaPlotnick_etal2015.pdf

Poblet, Marta; García-Cuesta, Esteban; & Casanovas, Pompeu. (2018). Crowdsourcing roles, methods and tools for data-intensive disaster management. *Information Systems Frontiers*, vol. 20, no. 6, pp. 1363–1379. https://doi.org/10.1007/s10796-017-9734-6

Pohl, Daniela. (2013). Social Media Analysis for Crisis Management: A Brief Survey. Retrieved from http://stcsn.ieee.net/e-letter/vol-2-no-1/social-media-analysis-for-crisis-management-a-brief-survey

Pohl, Daniela; Bouchachia, Abdelhamid; & Hellwagner, Hermann. (2015). Social media for crisis management: clustering approaches for sub-event detection. *Multimedia Tools and Applications*, vol. 74, no. 11, pp. 3901–3932. https://doi.org/10.1007/s11042-013-1804-2

ProspectMagazine. (2017). Open doors and Fake News: How People used Social Media after the Manchester Attack. Retrieved from https://www.prospectmagazine.co.uk/other/open-doors-and-fake-news-how-people-used-social-media-after-the-manchester-attack

Purohit, Hemant; Hampton, Andrew; Bhatt, Shreyansh; Shalin, Valerie L.; Sheth, Amit P.; & Flach, John M. (2014). Identifying Seekers and Suppliers in Social Media Communities to Support Crisis Coordination. *Computer Supported Cooperative Work (CSCW) – The Journal of Collaborative Computing and Work Practices*, vol. 23, no. 4–6, pp. 513–545.

Qu, Yan; Huang, Chen; Zhang, Pengyi; & Zhang, Jun. (2011). Microblogging after a Major Disaster in China: A Case Study of the 2010 Yushu Earthquake. In *Proceedings of the ACM Conference on Computer-Supported-Cooperative Work (CSCW)* (pp. 25–34). New York, USA: ACM.

Qu, Yan; Wu, Philip Fei; & Wang, Xiaoqing. (2009). Online Community Response to Major Disaster : A Study of Tianya Forum in the 2008 Sichuan Earthquake. In *Proceedings of the Hawaii International Conference on System Sciences (HICSS)* (pp. 1–11). Waikoloa, USA: IEEE Computer Society. https://doi.org/10.1109/HICSS.2009.330

Quarantelli, Enrico L. (1984). *Emergent Citizen Groups in Disaster Preparedness and Recovery Activities*. University of Delaware. Retrieved from http://udspace.udel.edu/handle/19716/1206

Quarantelli, Enrico L. (1988). Disaster Crisis Management: A summary of research findings. *Journal of Management Studies*, vol. 25, no. 4, pp. 373–385. Retrieved from http://udspace.udel.edu/bitstream/handle/19716/487/PP113.pdf

Quarantelli, Enrico L.; & Dynes, Russell Rowe. (1977). Response to Social Crisis and Disaster. *Annual Review of Sociology*, vol. 3, no. 1, pp. 23–49. https://doi.org/10.1146/ann urev.so.03.080177.000323

Rabin, Jack; Hildreth, W. Bartley; & Miller, Gerald. (2007). *Handbook of Public Administration*. Routledge. https://doi.org/10.4324/9781315093215

Reddick, Christopher G. (2012). *Public Administration and Information Technology*. Sudbury, USA: Jones & Bartlett Learning.

Reilly, W. Scott Neal; Guarino, Sean L.; & Kellihan, Bret. (2007). Model-Based Measurement of Situation Awareness. In *Proceedings of the 2007 Winter Simulation Conference* (pp. 1353–1360). Washington.

Renn, Ortwin; & Rohrmann, Bernd. (2000). *Cross-Cultural Risk Perception: State and Challenges*. https://doi.org/10.1007/978-1-4757-4891-8_6

Reuter, Christian. (2014a). Communication between Power Blackout and Mobile Network Overload. *International Journal of Information Systems for Crisis Response and Management (IJISCRAM)*, vol. 6, no. 2, pp. 38–53. https://doi.org/10.4018/ijiscram.201404 0103

Reuter, Christian. (2014b). *Emergent Collaboration Infrastructures: Technology Design for Inter-Organizational Crisis Management (Ph.D. Thesis)*. Siegen, Germany, Germany: Springer Gabler. https://doi.org/10.1007/978-3-658-08586-5

Reuter, Christian. (2018). Special Issue on Human-Computer-Interaction and Social Media in Safety-Critical Systems. *Journal of Contingencies and Crisis Management (JCCM)*, vol. 26, no. 1, pp. 1–199. Retrieved from http://onlinelibrary.wiley.com/doi/https://doi.org/10.1111/jccm.2018.26.issue-1/issuetoc

Reuter, Christian; Amelunxen, Christoph; & Moi, Matthias. (2016a). Semi-Automatic Alerts and Notifications for Emergency Services based on Cross-Platform Social Media Data –Evaluation of a Prototype. In H. C. Mayr & M. Pinzger (Eds.), *Informatik 2016: von Menschen für Menschen, Lecture Notes in Informatics (LNI)* (GI Edition, pp. 1805–1818). Klagenfurt, Germany: Gesellschaft für Informatik. Retrieved from http://subs.emis.de/LNI/Proceedings/Proceedings259/P-259.pdf#page=1806

Reuter, Christian; Backfried, Gerhard; Kaufhold, Marc-André; & Spahr, Fabian. (2018a). ISCRAM turns 15: A Trend Analysis of Social Media Papers 2004–2017. In *Proceedings of the Information Systems for Crisis Response and Management (ISCRAM)* (pp. 1–14). Rochester, New York, USA: ISCRAM. Retrieved from http://idl.iscram.org/files/christian reuter/2018/2122_ChristianReuter_etal2018.pdf

Reuter, Christian; Hartwig, Katrin; Kirchner, Jan; & Schlegel, Noah. (2019a). Fake News Perception in Germany: A Representative Study of People's Attitudes and Approaches to Counteract Disinformation. In *Proceedings of the International Conference on Wirtschaftsinformatik*. Siegen, Germany: AIS.

Reuter, Christian; Heger, Oliver; & Pipek, Volkmar. (2013). Combining Real and Virtual Volunteers through Social Media. In T. Comes, F. Fiedrich, S. Fortier, J. Geldermann, & T. Müller (Eds.), *Proceedings of the International Conference on Information Systems for Crisis Response and Management (ISCRAM)* (pp. 780–790). Baden-Baden, Germany: ACM. https://doi.org/10.1126/science.1060143

Reuter, Christian; Hughes, Amanda Lee; & Kaufhold, Marc-André. (2018b). Social Media in Crisis Management: An Evaluation and Analysis of Crisis Informatics Research. *International Journal on Human-Computer Interaction (IJHCI)*, vol. 34, no. 4, pp. 280–294. https://doi.org/10.1080/10447318.2018.1427832

Reuter, Christian; & Kaufhold, Marc-André. (2018). Fifteen Years of Social Media in Emergencies: A Retrospective Review and Future Directions for Crisis Informatics. *Journal of Contingencies and Crisis Management (JCCM)*, vol. 26, no. 1, pp. 41–57. https://doi.org/10.1111/1468-5973.12196

Reuter, Christian; Kaufhold, Marc-André; & Ludwig, Thomas. (2017a). End-User Development and Social Big Data – Towards Tailorable Situation Assessment with Social Media. In F. Paternò & V. Wulf (Eds.), *New Perspectives in End-User Development* (pp. 307–332). Springer. https://doi.org/10.1007/978-3-319-60291-2_12

Reuter, Christian; Kaufhold, Marc-André; Schmid, Stefka; Hahne, Anna Sophie; Spielhofer, Thomas; & Hahne, Anna Sophie. (2019b). The impact of risk cultures: Citizens' perception of social media use in emergencies across Europe. *Technological Forecasting and Social Change*, vol. 148, no. 119724. https://doi.org/10.1016/j.techfore.2019.119724

Reuter, Christian; Kaufhold, Marc-André; Spielhofer, Thomas; & Hahne, Anna Sophie. (2017b). Social Media in Emergencies: A Representative Study on Citizens' Perception in Germany. *Proceedings of the ACM: Human Computer Interaction (PACM): Computer-Supported Cooperative Work and Social Computing*, vol. 1, no. CSCW, pp. 1–19. https://doi.org/10.1145/3134725

Reuter, Christian; Kaufhold, Marc André; Spahr, Fabian; Spielhofer, Thomas; & Hahne, Anna Sophie. (2020a). Emergency service staff and social media – A comparative empirical study of the attitude by emergency services staff in Europe in 2014 and 2017. *International Journal of Disaster Risk Reduction (IJDRR)*, vol. 46, no. 101516. https://doi.org/10.1016/j.ijdrr.2020.101516

Reuter, Christian; Ludwig, Thomas; Friberg, Therese; Pratzler-Wanczura, Sylvia; & Gizikis, Alexis. (2015a). Social Media and Emergency Services? Interview Study on Current and Potential Use in 7 European Countries. *International Journal of Information Systems for Crisis Response and Management (IJISCRAM)*, vol. 7, no. 2, pp. 36–58. https://doi.org/10.4018/IJISCRAM.2015040103

Reuter, Christian; Ludwig, Thomas; Kaufhold, Marc-André; & Pipek, Volkmar. (2015b). XHELP: Design of a Cross-Platform Social-Media Application to Support Volunteer Moderators in Disasters. In *Proceedings of the Conference on Human Factors in Computing Systems (CHI)* (pp. 4093–4102). Seoul, Korea, Korea: ACM Press. https://doi.org/10.1145/2702123.2702171

Reuter, Christian; Ludwig, Thomas; Kaufhold, Marc-André; & Spielhofer, Thomas. (2016b). Emergency Services Attitudes towards Social Media: A Quantitative and Qualitative Survey across Europe. *International Journal on Human-Computer Studies (IJHCS)*, vol. 95, pp. 96–111. https://doi.org/10.1016/j.ijhcs.2016.03.005

Reuter, Christian; Ludwig, Thomas; Kotthaus, Christoph; Kaufhold, Marc-André; Radziewski, Elmar von; & Pipek, Volkmar. (2016c). Big Data in a Crisis? Creating Social Media Datasets for Emergency Management Research. *I-Com: Journal of Interactive Media*, vol. 15, no. 3, pp. 249–264. https://doi.org/10.1515/icom-2016-0036

Reuter, Christian; Ludwig, Thomas; & Pipek, Volkmar. (2016d). Kooperative Resilienz – ein soziotechnischer Ansatz durch Kooperationstechnologien im Krisenmanagement.

Gruppe. Interaktion. Organisation. Zeitschrift Für Angewandte Organisationspsychologie (GIO), vol. 47, no. 2, pp. 159–169. https://doi.org/10.1007/s11612-016-0317-7

Reuter, Christian; Ludwig, Thomas; Ritzkatis, Michael; & Pipek, Volkmar. (2015c). Social-QAS: Tailorable Quality Assessment Service for Social Media Content. In *Proceedings of the International Symposium on End-User Development (IS-EUD). Lecture Notes in Computer Science* (pp. 156–170). https://doi.org/10.1007/978-3-319-18425-8_11

Reuter, Christian; Marx, Alexandra; & Pipek, Volkmar. (2012). Crisis Management 2.0: Towards a Systematization of Social Software Use in Crisis Situations. *International Journal of Information Systems for Crisis Response and Management (IJISCRAM)*, vol. 4, no. 1, pp. 1–16. https://doi.org/10.4018/jiscrm.2012010101

Reuter, Christian; Mentler, Tilo; & Geisler, Stefan. (2015d). *Special Issue on Human Computer Interaction in Critical Systems I: Citizen and Volunteers. International Journal of Information Systems for Crisis Response and Management (IJISCRAM)* (Vol. 7). Retrieved from https://www.wineme.uni-siegen.de/paper/2015/2015_ijiscram-specialissue_hci-criticalsystems-i.pdf

Reuter, Christian; & Ritzkatis, Michael. (2014). Adaptierbare Bewertung bürgergenerierter Inhalte aus sozialen Medien. In M. Koch, A. Butz, & J. Schlichter (Eds.), *Mensch & Computer: Interaktiv unterwegs – Freiräume gestalten* (pp. 115–124). München, Germany: Oldenbourg-Verlag. Retrieved from https://dl.gi.de/bitstream/handle/20.500.12116/7536/Reuter_Ritzkatis_2014.pdf

Reuter, Christian; Ritzkatis, Michael; & Ludwig, Thomas. (2014). Entwicklung eines SOA-basierten und anpassbaren Bewertungsdienstes für Inhalte aus sozialen Medien. In E. Plödereder, L. Grunske, E. Schneider, & D. Ull (Eds.), *Informatik 2014 – Big Data – Komplexität meistern* (pp. 977–988). Stuttgart, Germany: GI-Edition-Lecture Notes in Informatics (LNI). Retrieved from https://dl.gi.de/handle/20.500.12116/2709

Reuter, Christian; & Scholl, Simon. (2014). Technical Limitations for Designing Applications for Social Media. In M. Koch, A. Butz, & J. Schlichter (Eds.), *Mensch & Computer: Workshopband* (pp. 131–140). München, Germany: Oldenbourg-Verlag. https://doi.org/10.1524/9783110344509.131

Reuter, Christian; & Schröter, Julian. (2015). Microblogging during the European Floods 2013: What Twitter May Contribute in German Emergencies. *International Journal of Information Systems for Crisis Response and Management (IJISCRAM)*, vol. 7, no. 1, pp. 22–41. https://doi.org/10.4018/IJISCRAM.2015010102

Reuter, Christian; & Spielhofer, Thomas. (2017). Towards Social Resilience: A Quantitative and Qualitative Survey on Citizens' Perception of Social Media in Emergencies in Europe. *Journal Technological Forecasting and Social Change (TFSC)*, vol. 121, pp. 168–180. https://doi.org/10.1016/j.techfore.2016.07.038

Reuter, Christian; Stieglitz, Stefan; & Imran, Muhammad. (2020b). Social media in conflicts and crises. *Behaviour & Information Technology (BIT)*, vol. 39, no. 3, pp. 241–251. https://doi.org/10.1080/0144929X.2019.1629025

Rexiline Ragini, J.; Rubesh Anand, P. M.; & Bhaskar, Vidhyacharan. (2018). Mining crisis information: A strategic approach for detection of people at risk through social media analysis. *International Journal of Disaster Risk Reduction*, vol. 27, pp. 556–566. https://doi.org/10.1016/j.ijdrr.2017.12.002

Rieder, Bernhard. (2013). Studying Facebook via Data Extraction: The Netvizz Application. In *Proceedings of the 5th Annual ACM Web Science Conference* (pp. 346–355). New York, USA: ACM. https://doi.org/10.1145/2464464.2464475

Righi, Valeria; Sayago, Sergio; & Blat, Josep. (2017). When we talk about older people in HCI, who are we talking about? Towards a 'turn to community' in the design of technologies for a growing ageing population. *International Journal of Human-Computer Studies*, vol. 108, pp. 15–31. https://doi.org/10.1016/j.ijhcs.2017.06.005

Ritter, Alan; Clark, Sam; Mausam; & Etzioni, Oren. (2011). Named Entity Recognition in Tweets: An Experimental Study. In P. Merlo, R. Barzilay, & M. Johnson (Eds.), *Proceedings of the Conference on Empirical Methods in Natural Language Processing (EMNLP)* (pp. 1524–1534). Edinburgh: Association for Computational Linguistics.

Rizza, Caroline; Pereira, Angela Guimarães Pereira; & Curvelo, Paula. (2013). Do-it-yourself Justice-Considerations of Social Media use in a Crisis Situation: The Case of the 2011 Vancouver Riots. In *Proceedings of the Information Systems for Crisis Response and Management (ISCRAM)* (pp. 411–415). Baden-Baden, Germany.

Robinson, AC; Savelyev, Alexander; Pezanowski, Scott; & MacEachren, Alan M. (2013). Understanding the Utility of Geospatial Information in Social Media. In *Proceedings of the International Conference on Information Systems for Crisis Response and Management (ISCRAM)* (pp. 918–922). Baden-Baden, Germany.

Rogers, Everett M. (2003). *Diffusion of innovation* (5th ed.). New York, USA: Free Press.

Rohde, Markus; Brödner, Peter; & Wulf, Volker. (2009). Towards a paradigmatic shift in IS: designing for social practice. In *Proceedings of the International Conference on Design Science Research in Information Systems and Technology (DESRIST)*. https://doi.org/10.1145/1555619.1555639

Rossi, C.; Acerbo, F. S.; Ylinen, K.; Juga, I.; Nurmi, P.; Bosca, A.; … Alikadic, A. (2018). Early detection and information extraction for weather-induced floods using social media streams. *International Journal of Disaster Risk Reduction*, vol. 30, pp. 145–157. https://doi.org/10.1016/j.ijdrr.2018.03.002

Rudolph-Cleff, Annette; Knodt, Michèle; Schulze, Joachim; & Engel, Alice. (2022). Crisis communication in a blackout scenario – An assessment considering socio-spatial parameters and the vulnerabilities of the population. *International Journal of Disaster Risk Reduction*, vol. 72, pp. 102856. https://doi.org/10.1016/j.ijdrr.2022.102856

Sackmann, Stefan; Hofmann, Marlen; & Betke, Hans J. (2014). Organizing On-Site Volunteers: An App-Based Approach. In *Proceedings of the 2014 Ninth International Conference on Availability, Reliability and Security (ARES '14)* (pp. 438–439). Washington, DC: IEEE. https://doi.org/10.1109/ARES.2014.66

Sagar, Vishalini Chandara. (2016). As the Water Recedes: Sri Lanka Rebuilds. *RSIS Commentaries*, vol. 141.

Sakaki, Takeshi; Okazaki, Makoto; & Matsuo, Yutaka. (2010). Earthquake shakes Twitter users: real-time event detection by social sensors. *Proceedings of the 19th International Conference on World Wide Web (WWW)*, pp. 851. https://doi.org/10.1145/1772690.1772777

San, Yee; Wardell III, Clarence; & Thorkildsen, Zoë. (2013). *Social Media in the Emergency Management Field: 2012 Survey Results*. National Emergency Manaagement Association. Retrieved from https://web.archive.org/web/20131028032920/http://www.cna.org/sites/default/files/research/SocialMedia_EmergencyManagement.pdf

Saroj, Anita; & Pal, Sukomal. (2020). Use of social media in crisis management: A survey. *International Journal of Disaster Risk Reduction*, vol. 48, pp. 101584. https://doi.org/10. 1016/j.ijdrr.2020.101584

Scanlon, Joseph; Helsloot, Ira; & Groenendaal, Jelle. (2014). Putting it all together: Integrating ordinary people into emergency response. *International Journal of Mass Emergencies and Disasters*, vol. 32, no. 1, pp. 43–63.

Schelfaut, K.; Pannemans, B.; van der Craats, I.; Krywkow, J.; Mysiak, J.; & Cools, J. (2011). Bringing flood resilience into practice: the FREEMAN project. *Environmental Science & Policy*, vol. 14, no. 7, pp. 825–833. https://doi.org/10.1016/j.envsci.2011.02.009

Schmidt, Arjen; Wolbers, Jeroen; Ferguson, Julie; & Boersma, Kees. (2018). Are you Ready2Help? Conceptualizing the management of online and onsite volunteer convergence. *Journal of Contingencies and Crisis Management*, vol. 26, no. 3, pp. 338–349. https://doi.org/10.1111/1468-5973.12200

Schütz, Alfred. (1932). *Der Sinnhafte Aufbau der Sozialen Welt*. Vienna: Springer Vienna. https://doi.org/10.1007/978-3-7091-3108-4

Schütz, Alfred; & Luckmann, Thomas. (2017). *Strukturen der Lebenswelt* (2nd ed.). Konstanz: UTB GmbH.

Semaan, B.; & Mark, G. (2012). "Facebooking" Towards Crisis Recovery and Beyond: Disruption as an Opportunity. In *Proceedings of the ACM Conference on Computer Supported Cooperative Work (CSCW)* (pp. 27–36). New York, USA. https://doi.org/10.1145/214 5204.2145214

Semaan, Bryan. (2019). "Routine Infrastructuring" as "Building Everyday Resilience with Technology": When Disruption Becomes Ordinary. *Proceedings of the ACM on Human-Computer Interaction*, vol. 3, no. CSCW. https://doi.org/10.1145/3359175

Sherrod, D. R. (1971). Selective perception of political candidates. *Public Opinion Quarterly*, vol. 35, pp. 554– 562.

Shklovski, Irina; Palen, Leysia; & Sutton, Jeannette. (2008). Finding Community Through Information and Communication Technology During Disaster Events. In *Proceedings of the ACM Conference on Computer-Supported-Cooperative Work and Social Computing (CSCW)* (pp. 127–136). San Diego, USA: ACM-Press.

Simão, João; Luís, Belfo; Schmidt, Silke; Rhode, Dieter; Freitag, Simone; Lück, Anja; … Villot, Emmanuelle. (2015). iSAR+ Guidelines: Online and Mobile Communications for Crisis Response and Search and Rescue. Retrieved from https://web.archive.org/web/201 71221232236/http://isar.i112.eu/downloads/files/D2271-iSARGuidelinesRoadmap.pdf

Simon, H. A. (1971). Designing Organizations for an Information-Rich World. In M. Greenberger (Ed.), *Computers, Communication, and the Public Interest* (pp. 40–41). Baltimore: The Johns Hopkins Press.

Smets, Peer; Younes, Younes; Dohmen, Marinka; Boersma, Kees; & Brouwer, Lenie. (2021). Social media in and around a temporary large-scale refugee shelter in the Netherlands. *Social Media + Society*, vol. 7, no. 2, pp. 1–11. https://doi.org/10.1177/205630512110 24961

Smith, William R.; Stephens, Keri K.; Robertson, Brett R.; Li, Jing; & Murthy, Dhiraj. (2018). Social Media in Citizen-Led Disaster Response: Rescuer Roles, Coordination Challenges, and Untapped Potential. In *Proceedings of the Information Systems for Crisis Response and Management (ISCRAM)*.

Soden, Robert; & Owen, Embry. (2021). Dilemmas in Mutual Aid: Lessons for Crisis Informatics from an Emergent Community Response to the Pandemic. *Proceedings of the ACM on Human-Computer Interaction*, vol. 5, no. CSCW2. https://doi.org/10.1145/3479862

Soden, Robert; & Palen, Leysia. (2014). From Crowdsourced Mapping to Community Mapping: The Post-Earthquake Work of OpenStreetMap Haiti. In *COOP 2014 – Proceedings of the 11th International Conference on the Design of Cooperative Systems* (pp. 311–326). Nice, France. https://doi.org/10.1007/978-3-319-06498-7

Soden, Robert; & Palen, Leysia. (2016). Infrastructure in the Wild: What Mapping in Post-Earthquake Nepal Reveals About Infrastructural Emergence. *Proceedings of the Conference on Human Factors in Computing Systems (CHI)*, pp. 2796–2807. https://doi.org/10.1145/2858036.2858545

Spence, Patric R.; Lachlan, Kenneth A.; Lin, Xialing; & del Greco, Maria. (2015). Variability in Twitter Content Across the Stages of a Natural Disaster: Implications for Crisis Communication. *Communication Quarterly*, vol. 63, no. 2, pp. 171–186. https://doi.org/10.1080/01463373.2015.1012219

Sprout Social. (2014). SproutSocial: Powerful, Approachable Software for Social Business. Retrieved from http://sproutsocial.com/features

St. Denis, Lise Ann; Anderson, Kenneth M.; & Palen, Leysia. (2014). Mastering Social Media : An Analysis of Jefferson County's Communications during the 2013 Colorado Floods. In *Proceedings of the Information Systems for Crisis Response and Management (ISCRAM)* (pp. 737–746).

St. Denis, Lise Ann; Hughes, Amanda Lee; & Palen, Leysia. (2012). Trial by Fire: The Deployment of Trusted Digital Volunteers in the 2011 Shadow Lake Fire. In L. Rothkrantz, J. Ristvej, & Z. Franco (Eds.), *Proceedings of the International Conference on Information Systems for Crisis Response and Management (ISCRAM)* (pp. 1–10). Vancouver, Canada, Canada: ISCRAM.

Stake, Robert E. (1995). *The art of case study research*. Sage Publications.

Stallings, Robert A.; & Quarantelli, Enrico L. El. (1985). Emergent Citizen Groups and Emergency Management. *Public Administration Review*, vol. 45, no. Special Issue, pp. 93–100. https://doi.org/10.2307/3135003

Starbird, Kate. (2013). Delivering patients to sacré coeur: collective intelligence in digital volunteer communities. In W. E. Mackay, S. Brewster, & S. Bødker (Eds.), *Proceedings of the Conference on Human Factors in Computing Systems (CHI)* (pp. 801–810). Paris, France: ACM. Retrieved from http://dl.acm.org/citation.cfm?id=2470769

Starbird, Kate. (2017). Examining the Alternative Media Ecosystem Through the Production of Alternative Narratives of Mass Shooting Events on Twitter. In *Proceedings of the Eleventh International Conference on Web and Social Media* (pp. 230–239). Palo Alto, CA: AAAI Press.

Starbird, Kate; Arif, Ahmer; & Wilson, Tom. (2019). Disinformation as collaborative work: Surfacing the participatory nature of strategic information operations. *Proceedings of the ACM on Human-Computer Interaction*, vol. 3, no. CSCW, pp. 1–26. https://doi.org/10.1145/3359229

Starbird, Kate; Maddock, Jim; Orand, Mania; Achterman, Peg; & Mason, Robert M. (2014). Rumors, False Flags, and Digital Vigilantes: Misinformation on Twitter after the 2013 Boston Marathon Bombing. In *iConference 2014*. Berlin, Germany. https://doi.org/10.9776/14308

Starbird, Kate; & Palen, Leysia. (2010). Pass It On?: Retweeting in Mass Emergency. In S. French, B. Tomaszewski, & C. Zobel (Eds.), *Proceedings of the International Conference on Information Systems for Crisis Response and Management (ISCRAM)* (pp. 1–10). Seattle, USA.

Starbird, Kate; & Palen, Leysia. (2011). Voluntweeters: Self-Organizing by Digital Volunteers in Times of Crisis. In *Proceedings of the Conference on Human Factors in Computing Systems (CHI)* (pp. 1071–1080). Vancouver, Canada: ACM-Press. https://doi.org/10.1145/1978942.1979102

Starbird, Kate; & Palen, Leysia. (2012). (How) will the revolution be retweeted?: information diffusion and the 2011 Egyptian uprising. In S. E. Poltrock, C. Simone, J. Grudin, G. Mark, & J. Riedl (Eds.), *Proceedings of the ACM Conference on Computer Supported Cooperative Work (CSCW)*. Bellevue, USA: ACM Press. https://doi.org/10.1145/2145204.2145212

Starbird, Kate; Palen, Leysia; Hughes, Amanda Lee; & Vieweg, Sarah. (2010). Chatter on the red: what hazards threat reveals about the social life of microblogged information. In *Proceedings of the Conference on Computer Supported Cooperative Work (CSCW)* (pp. 241–250). New York, USA: ACM Press. https://doi.org/10.1145/1718918.1718965

Starbird, Kate; & Stamberger, Jeannie. (2010). Tweak the Tweet: Leveraging Microblogging Proliferation with a Prescriptive Syntax to Support Citizen Reporting. In S. French, B. Tomaszewski, & C. Zobel (Eds.), *Proceedings of the Information Systems for Crisis Response and Management (ISCRAM)* (pp. 1–5). Brussels, Belgium: ISCRAM.

Statista. (2017). Anzahl der monatlich aktiven Nutzer von sozialen Netzwerken in ausgewählten Ländern weltweit im Jahr 2016 (in Millionen). Retrieved from https://de.statista.com/statistik/daten/studie/554504/umfrage/anzahl-der-monatlich-aktiven-nutzer-von-sozialen-netzwerken-in-ausgewaehlten-laendern-weltweit/

Statista. (2022). Ranking der größten Social Networks und Messenger nach der Anzahl der Nutzer im Januar 2022. Retrieved from https://de.statista.com/statistik/daten/studie/181086/umfrage/die-weltweit-groessten-social-networks-nach-anzahl-der-user/

Statman, Meir. (2008). Countries and Culture in Behavioral Finance. In *CFA Institute Conference Proceedings Quarterly* (pp. 38–44). https://doi.org/10.2469/cp.v25.n3.6

Stevens, Gunnar; Pipek, Volkmar; & Wulf, Volker. (2009). Appropriation Infrastructure: Supporting the Design of Usages. In V. Pipek, M. B. Rosson, & V. Wulf (Eds.), *Proceedings of the Second International Symposium on End-User Development (IS-EUD)* (pp. 50–69). Heidelberg, Germany: Springer, LNCS.

Stieglitz, Stefan; Dang-Xuan, Linh; Bruns, Axel; & Neuberger, Christoph. (2014). Social Media Analytics. *Wirtschaftsinformatik*, vol. 56, no. 2, pp. 101–109.

Strauss, Anselm L. (1987). *Qualitative Analysis for Social Scientists*. Cambridge, UK: Cambridge Press.

Strauss, Anselm L.; & Corbin, Juliet. (1998). *Basics of qualitative research: Techniques and procedures for developing grounded theory*. Thousand Oaks, CA: Sage Publications.

Sutton, Jeannette. (2010). Twittering Tennessee: Distributed networks and Collaboration Following a Technological Disaster. In S. French, B. Tomaszewski, & C. Zobel (Eds.), *Proceedings of the International Conference on Information Systems for Crisis Response and Management (ISCRAM)* (pp. 1–10). Seattle, USA.

Sutton, Jeannette; Palen, Leysia; & Shklovski, Irina. (2008). Backchannels on the Front Lines: Emergent Uses of Social Media in the 2007 Southern California Wildfires. In *Proceedings of the International Conference on Information Systems for Crisis Response and Management (ISCRAM)* (pp. 624–632). Brussels, Belgium: ISCRAM.

Sutton, Jeannette; Spiro, E. S.; Johnson, B.; Fitzhugh, S. M.; Greczek, M.; & Butts, C. T. (2012). Connected Communications: Network Structures of Official Communications in a Technological Disaster. In *Proceedings of the International Conference on Information Systems for Crisis Response and Management (ISCRAM)*. Vancouver, BC, Canada. Retrieved from http://idl.iscram.org/files/sutton/2012/214_Sutton_etal2012.pdf

Talabi, Felix Olajide; Aiyesimoju, Ayodeji Boluwatife; Lamidi, Ishola Kamorudeen; Bello, Samson Adedapo; Okunade, Joshua Kayode; Ugwuoke, Chinedu Joel; & Gever, Verlumun Celestine. (2022). The use of social media storytelling for help-seeking and help-receiving among Nigerian refugees of the Ukraine–Russia war. *Telematics and Informatics*, vol. 71, pp. 101836. https://doi.org/10.1016/j.tele.2022.101836

Tandoc Jr., Edson C.; Lim, Zheng Wei; & Ling, Richard. (2018). Defining "Fake News": A typology of scholarly definitions. *Digital Journalism*, vol. 6, no. 2, pp. 137–153. https://doi.org/10.1080/21670811.2017.1360143

Tapia, Andrea H.; & Moore, Kathleen. (2014). Good Enough is Good Enough: Overcoming Disaster Response Organizations' Slow Social Media Data Adoption. *Computer Supported Cooperative Work (CSCW) – The Journal of Collaborative Computing and Work Practices*, vol. 23, no. 4–6, pp. 483–512.

Tapia, Andrea H.; Moore, Kathleen; & Johnson, Nicholas. (2013). Beyond the Trustworthy Tweet: A Deeper Understanding of Microblogged Data Use by Disaster Response and Humanitarian Relief Organizations. In *Proceedings of the Information Systems for Crisis Response and Management (ISCRAM)*. Retrieved from http://idl.iscram.org/files/tapia/2013/993_Tapia_etal2013.pdf

Terpstra, Teun; Vries, A. de; Stronkman, R.; & Paradies, G. L. (2012). Towards a realtime Twitter analysis during crises for operational crisis management. In *Proceedings of the International Conference on Information Systems for Crisis Response and Management (ISCRAM)* (pp. 1–9). Vancouver, Canada.

Thomson, Robert; Ito, Naoya; Suda, Hinako; & Lin, Fangyu. (2012). Trusting Tweets: The Fukushima Disaster and Information Source Credibility on Twitter. In *Proceedings of the International Conference on Information Systems for Crisis Response and Management (ISCRAM)* (pp. 1–10). Vancouver, Canada.

Turoff, Murray; Chumer, Michael; van de Walle, Bartel; & Yao, Xiang. (2004). The design of a dynamic emergency response management information system (DERMIS). *The Journal of Information Technology Theory and Application (JITTA)*, vol. 5, no. 4, pp. 1–35. Retrieved from http://aisel.aisnet.org/jitta/vol5/iss4/3

Twidale, Michael; Randall, David; & Bentley, Richard. (1994). *Situated evaluation for cooperative systems Situated evaluation for cooperative systems*. Lancester, UK.

Twitter, Inc. (2014). TweetDeck. Retrieved from https://tweetdeck.twitter.com/

uberMetrics Technologies GmbH. (2014). uberMetrics DELTA. Retrieved from http://www.ubermetrics-technologies.com/en/product

UN Office for Disaster Risk Reduction. (2016). Terminology. Retrieved from https://www.unisdr.org/we/inform/terminology

United Nations. (2009). *2009 UNISDR Terminology on Disaster Risk Reduction. International Stratergy for Disaster Reduction (ISDR)*. Geneva: United Nations International Strategy for Disaster Reduction (UNISDR). Retrieved from https://www.undrr.org/public ation/2009-unisdr-terminology-disaster-risk-reduction

United Nations. (2015). Sendai Framework for Disaster Risk Reduction 2015–2030. Sendai, Japan. Retrieved from https://www.undrr.org/publication/sendai-framework-dis aster-risk-reduction-2015-2030

Utz, Sonja; Schultz, Friederike; & Glocka, Sandra. (2013). Crisis communication online: How medium, crisis type and emotions affected public reactions in the Fukushima Daiichi nuclear disaster. *Public Relations Review*, vol. 39, no. 1, pp. 40–46.

Valecha, Rohit; Oh, Onook; & Rao, R. (2013). An Exploration of Collaboration over Time in Collective Crisis Response during the Haiti 2010 Earthquake. In R. Baskerville & M. Chau (Eds.), *Proceedings of the Thirty Fourth International Conference on Information Systems (ICIS)* (pp. 1–10). Atlanta, GA, Italy: AISeL.

van Brakel, Rosamunde; Kudina, Olya; Fonio, Chiara; & Boersma, Kees. (2022). Bridging values: Finding a balance between privacy and control. The case of Corona apps in Belgium and the Netherlands. *Journal of Contingencies and Crisis Management (JCCM)*, vol. n/a, no. n/a. https://doi.org/10.1111/1468-5973.12395

van de Walle, Bartel; Brugghemans, Bert; & Comes, Tina. (2016). Improving situation awareness in crisis response teams: An experimental analysis of enriched information and centralized coordination. *International Journal of Human-Computer Studies*, vol. 95, pp. 66–79. https://doi.org/10.1016/j.ijhcs.2016.05.001

van de Walle, Bartel; & Turoff, Murray. (2008). Decision support for emergency situations. *Information Systems and E-Business Management*, vol. 6, no. 3, pp. 295–316. https://doi. org/10.1007/s10257-008-0087-z

van Esch, Stella; van den Homberg, Marc; & Boersma, Kees. (2021). Looking beyond the data: an assessment of the emerging data ecosystem of Nepal's Flood Early Warning Systems. In A. Adrot, R. Grace, K. Moore, & C. Zobel (Eds.), *Proceedings of the Information Systems for Crisis Response and Management (ISCRAM)* (pp. 282–293). Virginia Institute of Technology.

Veil, Shari R.; Buehner, Tara; & Palenchar, Michael J. (2011). A Work-In-Process Literature Review: Incorporating Social Media in Risk and Crisis Communication. *Journal of Contingencies and Crisis Management (JCCM)*, vol. 19, no. 2, pp. 110–122. https://doi.org/ 10.1111/j.1468-5973.2011.00639.x

Vieweg, Sarah; Hughes, Amanda Lee; Starbird, Kate; & Palen, Leysia. (2010). Microblogging During Two Natural Hazards Events: What Twitter May Contribute to Situational Awareness. In *Proceedings of the Conference on Human Factors in Computing Systems (CHI)* (pp. 1079–1088). New York, USA: ACM. https://doi.org/10.1145/1753326. 1753486

Vieweg, Sarah; Palen, Leysia; Liu, Sophia B.; Hughes, Amanda Lee; & Sutton, Jeannette. (2008). Collective Intelligence in Distaster: Examination of the Phenomenon in the Aftermath of the 2007 Virginia Tech Shooting. In F. Friedrich & B. Van de Walle (Eds.), *Proceedings of the International Conference on Information Systems for Crisis Response and Management (ISCRAM)* (pp. 44–54). Washington D.C., USA.

Viklund, Mattias J. (2003). Trust and Risk Perception in Western Europe: A Cross-National Study. *Risk Analysis*, vol. 23, no. 4, pp. 727–738. https://doi.org/10.1111/1539-6924. 00351

vom Brocke, Jan; Simons, Alexander; Riemer, Kai; Niehaves, Björn; & Plattfaut, Ralf. (2015). Standing on the Shoulders of Giants: Challenges and Recommendations of Literature Search in Information Systems Research. *Communications of the AIS*, vol. 37, no. 1, pp. 205–224. https://doi.org/10.1088/1464-4258/8/7/S10

Wachinger, Gisela; Renn, Ortwin; Begg, Chloe; & Kuhlicke, Christian. (2013). The Risk Perception Paradox—Implications for Governance and Communication of Natural Hazards. *Risk Analysis*, vol. 33, no. 6, pp. 1049–1065. https://doi.org/10.1111/j.1539-6924.2012. 01942.x

Wan, Stephen; & Paris, Cécile. (2015). Understanding Public Emotional Reactions on Twitter. In M. Cha, C. Mascolo, & C. Sandvig (Eds.), *Proceedings of the Ninth International AAAI Conference on Web and Social Media* (pp. 715–716). AAAI Press.

Wang, Ruo-Qian; Mao, Huina; Wang, Yuan; Rae, Chris; & Shaw, Wesley. (2018). Hyper-resolution monitoring of urban flooding with social media and crowdsourcing data. *Computers & Geosciences*, vol. 111, pp. 139–147. https://doi.org/10.1016/j.cageo.2017. 11.008

Ward, Jonathan Stuart; & Barker, Adam. (2013). Undefined By Data: A Survey of Big Data Definitions. *CoRR*, vol. abs/1309.5. Retrieved from https://arxiv.org/abs/1309.5821

Watson, Hayley; Finn, Rachel L.; & Wadhwa, Kush. (2017). Organizational and Societal Impacts of Big Data in Crisis Management. *Journal of Contingencies and Crisis Management (JCCM)*, vol. 25, no. 1. https://doi.org/10.1111/1468-5973.12141

We Are Social. (2014). Social, Digital & Mobile in Europe. Retrieved from w

Wendling, Cécile; Radisch, Jack; & Jacobzone, Stephane. (2013). The Use of Social Media in Risk and Crisis Communication. *OECD Working Papers on Public Governance*, vol. 24. https://doi.org/10.1787/5k3v01fskp9s-en

Western Cape Government. (2015). Disaster Management Definitions. Retrieved from https://www.westerncape.gov.za/general-publication/disaster-management-definitions

White, Connie; & Plotnick, Linda. (2010). A Framework to Identify Best Practices: Social Media and Web 2.0 Technologies in the Emergency Domain. *International Journal of Information Systems for Crisis Response and Management (IJISCRAM)*, vol. 2, no. 1.

White, Connie; Plotnick, Linda; Kushma, Jane; Hiltz, Starr Roxanne; & Turoff, Murray. (2009). An online social network for emergency management. *International Journal of Emergency Management (IJEM)*, vol. 6, no. 3/4, pp. 369–382.

White, Conny M. (2011). *Social Media, Crisis Communication, and Emergency Management: Leveraging Web 2.0 Technologies*. Boca Raton, FL: CRC Press.

White, Joanne I.; & Palen, Leysia. (2015). Expertise in the Wired Wild West. In D. Cosley, A. Forte, L. Ciolfi, & D. McDonald (Eds.), *Proceedings of the ACM Conference on Computer-Supported-Cooperative Work and Social Computing (CSCW)* (pp. 662–675). New York, USA: ACM Press. https://doi.org/10.1145/2675133.2675167

White, Joanne I.; Palen, Leysia; & Anderson, Kenneth M. (2014). Digital Mobilization in Disaster Response: The Work & Self – Organization of On-Line Pet Advocates in Response to Hurricane Sandy. In S. R. Fussell, W. G. Lutters, M. R. Morris, & M. Reddy (Eds.), *Proceedings of the Conference on Computer Supported Cooperative Work (CSCW)* (pp. 866–876). Baltimore, USA: ACM.

Whittaker, Joshua; McLennan, Blythe; & Handmer, John. (2015). A review of informal volunteerism in emergencies and disasters: Definition, opportunities and challenges. *International Journal of Disaster Risk Reduction*, vol. 13, pp. 358–368. https://doi.org/10.1016/j.ijdrr.2015.07.010

Wiegand, Stefanie; & Middleton, Stuart E. (2016). Veracity and Velocity of Social Media Content during Breaking News: Analysis of November 2015 Paris Shootings. In J. Bourdeau, J. Hendler, R. Nkambou, I. Horrocks, & B. Y. Zhao (Eds.), *Proceedings of the 25th International Conference Companion on World Wide Web* (pp. 751–756). New York, USA: ACM Press. https://doi.org/10.1145/2872518.2890095

Wilensky, Hiroko. (2014). Twitter as a Navigator for Stranded Commuters during the Great East Japan Earthquake. In S. R. Hiltz, L. Plotnick, M. Pfaf, & P. C. Shih (Eds.), *Proceedings of the International Conference on Information Systems for Crisis Response and Management (ISCRAM)* (pp. 695–704). ISCRAM.

Wittmann, Sebastian; Jurisch, Marlen; & Krcmar, Helmut. (2015). Managing Network Based Governance Structures in Disasters: The Case of the Passau Flood in 2013. *Journal of Homeland Security and Emergency Management (JHSEM)*, vol. 12, no. 3, pp. 529–569. https://doi.org/10.1515/jhsem-2014-0078

Won, Markus; Stiemerling, Oliver; & Wulf, Volker. (2006). Component-Based Approaches to Tailorable Systems. In H. Lieberman, F. Paternó, & V. Wulf (Eds.), *End-user Development* (pp. 115–141). Dordrecht, Springer.

Wong, Jeffrey; & Hong, Jason I. (2007). Making mashups with marmite. In *Proceedings of the Conference on Human Factors in Computing Systems (CHI)* (pp. 1435–1444). New York, USA: ACM Press. https://doi.org/10.1145/1240624.1240842

World Health Organization. (2002). *Disasters and Emergencies: Definitions*. Retrieved from http://apps.who.int/disasters/repo/7656.pdf

World Wide Web Consortium. (2016). Activity Vocabulary. Retrieved from https://www.w3.org/TR/activitystreams-vocabulary/

Wulf, Volker; Misaki, Kaoru; Atam, Meryem; Randall, David; & Rohde, Markus. (2013). 'On the Ground' in Sidi Bouzid: Investigating Social Media Use during the Tunisian Revolution. In *Proceedings of the Conference on Computer Supported Cooperative Work (CSCW)* (pp. 1409–1418). San Antonio, USA: ACM.

Wulf, Volker; Rohde, Markus; Pipek, Volkmar; & Stevens, Gunnar. (2011). Engaging with practices: design case studies as a research framework in CSCW. In S. Fussell, W. Lutters, M. R. Morris, & M. Reddy (Eds.), *Proceedings of the ACM Conference on Computer Supported Cooperative Work (CSCW)* (pp. 505–512). Hangzhou, China: ACM Press. https://doi.org/10.1145/1958824.1958902

Xu, W.; Ritter, A.; & Grishman, R. (2013). Gathering and Generating Paraphrases from Twitter with Application to Normalization. In *Proceedings of the Sixth Workshop on Building and Using Comparable Corpora* (pp. 121–128). Sophia: Association for Computational Linguistics.

Yang, Seungwon; Chung, Haeyong; Lin, Xiao; Lee, Sunshin; & Chen, Liangzhe. (2013). PhaseVis: What, When, Where, and Who in Visualizing the Four Phases of Emergency Management Through the Lens of Social Media. In T. Comes, F. Fiedrich, S. Fortier, J. Geldermann, & T. Müller (Eds.), *Proceedings of the Information Systems for Crisis Response and Management (ISCRAM)* (pp. 912–917). Baden-Baden, Germany: ISCRAM.

Yates, Dave; & Paquette, Scott. (2011). Emergency knowledge management and social media technologies: A case study of the 2010 Haitian earthquake. *International Journal of Information Management*, vol. 31, no. 1, pp. 6–13. https://doi.org/10.1016/j.ijinfomgt.2010.10.001

Yin, J.; Lampert, A.; Cameron, Mark; Robinson, B.; & Power, R. (2012). Using social media to enhance emergency situation awareness. *Intelligent Systemts, IEEE*, vol. 27, no. 6, pp. 52–59.

Yin, Robert K. (2014). *Case Study Research: Design and Methods*. California: SAGE Pub.

Zade, Himanshu; Shah, Kushal; Rangarajan, Vaibhavi; Kshirsagar, Priyanka; Imran, Muhammad; & Starbird, Kate. (2018). From Situational Awareness to Actionability: Towards Improving the Utility of Social Media Data for Crisis Response. *Proceedings of the ACM on Human-Computer Interaction*, vol. 2, no. CSCW, pp. 1–18. https://doi.org/10.1145/3274464

Zafarani, Reza; Abbasi, Mohammad Ali; & Liu, Huan. (2014). *Social Media Mining: An Introduction*. Cambridge University Press.

Zagel, B. (2012). Soziale Netzwerke als Impulsgeber für das Verkehrs-und Sicherheitsmanagement bei Großveranstaltungen. In A. Koch, T. Kutzner, & T. Eder (Eds.), *Geoinformationssysteme* (pp. 223–232). Berlin/Offenbach: VDE Verlag.

Zeng, Jing; Chan, Chung-hong; & Fu, King-wa. (2017). How Social Media Construct "Truth" Around Crisis Events: Weibo's Rumor Management Strategies After the 2015 Tianjin Blasts. *Policy & Internet*, vol. 9, pp. 297–320. https://doi.org/10.1002/poi3.155

Zhang, Cheng; Fan, Chao; Yao, Wenlin; Hu, Xia; & Mostafavi, Ali. (2019). Social media for intelligent public information and warning in disasters: An interdisciplinary review. *International Journal of Information Management*, vol. 49, pp. 190–207. https://doi.org/10.1016/j.ijinfomgt.2019.04.004

Zheng, Lili. (2017). Does online perceived risk depend on culture? Individualistic versus collectivistic culture. *Journal of Decision Systems*, vol. 26, no. 3, pp. 256–274. https://doi.org/10.1080/12460125.2017.1351861

Zipf, Alexander. (2016). Mit Netz und Geodaten. Katastrophen-Management Online. *Ruperto Carola Forschungsmagazin*, vol. 8, pp. 42–49.

Printed in the United States
by Baker & Taylor Publisher Services

Printed in the United States
by Baker & Taylor Publisher Services